WOMEN IN SOCIETY
A Feminist List edited by Jo Campling

D0186708

Editorial Advisory Group

Phillida Bunckle, *Victoria University, Wellington, New Zealand;* Miriam David, *South Bank University;* Leonore Davidoff, *University of Essex;* Janet Finch, *University of Lancaster;* Jalna Hanmer, *University of Bradford;* Beverley Kingston, *University of New South Wales, Australia;* Hilary Land, *University of Bristol;* Diana Leonard, *University of London Institute of Education;* Susan Lonsdale, *South Bank University;* Jean O'Barr, *Duke University, North Carolina, USA;* Arlene Tigar McLaren, *Simon Fraser University, British Columbia, Canada;* Jill Roe, *Macquarie University, Australia;* Hilary Rose, *University of Bradford;* Susan Sellars, *Centre D'Etudes Feminines, Université de Paris;* Pat Thane, *Goldsmiths' College, University of London;* Clare Ungerson, *University of Kent at Canterbury;* Judy Walkowitz, *Rutgers University, New Jersey, USA.*

The last 20 years have seen an explosion of publishing by, about and for women. This new list is designed to make a particular contribution to this continuing process by commissioning and publishing books which consolidate and advance feminist research and debate in key areas in a form suitable for students, academics and researchers but also accessible to a broader general readership.

As far as possible, books will adopt an international perspective incorporating comparative material from a range of countries where this is illuminating. Above all they will be interdisciplinary, aiming to put women's studies and feminist discussion firmly on the agenda in subject-areas as disparate as law, literature, art and social policy.

WOMEN IN SOCIETY
A Feminist List edited by
Jo Campling

Women and Crime

Frances Heidensohn

First published 1985 by
THE MACMILLAN PRESS LTD
Houndmills, Basingstoke, Hampshire RG21 2XS
and London
Companies and representatives
throughout the world

ISBN 0–333–36216–0 hardcover
ISBN 0–333–36217–9 paperback /ᵣₑ

A catalogue record for this book is available
from the British Library.

Printed in Hong Kong

Reprinted 1986 (twice), 1989, 1990, 1991, 1992, 1993

To all my family

Contents

Preface

In all the best books I have read, the introductory pages contain some of the most fascinating material. Here are to be found declarations of debts and commitments, both intellectual and personal, and often, the neatest précis of the author's argument which a busy reader can find. This one will not, I hope, prove disappointing.

In writing this text, I have analysed and presented major issues and debates in relation to women and crime. The framework within which this has been done consists of a series of propositions which derive from these discussions. These are that women have apparently no less a capacity than men for committing criminal acts, nor do they face formally different rules and laws, but their official criminality tends to be lower, less frequent and less serious. Moreover, convicted female offenders themselves resist and reject the label of criminal because of its damaging effects. When we examine the legal apparatus which is designed to deal with crime and criminals, we can clearly see how uneasily women fit into its categories and correctional system: they are not so much, when in court, police custody, or prison, in no-man's-land as in too-much-man's-land. Criminologists, too, for the most part, have dealt unfairly with women criminals, ignoring, and avoiding them and at best caricaturing their behaviour in clumsy stereotypes.

From these and further analyses we can, I suggest, derive some conclusions which can be further explored and tested. Briefly, it is not so much female criminality which seems to be distinctive, despite the efforts of a surprising coalition of authors to assert this, as the defining and controlling apparatuses which they face and which limit their public and private behaviour in gender-related ways.

ix

The study of women and crime has developed a great deal in the past twenty years, but there are still many unexplored areas and I hope that the ideas put forward in this book may stimulate others to take them further.

I have drawn mainly on British and North American sources and on easily accessible material, save where there are outstanding reasons for including unpublished or obscure sources.

The task of researching and writing a book is a curiously time-consuming, self-absorbed one which requires confidence and inspiration; for their encouragement and support in this work, I am especially grateful to Jo Campling, who persuaded me to write it, and to Gay Cohen, Evelyn Caulcott and Rita O'Brien. Eve Saville gave me invaluable help in many ways. Nigel Walker and the librarian and staff of the Institute of Criminology in Cambridge were most welcoming and helpful. David Downes and Paul Rock, while not involved with the present volume, have been my constant and cheerful criminological companions over many years and I owe them a great deal. Pat Arrowsmith generously gave me her time, many thoughts and ideas, and lent me copies of her poems and other writings. Iris Swain provided practical help with the manuscript, which Edmund and Lucy Pereira prepared with skill and efficiency.

At Goldsmiths' College, my undergraduate students in the Sociology of Sex and Gender, and the members of the postgraduate seminar in Women's studies helped to convince me of the need for such text.

It is customary to regret the burden and deprivations caused to families by authorship carried out in their midst. I should, however, like to record that, at least once in publishing history, this was not the case and that my sensible relatives, while pursuing their lives in uninterrupted fashion as I wrote this book, gained in a number of ways. These included acquiring an amusing topic of conversation, a dinghy sailing certificate, personal stereos and a portable television.

My parents and brothers were kind and enquiring; Christina and Martin Heidensohn worked on the references, collating and photocopying with zest and enjoyment. Klaus Heidensohn gave me happily every sort of practical and personal support. I am most grateful to them all for their humour and scepticism, their sense of reality and unstinted affection.

My thanks to everyone, but of course I am alone responsible for the contents of this book.

FRANCES HEIDENSOHN

Editor's Introduction

Female crime has attracted great interest, in personalities such as Ulrike Meinhof, the Price sisters and Patty Hearst, as well as from academics examining the 'new female criminal'. Yet, while there has been a considerable growth in publications on the topic, there is no comprehensive text to guide students, professionals and interested observers through the complex issues. *Women and Crime* aims to fill this gap. It provides a unique survey of topics, sources and theories. Lively, well written and often amusing, the material is presented clearly with guides to all the major debates which have raged over one of the most controversial areas of women's studies.

Is there a 'new female criminal'? Do the police and the courts extend a protective chivalry to women offenders? Are women more harshly or more leniently treated in prison than men? Why have male criminologists neglected female criminals for so long? This book attempts to answer all these questions. As a guide to the literature and research on this topic it is without parallel.

Frances Heidensohn also uses a range of autobiographical material and other sources to explore deviant women's own experiences and their reactions to them. From these she puts forward a new explanation of the form and pattern of female crime, using not only criminological studies but also historical and literary sources. She presents the key issues of female criminality as seen by society and by the women themselves. She deals with women and justice, women and the courts, women and prison, and images of deviant women. The book contains a full account of criminology's contribution to the study of women's crime. In a novel analysis of women and social control, Frances Heidensohn shows how women's behaviour is confined and controlled in private and in public.

This fascinating book is essential reading for professionals and students, but it is also compelling reading for those interested in feminism and its impact, and on the status of women in society today.

JO CAMPLING

1

Introducing women and crime

One of the most remarkable developments in publishing in recent years has been the growth in the number of books for, about and by women. In particular, handbooks and guides of every sort have appeared, encouraging women to realise themselves emotionally and educationally and imparting skills in everything from building to banking. There is too a growing range of women's studies – books designed to explain and analyse aspects of women's experience both for the concerned general reader and for the increasing numbers of students of women's studies or sex and gender courses which are now offered. This book will, I hope, share some of the characteristics of both these types. While it is not intended to be a how-to-do-it handbook for female criminals, I have included as comprehensive a selection as I could of what we know about women and crime, women and criminal justice, and women's experience of imprisonment. At the same time, I have tried to extend and develop an understanding of the deviance and conformity of women which will, I trust, prove useful both to students of women's studies and to the professional looking for a guide to the maze of assertions and counter-assertions about, for instance, the 'new' female criminal.

The plan of the book is as follows. In this chapter, I shall set out the main characteristics of women's contribution to criminality and the issues and problems associated with this. The next four chapters deal with the accounts women themselves have given of their experiences of crime and their reactions to these, with the impact on women both of the criminal justice system and of their imprisonment, and social reactions to female deviance. The subsequent three chapters present an account of developments in theorising

about women and crime and are followed by a chapter which analyses the social pressures to conform which affect women, through the images of deviant women and through the structuring of their social position. In short, the first part of this volume contains as full a description as possible of which women become officially defined as delinquent, how they feel about their stigmatisation, and what happens to them with the police and in court and in prison. The second section concentrates on presenting and analysing both conventional and feminist approaches to the understanding of female criminality and suggests some new perspectives.

The issues

There are probably two observations about female criminality with which many people will be familiar. First, and much the best known, is that over long periods of time and in many differing judicial systems, women have a consistently lower rate of officially recorded crimes than men. There are many ways of presenting this, but one clear one is given by Farrington (1981, p. 174) in estimating the accumulation of criminal convictions over a lifetime in England and Wales:

> This analysis shows 11.70 per cent of males convicted up to the seventeenth birthday, 21.76 per cent up to the twenty-first birthday, and 43.57 per cent at some time in their lives. For females, the corresponding figures are 2.10, 4.66 and 14.70 per cent.

In other words, females are not only much less criminal than males, they are so much less criminal that whereas convictions are, statistically at least, 'normal' for males, they are very unusual for females. Indeed Farrington predicts a lifetime prevalence for males by 1989 in excess of 50 per cent (Farrington, 1981).

The second observation which has been increasingly stressed by feminist and other commentators since the 1960s is that this low criminal-participation rate has not been sufficiently remarked upon nor studied. Feminists have seen it as another example of the characteristic 'invisibility' of women in social science or social policy, while several non-feminist writers have pointed out that any causal explanation of crime which does not include gender-related factors cannot be valid (Harris, 1977; Box, 1983). Female criminality is now a topic on the agenda and there have been very many more studies of it produced in the fifteen years up to 1984 than in any previous period. One purpose of this book is to present an accessible version of these findings.

While a 'hidden' group of women have, thus, to some extent, been rendered visible, this development does not, at first sight, seem to have the same broad relevance for all women as other parallel 'discoveries' have. The (re-) discovery of domestic violence in the early 1970s and the discussions of rape and of sexual harassment at work have been presented and analysed in ways which make them relevant to the oppression of all women and not just to those who are victims of these particular acts. Moreover, the first open consideration of all these issues led to a flood of revelations from women who had been silent sufferers before. In turn, there have been some changes in law, related social policies or trades union practices which acknowledge that these problems exist. Women's criminality, however, appears rather different. It does not look like a problem which connects with the experience of many women. I want now to look at what we know about female criminality and then to look at its main characteristics to see how we can understand them and make the topic a much broader and more widely relevant one than first it seems.

Crime and women

A cautionary note

Scepticism about both the validity and the reliability of criminal statistics is now more or less universal. The police themselves point to changes in recording procedures and public attitudes which can affect reporting of crime and the annual British *Criminal Statistics* publication makes a point of stressing the limitations of the data it presents (Home Office, 1983a, p. 218). The UK Home Office now undertakes a regular crime survey which gives a rather different picture from police records and surveys are increasingly used in Canada, the Netherlands, etc. Two principal features limit the official recording of crime: the iceberg effect and the dark figure.

While the tip of the iceberg – that is, the amount of reported and recorded crime – may be visible, there are many offences which go unobserved, unreported or unrecorded. Lack of a victim, or of witnesses or of sufficient evidence may all limit or prevent recording. The amount of unrecorded crime is not known, although attempts to measure it through victim and crime surveys or self-report studies all indicate that it is much larger than 'crimes known'. A further problem lies in the fact that the relationship between hidden and recorded crime can change, so that an apparent increase in crime may reflect an increase in offences reported and recorded rather than an increase in crimes actually committed. This, the Home Office itself suggests, is exactly what happened with offences of burglary and theft in a dwelling in the 1970s (Home Office, 1983a, p. 29) in England and Wales.

Even when crimes are known to the police, only a small proportion are 'cleared up' – that is, lead to arrest, conviction and sentence or other outcome which closes the case. There thus remains a dark figure of uncleared crimes about which very little detail is available, such as the sex, age or social characteristics of the perpetrator. In looking at available official data we must bear these general limitations in mind. There are also several factors which may have particular impact on the recording of female criminality. The only certain data on the sex of offenders comes either from police statistics of cautioning, or from judicial figures of those tried in the courts, in other words, at a fairly late stage in the process from commission to conviction, and it is a criminological truism that the further away one is from the act itself the more selected is the sample of people and events. Many early studies, for example, were seriously flawed by their exclusive use of incarcerated offenders as samples of criminals.

A further difficulty lies with the unknown dimensions of possible bias in reporting and recording offences by girls and women. It has often been suggested (see Chapter 3) that there is an innate 'chivalry' which protects women from the full rigours of policing and the courts, although as evidence put forward in that chapter shows, this is a doubtful contention. However there may be special features which affect the reporting of crimes committed by women. Pollak (1961) suggested that women's hidden crimes were massive, but he gave neither serious evidence for this contention, nor explanation for the tolerance of widespread female crime (see Chapter

6). It has also been contended that woman, especially young girls, are brought before the courts for trivial activities which would be tolerated in boys (see Chapter 3). All we can say is that the propensity to report women's crimes may differ from the propensity to report those of men but to what degree we cannot say. Two further rather technical points of interpretation also need to be stressed. First, since the numbers of women convicted of serious offences tends to be fairly small, a small numerical increase can mean a very large percentage change which should be interpreted with great caution. Second, the small numbers involved mean that various forms of analysis routinely applied to figures for males may either not be used on females or need to be treated with scepticism because of the small numbers. Thus the 1982 *Criminal Statistics* for England and Wales devote fourteen lines to variations in known offending by male juveniles in different police force areas and only four and a half to the same phenomenon in girls. With all these reservations in mind we can now look at official crime and delinquency by females.

The female share of crime

As I have already noted, the one thing most people know about women and crime is that women's contribution to total criminality is modest. Indeed this is an area of public achievement where women hardly compete with men.

In the analysis in this section I have used recent data for England and Wales. This data provides a reasonable example and has the advantage of coming from a single jurisdiction with a reasonably standard system of reporting and recording. Similar analyses for the USA can be found in Leonard (1982) and Simon (1975). Figures for the USA are complicated by the existence of State and Federal jurisdictions and the considerable variations in criminal law and in recording violations of it to which these lead. This presentation is therefore intended to be merely an example; while there are recent changes and local variations the patterns we shall find in recent British experience have a remarkable robustness and stability.

If we take the most recent year for which figures are available, 1982 (all the figures in this paragraph are from Home Office, 1983a) some 2 million offenders were found guilty by all courts in England and Wales. More than 1 million were found guilty of summary motoring offences. Of all those found guilty 1 in 9 was female (11 per cent). For indictable offences (that is, broadly, more serious offences) 1 in 7 was female (14 per cent). However, when figures of cautions are included – that is, where a formal warning was given and recorded by the police – the picture changes somewhat, as females are more likely to be cautioned. Thus in 1982 as in previous years a higher proportion of female offenders – 34 per cent of females but only 17 per cent of male offenders were cautioned for indictable offences. Therefore 83 per cent of those found guilty of, or cautioned for, indictable offences were male and 17 per cent female. These represent nearly half a million males and nearly 100 000 females of whom about a third of both sexes were juveniles. For both sexes the peak age of offending is very young and related to the period of compulsory schooling – at 15 years of age for boys and 14 for girls. This proportionate share of crime has remained fairly stable during the past decade.

These ratios, although they suggest that women now take a larger part in crime than they did in the past, or in some other societies, are not very dissimilar from historically observed trends (Mannheim, 1965, pp. 678–89). Indeed women's low level of performance in crime has been regularly cited as the reason for the lack of attention given to them by criminologists, both because they seemed not to pose a problem (Smart, 1977) and because their small numbers made study difficult (Mannheim, 1965). However in recent years there has been something of a moral panic created about the allegations that women's share of crime was rising faster than that of men and rising particularly fast in unfeminine and untypical offences such as robbery and violence. This phenomenon was linked to the movement for women's liberation which, it was suggested, was leading to the emancipation of women into taking a bigger share of crime. (See Adler, 1975; Simon, 1975; and for a review, Box and Hale, 1983.) Box and Hale analysed trends over the past thirty years and showed that there had been overall a fairly stable ratio of female to male convictions since 1951 in England and Wales, although property crimes had shown some convergence, while for crimes of violence, the female contribution remained static. In reviewing the extensive popular and academic concern, they point out that most studies used absolute increases in female crime, rather than relative share and that this leads to an exaggeration of the female contribution.

Crimes women and girls commit

Females contribute to the officially recorded tariffs of all known offences. Even where there are legal requirements, as with rape, which women cannot fulfil, they may be charged as accomplices to a crime. Certain offences relate only to women: it is only mothers who can be charged with infanticide and offences by prostitutes involve soliciting and similar actions by females. Male homosexual relations are still much more heavily restricted by criminal sanction. But the overwhelming majority of offenders are charged with motoring offences or theft, relatively few with those where there is a discriminatory factor in the law. It is therefore interesting to note that women's participation in different offence categories does vary considerably. Thus in England and Wales for every year from 1972 to 1982 some 200 women were convicted or cautioned for robbery while the numbers of men rose over the same period from 3500 to 4300 while for shoplifting in 1982 there were over 48 000 convictions of males and just over 32 000 for females (Home Office, 1983b). Shoplifting is in practice the only major category of crime to which women make a significant contribution. Even so, the rate of convictions in relation to population at risk has been higher in recent years for men than women (Smart, 1977, p. 9) and in an earlier study Gibbens and Prince (1962) suggested that men stole more expensive items. Mayhew has suggested that shoplifting is one activity in which women's opportunities to commit crime are greater than any other since shopping is a legitimate and indeed essential public activity for women. She quotes three surveys from the USA and Ireland which recorded similar rates of observed shoplifting in male and female shoppers (Mayhew, 1977). However, her analysis is not borne out by a more recent and methodologically much more exacting British study. In observing a sample of shoppers who entered a small department store, Buckle and Farrington (1984, p. 70) found that 'men are proportionally twice as likely to shoplift as women'. Moreover, men stole about five times as many items as did women and these were items of considerably greater value.

Women can be found in all other offence categories and so it would be wrong to say that there are 'sex-specific' crimes (Smart, 1977) or 'masculine' crimes (Adler, 1975). Rather criminal activity as officially recorded is by and large a masculine activity, but one in which women do participate. In Britain and the USA more women have been participating in the past decade, with their age-related rates growing slightly faster than those for males (2–3 per cent) while for females they averaged 3–4 per cent between 1971 and 1981 (Home Office, 1982c, p. 84). But this shift, while it increased the numbers of women going to prison, did not result in women taking a noticeably larger role in recorded criminality.

While official data is not very helpful on this, it does seem that women commit fewer serious crimes and are rather less likely to be recidivists. Men predominate in homicide – 176 : 8 in 1982 – and the infanticide figures hardly change the picture (three cases in 1982) (Home Office, 1983b). Studies of cautioning and sentencing procedures suggest, for the UK at least, that the lesser showing of women is due to the more trivial nature of their offences and their comparative lack of 'form' (see Chapter 3).

Earlier in this chapter, I listed some of the dangers in using official records of crime, and these must be stressed again in interpreting the data set out above. It is possible, for example, that there have been 'real' increases in property crime and violence amongst women in the past few years. Or agencies such as the police or the management of stores may have changed their policies on prosecution (Hindelang, 1974; Morris and Gelsthorpe, 1981). Or again, while the volume of offending may not have changed, tendencies to report it may have altered (Home Office, 1983a) and specifically perhaps, willingness to report women, partly because of changed perceptions of female offenders (Morris and Gelsthorpe, 1981; Simon, 1975; Gibbens, 1981).

With the defects of criminal statistics so well-known, attempts have been made by both policy-makers and academics to supplement and correct them. These attempts are of two main kinds: crime surveys and self-report studies. Crime surveys can either be large-scale attempts to measure the volume of perceived offences by questionnaire or interview, as in the British Crime Survey, or smaller studies, such as the observations of shoplifting reported above. The former are not very helpful to us since obviously, unless the victim of a crime actually saw the individual who burgled his home or picked his pocket, there would be no evidence on that individual's sex. The shoplifing studies suggest on the whole that, while official figures greatly under estimate the *incidence* of shoplifting by women they also do so in relation to men, if anything, rather more so. Pratt's study of mugging in London, based not on a sample survey of victims but on police records of details reported by victims of their attackers showed that 'the vast majority of assailants are male. In less than 2 per cent of cases were females alone involved' (Pratt, 1980, p. 89).

Victim surveys in the USA have a longer history than in Britain, probably because of even greater discontent with official data. Hindelang reviewed a series of such studies to see how different a picture they gave from arrest or court data. He found that basically, there was no real difference, reported and observed female involvement was 'strikingly similar to that portrayed in arrest data' (Hindelang, 1979, p. 152).

Self-report studies are a more rewarding area to examine, since the purpose of many has actually been to correct for the supposed 'bias' in under-reporting female crime. This was a claim made by Pollak which has been sustained by generations of criminologists ever since (see Chapter 6). Self-report studies are questionnaires administered anonymously and confidentially to various population samples which ask respondents which of a list of offences they have ever, or frequently committed. Most of them have been conducted on rather youthful groups who tend to be conveniently available, *en masse* in schools and colleges and also, of course, tend to be in the age ranges in which the peak rate of offending is found. As with victim surveys, most of the studies have been conducted in North America, as Mawby points out 'in Britain ... the three major self-report studies currently available are all confined to male respondents' (Mawby, 1980, p. 525). Mawby's own study in Sheffield showed:

clearly that, despite a narrowing of the sex differences found in recorded crime data, there is still considerable difference between the sexes. Although girls were more likely to truant, on sixteen of the items in the crime check list, boys were significantly more likely to offend (Mawby, 1980, p. 541).

Mawby's findings also demonstrate that boys commit more offences than girls (Mawby, 1980, p. 535) and that class cannot alone explain the sex difference.

Mawby's results confirm those of most North American researchers. Gold, for instance, in a carefully researched study of teen-agers in Flint, Michigan found that:

> the Flint boys behaved more delinquently than the girls according to our measures of delinquent behavior ... a comparison of the figures shows that girls are especially less delinquent than boys when seriousness of offenses was taken into account (Gold, 1970, p. 61).

In short, 'the boys as a group were significantly more delinquent than the girls' (Gold, 1970, p. 121). Smith and Visher, in a massive review of the self-report literature conclude that, while the involvement of young girls in delinquency appears to be somewhat under-reported, official and self-report data run in a remarkably parallel fashion (Smith and Visher, 1980). There are in short, no great untapped wells of female deviance protected from police prospectors by the curious conspiracy alleged by Pollak. As Box notes, 'this is an ironic conclusion' since the point of many of these studies was to try to prove just that (Box, 1983).

Of course, self-report studies have limitations, just as criminal statistics do. Respondents may lie, although lie-detecting questions are built-in. Girls may feel more shame and boys be more inclined to boast about past delinquencies. In any case, respondents' perceptions of an offence may be incorrect, they may misjudge their own behaviour which might not in any case, have been defined as a crime had it ever been detected. Despite these reservations, self-report studies, like criminal statistics, do measure certain aspects of deviance, even though they may not give the whole picture. What is of lasting interest is what we learn from them, which confirms very largely what we know from official sources and from surveys about women offenders. Women commit very little crime; most of their offences (about 80 per cent at present) relate to property or to fraud and forgery. They are convicted of physical harm or damage infrequently and they are in general petty and trivial offenders. Since very few are found in organised crime, or at the top of large organisations, they are, as Box points out, if anything *over-represented* in official statistics, since these serious and costly 'crimes of the powerful' are hardly recorded at all (Box, 1983, p. 169). While more women have been active in crime in recent years, this seems to match overall developments in criminality rather than a distinctive pattern of new 'liberated criminality'.

Finding a place for female crime

If we were to try to draw a portrait of a 'typical' female offender at this stage she would be a young girl, a first offender charged with shoplifting, and her likely destiny would be a caution or a non-custodial sentence. There are, of course, small groups of women who deviate from this: the regular drunk with a string of convictions, or the prostitute regularly fined for soliciting, as well as a sprinkling of women convicted of serious crimes such as murder, and offences associated with terrorism. However, while a very few female offenders have attracted unusual popular attention (see Chapter 5) the picture is not on the whole an exciting one. 'Monster' murderers or big-time gangsters are scarcely found amongst the ranks of women offenders. There is little evidence of the drama of juvenile gang activity between girls of the kind which has excited the interest of several generations of sociologists.

It is because of their lack of glamour as well as their low social threat, that as several commentators have suggested, female criminals have received so little consideration in the immense literature from sensational to serious which has been generated on the topic of crime (Smart, 1977; Millman, 1982). Yet I believe this cannot be the complete explanation. Even though women criminals may have seemed boring under-achievers compared with their male counterparts, the pattern of sex crime ratios – that is, the relative share of males and females in crime – was far too serious an issue to ignore for so long (Heidensohn, 1968; Harris, 1977). Baldly, no theory of criminality which ignores the overwhelming importance of gender can be valid. *Sex differences in criminality are so sustained and so marked as to be, perhaps, the most significant feature of recorded crime.*

In later chapters of this book I shall examine why female crime was neglected for so long and how, in the end, a feminist approach was necessary to free it from this invisible state. At this stage I simply want to point out that, paradoxically, an examination of female criminality and unofficial deviance suggests that we need to move away from studying infractions and look at conformity instead, because the most striking thing about female behaviour on the basis of all the evidence considered here is how notably conformist to social mores women are. There is no evidence that this is somehow innate in women, a feature of their sweeter 'better' natures, not as the nursery rhyme has it that little girls are 'sugar and spice and all things nice' while boys are 'snaps and snails and puppy dogs tails'. In fact some women can and do commit offences of the same kind as men, save where legal or technical barriers exist, but they do so in very much smaller numbers, at less serious levels and far less often. In consequence, there are far more men than women in prison (see Chapter 4).

I shall therefore devote some space in this book to the pressures to conform and the patterns of social control experienced by women and to show how these are related to female crime. It is at this point that I think the wider relevance of female criminality to women in general can be seen. Only a few women are ever defined as criminal, but the control system which subtly, and with their compliance, inhibits the rest affects most women. Criminologists and even the more broadly interested sociologists of deviance have been uncomfortable with the study of female criminality because, logically, it leads to the superficially dull topic of conformity and not to the excitements of deviance.

The growth of a feminist appreciation of social divisions and forces enables a reappraisal. It is possible to break conventional moulds and link different approaches to the topic, it also means that we no longer take for granted long-current assumptions about the world. Thus I have used feminist analyses of family life to show how these have a bearing on the social constraints experienced by women. In what follows I have deliberately mixed résumés of scholarly researches with more direct descriptions by individuals and popular accounts. Crime is not just for experts who have, in any case, no purpose to their existence if they cannot convey their findings to wider and less specialised audiences. At times, therefore, the argument I convey is direct and simple. It is meant to be challenging, and I hope, arresting. There are, of course, reservations and caveats as with all such contentions: real life is far more complicated than any description or analysis can reasonably portray. The main aims that I have followed have been to convey as fully and faithfully as possible the experiences undergone by women offenders through their own and society's reactions and in the courts and prison. The questions raised by these experiences are then analysed and as far as possible, answered in a coherent fashion. There should be here something of interest and relevance and certainly to argue about for professionals who encounter female offenders and for students.

2

The experiences of women and crime

In the last chapter we looked at the problems and issues connected with female criminality. These were conceptualised in formal, official terms using statistical records and academic techniques. But how do women involved in crime see the issues? Do they try to make sense of the world and seek causal explanations in the way that professional carers or social scientists do? In this chapter I want to present some personal accounts by women criminals. Not surprisingly, since we saw that women's criminal achievements were modest and mundane, there are not really any villains' autobiographies nor have many studies recorded the perceptions of deviant women.

If women criminals are reluctant to publicise their activities, they are also often inaccessible to researchers wanting to record their histories. Player (1981) has described her difficulties in gaining acceptance by a group of black girls involved in a delinquent subculture. Important studies of female crime have been published which contain no case study or equivalent material (Smart, 1977; Leonard, 1982). Of course women are not only scarcely criminal, they are – even when criminal – rarely recidivist so that it is possible to argue that the natural history, or moral career of a woman deviant fails to develop in the way a man's would. Far fewer women with convictions then will have a dominant deviant identity.

Women nevertheless do commit crimes and contribute to the tariff of most offence categories. Their crime rates have been rising, in some cases faster than men's. The full panoply of law, justice and the penal system can be used against women, sometimes even more harshly than it is against men, so the views of those women who have been involved in crime could be worth hearing.

13

In his introduction to the autobiography of Walter 'Angel face' Probyn, Stan Cohen has stressed the importance and validity of such stories. They can be useful in 'unmasking, debunking, reading between the lines' (Cohen, 1977, p.12) and also because they can make the connection between private troubles and public issues. There seems to be no real female equivalent of the 'famous villain tells all' type of story, with its obligatory celebration of violence and villainy. As we shall see, famous female criminals tend to produce romances rather than thrillers. In seeking to present the voices of women who have been involved in crime in this section I shall draw on a few autobiographies and authorised biographies as well as research studies which report personal accounts. I begin with the history of 'Rosa', a serious offender with plenty of form, whom I first knew before her criminal career really developed. I shall then examine some other voices of delinquent girls and women and consider what they tell us about the key issues we have already raised.

Rosa

[I first knew Rosa when she was an art student. She discussed her earlier life with me and later gave me this account of her career. I have added extracts from her letters and a few explanations].

I was born working class. On a big estate – slum clearance – in the North. It was pretty rough and my mum watched us. Well, I was watched more. Like when I started to grow up, she said 'Come inside, don't play out'. She wouldn't let me play out any more. I had to stay in. My brother was allowed out. He'd cycle round and round the estate on his bike and I'd stay in. So of course I did my homework, nothing else to do. I wasn't clever. [Rosa had passed her 11+ and gone to a grammar school]. I was a big girl and I could fight, but the boys were scared. They were all too small.

I went on to art college. It was a fantastic scene – drugs, sex, the lot – but I missed out on it all then. Just worked and well, a bit of the other. Nothing great. I was a gawky thing and slow too. Then I got this stall. In the antique market. Shawls, lace, any old bric à brac. Some of it was lovely and of course you didn't ask where it came from. I was living with Shane then and it was really his business.

[Rosa had left home and was living with a man a few years older than herself. She was still an intermittent student but was also involved in a market stall. She became known to the police because of a series of rows over the siting of the stall and allegations over handling stolen goods. Eventually she was charged with the latter offence, covicted and fined].

I never even realised what it was, when the court case came up. I was confused about the stall and the licence. I thought the police had come about that. Shane could have helped, but he kept out of the picture – too well-known to the police.

Well I was scared then. Went straight for years. The court and the police had upset me. And the shock. A glimpse over the edge really. I got the job on the magazine and then the advertising one then. Very respectable and good money. Shane went then. I got fond of my own way. I was sure I didn't want kids, marriage, that sort of thing. Funny, though, I had several abortions, and knew some rotten men. Worse than married, really, some of them. Well, Jeff, well he could be brutal. But I had my own place then and I could kick him out. And then Steve was marvellous.

[Rosa worked for several years in graphic work. Then she linked up again with an artisitic group and met Steve, a younger man who depended on her a good deal. Her flat was raided during a party and marijuana was found. Rosa was charged with illegal possession and threatened with possible 'pushing' charges.]

It wasn't even my party. Boring people. I think I'd gone to bed. Well, it was my flat and I was older. But it was what counted later. It was the start really.

Then I wanted a fresh start. That's why we went away to India. New start. Contemplating yourself. Who you are. I was Rosa and I didn't intend to change much, but I did want out for a bit.

[Rosa and Steve travelled to India and Nepal. Steve stayed in India and Rosa eventually came back, having allegedly acquired skills as an acupuncturist in the Far East].

Well, I knew then what I wanted to do. No more drugs, distortions, that kind of thing. And I was into feminism too. No more men. No sexist crap. Well I was always bisexual really.

[Rosa joined women's groups and had a girl-friend who had been a drug addict].

> It was pressure really. I wanted money for myself and Marie. No money in the acupuncture. Well drugs were easy. I knew them. But I needed cash quickly to set up in that line of business. That's when we set up the fiddle.

[Rosa became involved in a complex fraud, planned to obtain funds for a venture into pushing soft drugs. She was caught and remanded for reports.]

> I got a great doctor. He's going to plead my health and my state. I mean it's ridiculous to say all this is big crime stuff. Titchy amounts. No one was hurt. Except me. I'm the one who'll suffer. And I was doing fine. I told him about the acupuncture. He was really interested.

[Rosa got a custodial sentence this time. After her release she obviously became more involved with a group of people whom she knew through prison contacts. She was arrested once in connexion with pushing hard drugs but medical examination revealed that she was very seriously ill and charges were dropped. Rosa died some months later].

Rosa's story contains some of the main themes that we can find in women's own accounts of their involvement in crime. Some of these descriptions have, of course, been ghosted by professional writers and therefore hardly correspond to Cohen's criterion of 'good sociology – not messed up'. Nevertheless, even stereotyped presentations tell us something about the subject's self-concept.

Some women resist deviant identities

Matza has noted what he called 'techniques of neutralisation' amongst delinquents about their offences and one of these was 'denial of the offence' (Matza, 1964). Adult male criminals also, of course, deny their offences and claim to have been 'framed', but it seems that some women reject a criminal identity with especial rigour. Even a professional thief and prostitute 'Chicago May' who had to 'acknowledge that I am a recidivist' was nevertheless very anxious to set the record straight and deny that she had 'been convicted of being a common prostitute' (Churchill Sharpe, 1928, p. 16).

Patty Hearst (whose sentence was later commuted by President Carter) described in great detail her imprisonment and brainwashing by her kidnappers and how she came to find herself joining in their bank robbery and shoot-outs:

> Why did I do it? . . . The only answer I could find that satisfied me . . . was that I acted instinctively, because I had been trained and drilled to do just that, to react to a situation without thinking just as soldiers are trained and drilled . . . without thinking. By the time they had finished with me I was in fact a soldier in the Symbionese Liberation Army (Hearst, 1982, p. 216).

One of the doctors who saw her after she had been taken into custody diagnosed her as successfully brainwashed 'Dr West repeatedly tried to reassure me that I had no reason to feel guilty or humiliated' (Hearst, 1982, p. 401).

> They [the doctors] kept trying to explain the necessity for me to repent, and in effect, to ask the court for mercy. But that meant admitting guilt, admitting that I had acted unwillingly and not under duress and that I refused to do. *I was confident that my conviction would be overturned. I would* be found innocent of any crime (Hearst, 1982, p. 442, emphasis added).

Cynthia Payne, who was convicted after the famous 'Luncheon Vouchers' case of controlling prostitutes and of keeping a disorderly house, claimed 'I provide a useful service' (Bailey, 1983, p. 134) and is quite clear what kind of role she sees herself playing and the appropriate analogy for the service she provided:

> I have this bloody wonderful dream . . . It's my ambition to open a home for the elderly – men and women. I'd be matron. There would be special wards for the disabled. If people wanted sex, they could charge it to the National Health – the ones who can't afford it, I mean. I'd have slaves to do the cleaning and Mistresses to see that they don't cut corners (Bailey, 1983, p. 166).

Yolande McShane was sentenced to two years imprisonment after a very unusual case in which police had secretly filmed her conversations with her elderly depressed mother. In her 'Daughter of Evil' (McShane, 1980) she stresses her own lifelong affection for her mother and her stunned reaction at being convicted and sentenced. Similarly, in Frances Farmer's horrific account of her own progress from minor traffic offence through to commital to a ghastly state mental institution, she insists on her own innocence and her victimisation both by her own family and by the system (Farmer, 1974).

Tony Parker's skilfully presented interviews with five women criminals contain illustrations of this too, especially in the cases of the highly respectable confidence trickster and the pathetic Janey, the sad old woman who had accepted an identity as a petty offender as a cover for the secret of her appalling past – an incestuous liaison with her father (Parker, 1965). Pat Carlen in her interviews with women in Cornton Vale in Scotland found a common pattern of women, caught in unsatisfactory marriages and often drawn to drink, prostitution or theft in an attempt to sustain family life.

[They] blamed their husbands directly for their law-breaking activities (though many more felt that their domestic situation in general was indirectly to blame for their being in prison) ... Thelma Thompson described a situation, 'Twice I've been in trouble because of his gambling. It was only because he promised that he would work and I'd get my fair share of the housekeeping that I went back to him and I ended up stealing and selling the stuff to get money for to pay my electric bill, to pay my light, my rent ... where do I land? Nine months imprisonment. ... *they wouldn't let my husband go up and speak and say it was his fault* that I was in prison' (Carlen, 1983, p. 56, added emphasis).

Woodside also interviewed women in prison: these were women abortionists imprisoned in Holloway for whom prison was an accepted hazard of helping people. A few were 'professionals' but most saw themselves as innocent aids: 'There is no doubt that compassion and feminine solidarity were strongly motivating factors among women who had acquired this skill' (Woodside 1963, p. 100). Simms quotes from the life-story of a woman imprisoned for an illegal abortion:

What I done I done with a good heart and was only too glad to help out and see them happy and free from worry (Simms, 1981, p. 180).

It can, of course, be argued that all these women are merely seeking to justify and rationalise their actions and that their denials of their own criminality are only to be expected, but this misses the central point that an admission of guilt, an acceptance of criminal labels, appear to be very vigourously resisted by some women, even when they have considerable criminal records. Many of these personal accounts emphasise the non-criminal aspects of the subjects' lives: Patty Hearst describes her strict and orderly childhood, Yolande McShane her lively and loving family life, and Cynthia Payne the eccentricities of her customers and her cheerful inventive attempts to meet their needs. If they had all read text books on 'labelling' theory in criminology, they could hardly have made more successful attempts at minimising rather than amplifying their deviance. Frances Farmer is the one exception to this, stressing as she does her radical politics and her flouting of the Hollywood system. Even she stresses how she achieved respectability in her last years, having rehabilitated herself from alcoholism and violent behaviour.

Cameron (1964) suggests that there are two types of delinquency: subcultural and peripheral. In the former there is support for deviance and reinforcement of delinquent values and behaviour; in the latter, deviance is isolated and incidental and receives no subcultural support and there is little recidivism. She applies these terms to shoplifting – 'the booster' is a commercial shoplifter, the 'snitch' a mere pilferer – and links them to social class. These categories can, I think also be applied to gender: on the whole crime is more peripheral to women's lives just as they are to crime. Similarly, delinquent subcultures, or at least, community support for deviance, tend to be both more public and more popular for males than females. The strong denials of their criminality by some women is probably, then, linked to 'appropriate' gender-role behaviour.

Cameron's observation of one shoplifter protesting innocence gives some indication as to why this should be so:

I didn't intend to take the dress. I just wanted to see it in daylight [she had stuffed it into a shopping bag and carried it out of the store]. Oh what will my husband do? I did intend to pay for it. It's all a mistake. O my God, what will my mother say! I'll be glad to pay for it. See, I've got the money with me. Oh my children! They can't find out I've been arrested! I'd never be able to face them again' (Cameron, 1964, p. 104).

Delinquent girls and delinquent subcultures

As we shall see in a later chapter, it was accepted wisdom for a long time that girls did not join gangs. Whereas boys joined street gangs and absorbed delinquent values while learning to perform delinquent acts, girls were at home and were definitely not participating. More recent researchers have challenged these assertions and we now have a number of accounts which present the voices of girl delinquents who give a different version.

Shacklady Smith found her respondents did belong to gangs, did get into fights and did have serious involvement in the subcultural world:

Well since I was about fourteen I was a member of the Skinheads and liked the sort of bother Skinheads made and I liked all the news they got ... we've got a bad name with everyone round here ... If anyone hit any one of us there would be war ... You've got to be a good fighter or you're not really one of the gang (Shacklady Smith, 1978, p. 85).

I reckon we fight as seriously as the boys. You know if anybody comes up to us we'll smack a bottle in their faces ... I always carry a knife or bog chain when I go down there (Shacklady Smith, 1978, p. 86).

Campbell's subjects emphasised their fighting spirit too:

I've been in lots of different fights cos've got a quick temper ... I threw my drink at her and messed her clothes up (Campbell, 1981, p. 174).

And the girls she interviewed were ready to attack boys:

The teacher went out of the class and I started fighting with this boy. So the teacher came in and he was sitting with his face burst open and blood all over his face (Campbell, 1981, p. 176).

Campbell points out, however:

that girls are more willing than boys to acknowledge the relative harmlessness of fighting. Machismo seems to be gained by girls merely by virtue of being *willing* to fight (Campbell, 1981, p. 179).

Welsh, in a study of 'The Kids', an East End teenage gang based in Bethnal Green, London, found that there were both boys and girls in the gang. In order to alleviate boredom, 'The Kids' committed minor delinquencies to attract police attention and manufacture excitement. In two main events mentioned by Welsh it is girls who take the lead (Welsh, 1981).

In her study of delinquent girls in a Northern city, in the UK, Wilson found that her subjects had even adopted and adapted that central mark of a successful subculture: a slum sex code. The girls classified both girls and boys by the code, although they disagreed with Whyte's typology of 'good girls' and 'lays' (Whyte, 1955). They defined boys as well, as:

1. untouchables
2. nice boys
3. boasters

and all wanted 'nice boys'. Wilson notes that it was the girls themselves who upheld and enforced the sex code:

The girls seemed unable to express sexuality without the presence of love ... seen as a natural ... precondition for marriage. *Any deviation by a girl ... resulted in a rejection by her peers* (Wilson, 1978, p. 71). [But see also Chapter 9.]

Girls in delinquent subcultures have been studied very little (see Chapter 7). Lack of serious evidence has not stopped various commentators from announcing the arrival of a new female criminal (see Chapter 8):

More and more angry young damsels have slowly made their debuts into organised deviance (Adler, 1975, p. 100).

Adler goes on to claim that 'female gangs have become a problem of major proportions for the British police who blame them for the substantial increase in the rate of muggings in London' (*sic*) (Adler, 1975, p. 100). But violent girls, extensively involved in delinquency are not a new phenomenon. In a study of seventy-seven delinquent girls I found considerable evidence of criminal connections and links to gangs.

'Jeanne' had convictions for robbery and assault:

I was in a gang. We went down the shops on Saturdays. Nicking things and that. I got put on probation and I went straight for a while. Me rich boyfriend kept me. He used to take me to smashing places, had a super car, we'd go to these posh pubs. He got into trouble with the police and went away. He's sending for me (Heidensohn, 1967).

Like Campbell I found that many of these girls, having had bad experiences with men, were contemptuous of them and envisaged a form of bachelor motherhood. Several in both groups were lesbian, some because they had formed such relationships in approved school or Borstal. The story of one of Campbell's subjects encapsulates the violence and cynicism of these girls:

That bloke that I'm in for. He picked me up at a bus stop and we went and he had a shop and at the time I was really bad on drugs and everything and I really needed money. Money, that's what I was thinking about. And he was really drunk at the time and this bloke, he'd said, 'do him' – you know what I mean? I got a monkey wrench and I bashed him over the head and this bloke turned round and said 'What are you trying to do?' So I hit him again a bit harder ... It was like a slaughter movie (Campbell, 1981, p. 185).

These girls, unlike the women whose accounts were discussed earlier, tended to accept their delinquent status but saw it, to some extent as damaging:

I'm too bad a girl for anyone to want ... you don't think when you're a kid ... you think no one will want you ... a bad record gives you a bad reputation (Heidensohn, 1967).

Hence, probably, the concern of several to achieve independence on their own or as single mothers. Most of them still assumed that marriage and having children were the appropriate goals for women even if they might not achieve them because their feminine identities had been 'spoiled'.

The search for the authentic voices of women and girls involved in crime is difficult. So often those voices have been silent or more concerned to demonstrate their lack of criminality than to illuminate their actions, although these attitudes are, of course, enormously revealing about the status of deviant women in our society and societal reaction to them. In the next section I want to look at several accounts by women who have had encounters with the criminal law among them some who have been imprisoned but who would not regard themselves as criminal. Their views provide some very interesting counterpoints to those we have looked at so far.

Women who defy man-made laws

Several very different groups of women have found themselves in conflict with what they have described as man-made laws. Since they have chosen, or found themselves forced into, defiance of the law, they have advertised their views on the law and often on the courts, the police, judges, prisons in a way that most ordinary criminal women have not. Most, of course, have been middle class and articulate but at least one important group is not. I shall deal with political protesters and organised prostitutes separately, but it is interesting to see to what extent they share a common feminist rhetoric and analysis.

Political protesters

In Britain in the early years of the century the Women's Social and Political Union ('the suffragettes') not only developed a strategy which used violence – breaking windows, setting pillar boxes alight, damaging paintings – but also produced a theoretical justification for their actions. The WSPU's motto was 'Deeds not Words'. Christabel Pankhurst clearly recognised the accepted standards of feminine behaviour of her day, and justified defiance of them:

> It is fight for [us] to be fierce as well as mild, to be strong as well as gentle ... [we] must be fierce and strong before [our] enemies and all who despitefully use them ... It is not right for women any more than for men, to have characters of tepid milk and water to be incapable of a divine rage and to be impotent to resist oppression (Pankhurst, 1913).

> A suffragist who becomes militant wins a new freedom and strength of spirit (Pankhurst, 1912). Men will ... admit other men's rights to rebel. It is only to women that they deny that right. That is to say women may not vote and they may not even fight for the vote (Pankhurst, 1913).

The history of the suffragettes' campaigns is very well known and recorded (Strachey, 1979). Their interest for us in this context lies in the way they used guerilla tactics and recognised that their actions were both crimes and challenges. Not surprisingly, the government of the day reacted to the challenges by trying to break the women with first, fairly repressive police responses and later the notorious 'Cat and Mouse' Acts, whereby the women were imprisoned, then having become weakened by hunger strikes and by the hideous process of forcible feeding were released only to be rearrested once their health had improved. The suffragettes were determined to expose the double standard:

> The Government use brute force to keep women in subjection. The anti-militant women bow down before brute force. The women in prison refuse to let brute force rule the world. They defy and by defying they are conquering it (Pankhurst, 1914).

Emmeline Pankhurst and Constance Lytton spoke out about conditions in Holloway and Lady Lytton's protests led to cells being made more comfortable (Smith, 1962, p. 144). But the suffragettes recognised their good fortune in life as compared with ordinary women prisoners, and this was epitomised in Mrs Pankhurst's plea from the dock for the 'poor wretches' she had seen in the Holloway hospital. However, what differentiated the suffragettes much more sharply and significantly from their criminal sisters was their resistance to criminalising. Although some were frequently sent to prison (Emmeline Pankhurst was sent to Holloway eight times) and vilified and abused in the Press and by public opinion, they fought back constantly and obviously embarrassed the politicians of the day to some extent. Emily Davidson died under the hooves of the King's horse. Constance Lytton's health was impaired by the hunger strikes, but on the whole, most of the militant suffragettes resumed their respectable bourgeois lives after the First World War.

Like Josephine Butler a generation earlier, WSPU members were trying to expose the paradoxes of 'dual morality'. They chose to attract public attention and demonstrate contradictions in justice and the law by criminal acts. They were the first group of women to do this in a collective and highly conscious fashion. As such, their histories deserve special consideration and raise further questions. Are women's crime and women's liberation inextricably linked? Are acting violently or aggressively role-breaking as well as rule-breaking, acts for women?

Since the fight for the suffrage, numbers of women have been prominently involved in political protests which have led to their conviction for offences such as obstruction or incitement and their commital to prison for refusing to pay fines or be bound over. Buxton and Turner described their months in Holloway in 1960 after CND and Committee of One Hundred anti-nuclear protests. Their 'straight' identities survived remarkably well in prison, despite the squalor and petty restrictions they describe, and, despite their sympathy for fellow prisoners, it is clear with whom they identified:

When we stopped at traffic lights people on the pavements stared in at us . . . slightly embarrassing at first to a normally law-abiding citizen. But we couldn't call out 'Ban the Bomb' or display our CND badges to show that we were not really criminals (Buxton and Turner, 1962, p. 2).

It seemed so funny that all I had done was take part in an extremely well-mannered demonstration against nuclear weapons; yet here I was under lock and key, in the custody of the

State and presumably in the company of many of the worst criminals in Britain (Buxton and Turner, 1962, p. 3).

Pat Arrowsmith has had numerous arrests and spells of imprisonment as a pacifist campaigner. She, like Buxton and Turner, has been able to express her feelings about imprisonment in writing: in poems, articles and a novel. She has also drawn and painted pictures of her experiences. In interviewing her, one is conscious of her considerable knowledge of the 'system' and her detailed recollection of all her sentences, complete with the campaigns she has waged against the authorities. In 'Somewhere Like This', she shows a variety of women prisoners: a bewildered mother, an unsociable, unstable girl, a sophisticated con artist. While she herself has been part of prison life, she has remained distinct from it, despite having 'loads of form'. None of the punishment has deterred her from her purposes:

For I don't believe that I shall change my mind after starting on a struggle of this sort or turn my head and look behind but go right on until the end (Arrowsmith, 1974).

The Greenham Common women protesting against the siting of US missiles in Britain, have produced very interesting accounts of their actions and they have, of course, been widely reported and represented on all the mass media. In their own words they show that they are putting into practice feminist theories and analyses of the world especially the world of male power exemplified in defence strategy and in the courts:

Women's action ... is so, women have been kept out of politics and all walks of life for so long, who've been pushed back into the home and been told that they can only function in one small closed-in area to do with children and nurturing ... can come out of those areas and take part in politics and actually begin to affect and change the world (Cook and Kirk, 1983, p. 80).

Women are treated badly by the courts ... not openly, but in all the male assumptions about how business in court should be conducted. It is so easy and comfortable for men to assume and exercise power and superiority over women, and given that courts are all to do with the legitimate exercise of power, women tend to come off very badly ... What did happen ... has changed all my feelings about courts. We took control of that environment away from the men, however briefly ... women did it by poems by singing and some cried while they spoke. Even policewomen were moved to tears. Every where there were flowers (Cook and Kirk, 1983, p. 118).

In one sense, the Greenham women are quite different from all the others quoted so far in this chapter. They live in a post-feminist world. They are well aware of the aspects of women's oppression which they are likely to find in the courts and of the notion of 'separate spheres' for men and women. None of their experiences with police, courts and magistrates are likely to be as surprising and bewildering to them as they were to earlier women for whom the ambiguous reaction of society to deviant women was only revealed at a very late stage.

Prostitutes organise

'One of the difficulties we had while the Departmental Committee was sitting was to get a first-hand account of the life and attitude of the prostitute herself.' Thus wrote Sir John Wolfenden, chairman of the committee whose report on homosexuality and prostitution bears his name. If autobiographical accounts by prostitutes were rare then, there have been a number since which deal explicitly with the operation of the law in relation to prostitution. The anonymous author of *Street Walker* described street prostitution just before the Street Offences Act was passed. She painted a picture of a drab, sordid, guilt- and violence-ridden life, in which she was overwhelmed by shame and tied helplessly to a cruel and abusive ponce. Despite this rather stereotyped view of the sorrows and terrors of a fallen woman the author had some very perceptive things to say about society's reactions to women like her:

It is part of the penalty we pay for our easy money that although we ask for no trial, we are tried and condemned without advocate or a chance to bear witness, by people schooled to spit on us in public while using us in private for their various ends. And this condemnation the hypocrisy of which we can hardly overlook, is perhaps the reason why we are, in the majority, so blatantly prostitutes in speech and dress, so actively on the defensive that we easily become offensive in street and café scenes; perhaps this is why we talk so loud, swear so hard and laugh so coarsely (Anon, 1959, p. 132).

By the time a Parliamentary sub-committee sought evidence on prostitution some two decades after Wolfenden, matters had changed a great deal. Not only did two prostitutes give evidence to the sub-committee, but three organisations also presented carefully argued memoranda to it, outlining their objections to the present legislation. Their analyses clearly draw on recent feminist views on women's rights:

The laws on prostitution ... clearly contradict the Sex Discrimination Act. The laws not only fail to protect prostitute women, but attack *prostitutes* not prostitution. In other words this crime is not that a woman gives her body but that she sells it for a specified time at a price many times higher than Woolworths pays by the hour. Women should have the right to control their own bodies (Expenditure Committee, 61–xiv, p. 288) (Original emphasis).

It is very clear that here we have campaigns by and on behalf of prostitutes to de-stigmatise their profession and de-criminalise the activities associated with it so that prostitutes can get on with their essentially ordinary, mundane lives. Helen Buckingham made an eloquent plea for the un-labelling of prostitutes that denies all the heavy past emphasis on the psychopathology of prostitutes and their perverse and deviant natures (e.g. Rolph, 1955).

Most prostitutes are not people with criminal intention; they are simply women looking for money. Women's jobs pay extremely badly ... The majority of prostitutes are perfectly normal women of very sound mind who are doing a very obvious and straight forward thing, they are going to look for money to keep their families (Expenditure Committee, 61–xiv, p. 298).

These claims follow similar moves by prostitutes in the USA and in France in recent years which have led to prostitutes organising themselves for rights and protection.

Eileen McLeod who has worked with Programme for the Reform of the Law on street offences. (PROS) gives a very interesting account of prostitutes' campaigns in the 1970s and 1980s to change the laws on prostitution and also to organise prostitutes in the community and gain public support for them (McLeod 1982, p. 122).

McLeod's study includes lengthy interviews with prostitutes and with some of their clients and she obviously had established exceptional rapport with the women whose responses are frank and thoughtful:

I do it purely for money ... I think once a prostitute always a prostitute. If one day you find out you're flat broke ... if you've been a prostitute you'll know where you can get the money from and you'll go back to it ... even if you only do the one client (McLeod, 1982, p. 26).

Inevitably, these prostitutes object to the present laws and the constraints and anomalies they impose on them.

The law gets me down. It says being a prostitute isn't illegal. They can even make you pay tax on it. But having said that 'OK you can be a prostitute', they then proceed to make it as difficult as possible for you. You can't advertise ... If you live with someone they can be done for living off your immoral earnings. If two of you share a house or flat it's a brothel (McLeod, 1982).

Groups of prostitutes are now working together both to provide self-help and support for their members and also to campaign for their rights, especially the right to work freely. They also seek – in what is to any criminologist a fascinating project – to increase public sympathy for their profession and to improve its image. Much of what they are about has to do with challenging stereotypes of female behaviour and women's role: a central and curious paradox for members of an ancient profession, generally supposed to be dedicated to the furtherance of the most basic of sexual stereotypes.

Some concluding thoughts

The views and interpretations of women involved in crime have rarely been given or sought. I have tried in this chapter to assemble a range of such contributions for readers to analyse and compare. This is in no sense a proper sample, but I think a few conclusions can be offered about the subjects of this chapter and women like them:

1. They all theorise, to some extent about crime and criminality: in other words they do not take it for granted as a usual activity as some males may do.
2. Several significant groups of women seek to object to the judicial, police or other processes in which they became involved.

Some seek *personal* de-criminalisation and rehabilitation, others have a more fundamental objection to man-made laws and courts as such. Perhaps because *men* made them? It is very interesting to see how, over the years, women have themselves mounted campaigns and projects directed towards changing assumptions about their roles and their work. We do not have a comprehensive picture of the past nor of today, but I hope that this selection of personal accounts will at least be interesting and lessen reliance on hunch and hearsay. Lady Vickers summed up very succinctly the alternatives for policy-maker and professional researcher:

> Lord Wolfenden told me that he could not get any prostitutes to give evidence so it was all done on hearsay ... This report was all done by officials and I gather that they did not have any contact with the actual people (Expenditure Committee, 61–xiv, p. 302).

3

Women and justice

In order to be defined as 'delinquent' or 'criminal' a girl or a woman has to have some interaction with the legal system. To become an 'official' criminal with a record is quite a complex process; at the very least it usually involves contact with the police, or other agencies, and the lower courts and lay magistrates. Probation officers may also become part of the process as may legal representatives, judges, juries and the higher courts. In this chapter I want to examine what is known about criminal justice and law enforcement as they affect women. These areas are unevenly researched and documented and for some topics material is very thin indeed. That, however, though serious, is not the most difficult task to be faced in interpreting these issues. The central problem is to determine the level at which evidence on women and justice should be analysed.

As we saw in Chapter 1 and as every sensible student of crime knows by now, criminal statistics are highly problematic data. No one, least of all the police who are involved in their compilation, trust them as 'true' records. Interpreting the law and its operation is subject to even more caveats: after all, the courts and the legal system are centuries old and are run in deeply traditional ways and these need to be taken into account if we are to understand their operation. Let me give two examples: the criminal law of England and Wales (with a few exceptions such as male homosexuality, rape, infanticide and street offences by prostitutes) does not differentiate between men and women today (Heidensohn, 1970). But this was no always so. English law used to recognise a defence of 'marital coercion' of wives by husbands in certain crimes. This was only repealed in 1925. A series of Laws, the infamous Contagious Diseases Acts of 1864, 1866 and 1869 were introduced to 'control' the spread of venereal disease amongst soldiers and sailors. Under these Acts, the police had wide powers to arrest women *suspected* of prostitution and to enforce medical examination and treatment. Failure to comply led to a prison sentence (Petrie, 1971). How far do these past, but perhaps not forgotten, laws affect the operation of laws today?

Smart has suggested that it is to the conceptions of women and girls found in the law that research on female criminality should turn (Smart, 1980). However, it is not so much the criminal law and the police as they affect women offenders which have been investigated, rather, it is the civil law with its impact on and definitions of family life, the role of women, proper child-care, etc. (see Smart, 1981; Wilson, 1977; Land, 1976) or the police as they treat women victims of crime (Dobash and Dobash, 1979; Toner, 1977).

In this chapter I shall try to analyse the law, the police and the courts as they are experienced by criminal women and delinquent girls on three levels:

1. the formal: what the law or the rules actually say;
2. the ideological: what values, beliefs and morals are held and/or expressed not only by all the 'agents of control' the police, judges, lawyers etc. but also by the women themselves;
3. the practice: what happens in daily practice, rather than ideological theory, within the system.

In doing this I shall consider some propositions which are widely asserted about women and the criminal justice system. These are:

1. the system is 'chivalrous' – women are especially protected from its full rigours and receive lesser punishments and lighter treatment;
2. the system is deeply sexist: it reinforces sexually stereotyped notions of role behaviour and specifically punishes women by its sanctions against sexually deviant women;
3. by attempting to 'protect' women from themselves or from the harshness of the law, courts can actually be more punitive to women through 'kindly coercion'.

The law

As I have already suggested, our criminal laws do not at a formal level discriminate very much between males and females. Only men can be convicted of rape (which requires penetration) although a woman may be an accomplice; only male homosexuality has ever been the subject of criminal sanctions. A female can be charged with an indecent assault on another female. Infanticide – in this country, legally defined as the killing of an infant by its mother while disturbed by the mental and physical upheaval of pregnancy and childbirth – is an offence with which only women can be charged. Only women can be cautioned under the Street Offences Act 1959 as 'common prostitutes' and charged with soliciting. With the exception of offences by prostitutes these are obviously trivial differences which can have no noticeable impact on recorded crime.

But this begs the key questions. Why are some activities covered by criminal law and others not? Some writers (notably Land, 1976; and Wilson, 1977) have argued that the state 'privatises' the control of women to the domestic sphere. (I explore this persepective more fully in Chapter 9). McIntosh has extended this argument in order to suggest that a particular type of 'chivalry' by benign neglect is inherent in the criminal law:

> The general pattern of non-interference and relative benevolence comes out most clearly in the exercise of the criminal law. Most laws apply to men and women alike – yet far more men are convicted of crimes than women ... the differences are so gross that there can be no doubt that the main reason is that *there are more laws against the kinds of thing that men and boys do than against the kind of thing that women and girls do* (McIntosh, 1978, p. 257, emphasis added).

She goes on to argue that the 'policing' of deviant women is undertaken by non-criminalising agencies and in other settings. It is impossible to prove or disprove McIntosh's assertion. We can, however, look at the law to see just how much of a 'man's world' it is and if this perhaps shapes its attitudes to women and crime.

It can be argued that laws are made by and for men. The

overwhelming majority of legislators are men, as are the over-whelming majority of ministers and indeed as are all the Permanent Secretaries in Britain who head government departments. In 1982 13.9 per cent of solicitors and 10.8 per cent of barristers were women. Three (of seventy-seven) High Court judges are women and ten (of 339) circuit judges. No Law Lord is a Lady so far although there is a woman Supreme Court judge. But of course it is more complicated than these figures suggest. Women are not excluded from the provisions of criminal laws even if they are to a large extent excluded from framing those laws. It can, however, be argued that it is largely men, and middle-aged and elderly upper-class men at that, who set the agenda of law-making as well as administering it. We have really very little evidence about that agenda setting. What we can examine are two sources: first, those few examples of the debates about the coverage of criminal law and second, the attitudes of lawyers and law-makers to women and to men in relation to criminal law as expressed in a variety of public contexts.

Most debates about the range of behaviour covered by the law have perhaps inevitably focussed on sexual activities. In the nineteenth century the Contagious Diseases Acts were initially passed with little comment, but were later the subject of twenty years of sustained campaigning by Josephine Butler and the Ladies National Association. Butler was quite clear from the outset what was at stake as her Declaration of Policy shows:

> The Law, in safeguarding individual liberty outside the home had not, hitherto, discriminated between men and women. The Acts, however, constituted just such a discrimination (Butler quoted in Petrie, 1971, p. 93).

She was also convinced that she knew the reasons why a double-standard which penalised women but not men for the same act was being legally enforced:

> The real reason why men are not treated in the same way as women is that Parliament would not endure that men should be put in prison for solicitation on such slight evidence before a summary court as is the case with women; for the men of the upper classes would be laid hold of by the Bill and it *would be a*

terrible thing indeed to the hearts of our present legislators to think that one of themselves or their sons might be touched (Butler quoted in Petrie, 1971, pp. 122–3, emphasis added).

The response of the Royal Commission on the Contagious Diseases Acts confirmed her fears precisely:

We may at once dispose of [any recommendation] founded on the principle of putting both parties to the sin of fornication on the same footing by the obvious but not less conclusive reply that there is no comparison to be made between prostitutes and the men who consort with them. With the one sex the offence is committed as a matter of gain; with the other it is an irregular indulgence of a natural impulse (cited in Thomas, 1959).

There were attempts at about this time (in 1883 and again in 1885), supported by Lord Shaftesbury which would 'render men as well as women liable to punishment for loitering for immoral purposes'. But they were defeated, and Lord Dalhousie expressed a fear of unfair stigmatisation for men which was to be echoed by the Wolfenden Committee seventy-five years later:

It would enable any woman of bad character to bring charges for the purpose of extortion against male passers-by (Wolfenden, 1957).

The Wolfenden Committee were concerned to get rid of 'the visible and obvious presence of prostitutes in the public streets'. By this they only appear to have meant women. They did discuss the nuisance of kerb-crawling but only to echo Victorian concerns with a twentieth-century slant. No new offence should be created because:

The difficulties of proof would be considerable, and the possibility of a very damaging charge being levelled at an innocent motorist must also be borne in mind (Wolfenden, 1957, p. 267).

In very recent times, however, attitudes have begun to change. The Criminal Law Revision Committee produced a Green Paper in 1982 which proposed to make it illegal for a man to accost a woman from a car for sexual purposes so as to put her in fear, or cause her annoyance, or for prostitution. Meanwhile, police in Britain do seem to be responding, albeit in a haphazard way, to local pressures to control kerb-crawling, by charging men either under the Justice of Peace Act 1361, or the 1839 Metropolitan Police Act. Clearly, in this long-drawn-out history, while it is primarily the activities of women which have been the subject of legal sanction it has not been impossible to include men under legal control, although there has been enormous resistance to criminalising them in this way.

With homosexual behaviour, however, the opposite has been true. While the Criminal Law Amendment Act of 1885 made even acts between consenting adult males an offence, such acts between women have never been an offence. A popular legend that has it that Queen Victoria could not bring herself to believe in the possibility of lesbianism and that it was therefore excluded is probably just myth (Pearsall, 1969, p. 576). But her alleged views were certainly held by others in positions of influence in law making:

> In 1913 an MP tried to bring the existence of sexual activity between females to the attention of the House. The Home Secretary refused to consider any amendment incorporating sexual acts between women and so turned down the proposal even before it appeared on the order Paper (Edwards, 1981, pp. 43–4).

An amending bill was defeated in the House of Lords in 1920 and Lord Desart summed up prevailing opinion:

> I am sure that a prosecution would really be a very great public danger. Is there any necessity for it? How many people does one suppose really are so vile, so unbalanced, so neurotic, so decadent as to do this? You may say there are a number of them – but an extremely small minority – and you are going to tell the whole world that there is such an offence, to bring it to the notice of women who have never heard of it, never thought of it, never dreamed of it (quoted in Hyde, 1972, p. 204).

As a result and after considerable debate and delay of the Wolfenden Committee Report, sexual relationships between consenting adult males in private were decriminalised; this of course was a much narrower proscription than for females. So in these instances, judgement of the scope of the law in regard to male and female actions is unclear. It is difficult for example, to sustain in relation to Edward's argument to prostitution that 'passive female sexuality' seemed to be the norm 'to the nineteenth-century mind' (1981, p. 23). On the contrary it was *men* who were perceived to be the helpless victims both of their own carnal (but natural) lusts when tempted by whores and then of the diseases which the women allegedly transmitted to them. It does seem possible to suggest, however, that certain differing assumptions about the roles of men and women underlie the law even if, when laws are framed, their impact is more complex.

Both Smart and Edwards have, for instance, pointed out that the British 1956 Sexual Offences Act is 'little more than a legal representation of actual sexual politics' (Smart, 1981, p. 55) with the whole emphasis of the Act on women as victims who are vulnerable and in need of protection and men as perpetrators, requiring control. Yet, as Smart points out:

a major consequence has been the growing legal as opposed to moral, concern over the sexuality of young women. Persistent promiscuity or public prostitution even though the female subject is defined as the victim, invariably leads to some form of restriction or incarceration for young women (Smart, 1981, p. 56).

Her summing-up can very usefully stand for an overview of this very complex topic:

Feminists have long been aware that legislation at the Parliamentary level does not necessarily produce expected results in court or elsewhere. The practice of law can therefore be more subtle and obscure than an initial reading of statutory legislation would imply (Smart, 1981, p. 58).

A cynic might sometimes be tempted to think that certain British judges were competing for entry into a dictionary of eccentric quotations. But she/he would certainly be wrong. When judges and magistrates do animadvert on sex differences, sex-role-appropriate demeanour and dress they are obviously sincere in believing themselves to be expressing genuine public opinions and influencing consensual views on these topics. Sachs and Wilson have extensively analysed the role of the judiciary in the nineteenth century in defining women as 'non-persons' in such civil issues as standing for local councils and obtaining access to the legal and medical professions (1978). It is in fact in civil proceedings as well as in cases in which women are the victims of criminal offences, that some of the most publicised judicial statements on sex roles have been made:

> It would be very wrong to my mind, if the statute were thought to obliterate the differences between men and women or to do away with chivalry and courtesy which we expect mankind to give to womankind.

This statement, by Lord Denning (as master of the Rolls in the Court of Appeal in Peake *v* Automotive Products Ltd) is perhaps the most complete modern expression of the view that the law should rightly and appropriately both differentiate between men and women and treat women protectively. In practice Lord Denning did try to use family law in a chivalrous manner:

> Denning and the Court of Appeal stretched statutory enactments to provide some protection for wives. His generous interpretations of the law which recognised the plight of a number of wives were eventually overruled by the House of Lords in 1965. The Court of Appeal was therefore acting in an independent fashion (Smart, 1980, p. 29).

Some writers (for example, Scutt, 1981; Chesney-Lind, 1980) have identified a crude sexist conspiracy in both the 'protective' attitudes expressed by some judges and lawyers as well as the discriminatory effect of some law. They argue that civil and criminal laws and lawyers combine to reinforce a stereotypical notion of what a 'proper' woman is and does: that she should be chaste and demure, a good mother and not primarily a worker:

> Our laws are administered by predominantly white, middle-class, middle-aged males who, in their professional lives, often express stereotype notions about women and show little understanding of the nature of women's lives (Patullo, 1983, p. 37).

There is undoubtedly a good deal of truth in this but it is not the whole truth.

Conspiracy theories are far too simple. It is, in any case, impossible to define a consistent set of masculine interests served by such stereotyping. It also becomes impossible, since this argument is largely a functionalist one, to explain legal changes. Thus Sachs and Wilson (1978) suggest that the common basis for the judiciary's 'suppression' of women's rights in the nineteenth century was the need to keep in their places a class of domestic servants who would not compete in the market-place. But this does not explain why changes did then occur in women's legal rights (Smart, 1980, p. 10). We could go on to suggest that shifts in the labour market, brought about by war and perhaps demography were influential, but we do have to explain the decline in patriarchal hegemony, or else show that it had shifted elsewhere.

It is possible to find examples both of sheer sexist prejudice against women embodied in the law – the laws on prostitution are probably the best example – and also of forms of 'protection' which have benefitted women even while stereotyping their behaviour – the assumptions that render female homsexuality innocuous and sexual aggression of women against men improbable. As we shall see in looking at the courts, it is also possible to find examples of 'protectiveness' which leads to excessive punishment. Women's position under criminal law is theoretically equal. In practice, one cannot divorce law and lawyers from the society in which they operate with its enormous cultural heritage and traditions. All the early feminists believed passionately in removing legal inequities, as a goal in itself and as a way to political power. In J. S. Mill's words:

> The legal subordination of one sex to the other – is wrong in itself, and now one of the chief hinderances to human improvement; ... it ought to be replaced by a principle of perfect equality, admitting no power or privilege on the one side, nor disability on the other (Mill, 1929, p. 220).

'Perfect equality' is still far away, not only for women, but for many other social groups. Our criminal law seems to operate at best on a series of dual assumptions about women some of which are sometimes lamentably confused: virgin and whore, witch and wife, Madonna and Magdalene. However women are defined in law, it is still of course mainly men who do the defining.

The courts

Courts tend to present a 'dramatisation of deviance'. In the English adversarial system that tendency is heightened. Many accounts of famous trials, and the daily fare of newspapers illustrate the amount of drama, comic and tragic, which can be culled from courtroom scenes. (In reality of course, many criminal trials are long and boring, taken up with tedious technical evidence or sordid and sickening details.) But the courts do provide dramatic material other than to satisfy curiosity and emotion; from the study of their procedures, the way in which cases are handled, defendants convicted and sentenced, we can learn a good deal, not least about the ways in which women experience criminal justice in them. Fortunately, court proceedings are in public and are a matter of record; there are a number of studies which make use of surveys of court cases, as well as some interviews and observation-based accounts. How then do women and girls experience the administration of justice in the courts and how are they treated by them?

Several accounts suggest that women find courts particularly bewildering, alien and unfair:

A large proportion of the girls did not understand what was happening during the proceedings; they were not clear who the people were in court, some could not understand the language and some did not understand the court's decision. Many girls, for example, mentioned that they had thought that the clerk of the court was presiding and had initially addressed their remarks to him rather than to the magistrates. Likewise the girls were rarely able to distinguish between costs, compensation and fines and viewed them all as 'punishments'. Most girls were also confused by the rules of court procedure regarding, for example, when they should speak and when they should sit down or stand up (Davies, 1975, p. 50).

And Dell, whose study might well be retitled 'Bewildered Afraid and Silent in Court' gives these accounts of women who had been committed to Holloway Prison although they had not been legally represented in court:

One remanded girl, when asked by the interviewer whether she had asked for bail in court, replied 'What is bail? Is it the same as legal aid?' . . . one girl put it, 'I kept being told to get up and sit down'. It is not easy in such circumstances to do justice to one's own defence . . . Frequently the women said that they had not been able to catch what was being said. One woman described her feelings when she was invited to speak in court and failed to respond, much as she wished to: 'I was too overawed and frightened . . . I didn't want to make a fool of myself – I would only have cried' (Dell, 1971, pp. 17–19).

It can, of course, be argued that court appearances are designed to degrade and humiliate the defendant (Carlen, 1976) whether female or male. There are grounds however for believing that the experience can be more traumatic for women and girls. Females are more likely than males to be first offenders and thus literally inexperienced in court affairs. Parker and his colleagues, in one of the few studies comparing male and female juvenile offenders before the courts noted a number of differences in their reactions and perceptions. Girls experienced much lengthier delays than boys in being charged and this added to their sense of injustice and confusion (Parker *et al.*, 1981, p. 100). More of the girls, too, although their 'offences were more trivial' were persuaded to plead guilty by their solicitors against their own inclinations and in consequence bore a feeling of unfairness (Parker *et al.*, 1981, p. 104):

Moreover passivity may be expected from girl defendants viewed as appropriate behaviour and even encouraged by some court workers . . . Girls may find it doubly difficult to break through this ascribed passivity and speak out in the juvenile court, the more so *since a shame at being on view* and weighed up in the eyes of unknown others featured in these girls' reflections on their juvenile court hearing (Parker *et al.*, 1981, p. 106).

In contrast, while many of the boys found the court personnel and atmosphere 'sympathetic':

These boys' feelings were not echoed by the . . . girls we talked with. Rather, for girls the overall impression, it seems was one of feeling 'scared' and 'frightened' and . . . few seemed to take in what was being said in court because their minds ran on fatalistically to their chances of being 'put away' (Parker *et al.*, 1981, p. 108).

Not only did these girls experience and perceive the juvenile court in a different way, they were expected and advised by their solicitors to play a different role from boys:

> Girls, in particular, tended to remember their solicitor advised mute passivity . . . whereas one or two boys say they were encouraged to assert themselves (Parker *et al.*, 1981, p. 111).

The juvenile court, with social workers and education officers present is rather less likely than a magistrates' court to be a predominantly male environment which some women find particularly intimidating:

> Women are treated badly by the courts – not openly, but in all the male assumptions about how business in court should be conducted (Cook and Kirk, 1983, p. 117).

Carlen, in her study of incarcerated women offenders in Scotland noted their feelings of injustice and exclusion. The women in Cornton Vale prison felt that their legal representation had been poorly prepared, their chances of acquittal very poor because the courts were biased towards the police. But most of all 'what had embittered them was their exclusion from the judicial process' (Carlen, 1983, p. 129). Several of these prisoners felt especially anxious because the judges and lawyers seemed neither to appreciate that they had children, nor to consider who would care for the children if the mother were imprisoned. Some female defendants certainly find their court appearances especially humiliating and oppressive; there is evidence that the trauma can be greater for them than for males although, ironically, their offences tend to be less serious and repeated less frequently. But how do the courts react to women offenders? Is there evidence of sexism or of chivalry?

There are two major themes to be drawn out in this discussion which polarise it to some extent at opposite points. The first is summed up by Mannheim:

It can, of course, be taken for granted that the female offender – if punished – meets on the whole with greater leniency on the part of the courts than the male. Speaking generally, the percentage of women decreases in conformity with the severity of the particular method of penal treatment (Mannheim, 1940, p. 343).

Courts, in short, are especially kind and indulgent to women. On the other hand there is the view that, especially in regard to young women and to sexually deviant women, the courts are actually harsher:

> The reason why girls appear to be penalized, then, is associated with society's concern with female sexual behaviour (Campbell, 1981, p. 207).

> My observations suggest that our juvenile court functions as a management tool, equipped to correct and survey female behaviour which ... flaunts normative expectations by challenging family authority and threatening truancy and sexual promiscuity (Casburn, 1979, p. 21).

On the former theme, there is a certain amount of material, on the latter a welter of studies, many of them American.

It must be stressed that consistency in sentencing, logically perhaps a key attribute of justice, does not in practice prevail, whatever the sex of the defendant. Hood's study of sentencing in magistrates courts is actually subtitled 'A study in *variations* of policy' (Hood, 1962) while Baldwin and McConville have documented the vagaries of juries' decisions (Baldwin and McConville, 1980).

Several American studies suggest some support for the 'chivalry' hypothesis for adult women. Kalven and Zeisel in their study of juries found that, if the defendant was a woman, this made a difference to the jury's decision. It seems clear, however, in this study, that what counted was whether or not the defendant was a normal, conventional woman since her femaleness could not be separated from her femininity. It was impossible:

> To isolate the circumstances that the defendant is a woman from the circumstances that she can also be a widow, a mother,

attractive, or may cry on the stand (Kalven and Zeisel, 1966, p. 201).

In a series of papers, Nagel and her colleagues in both empirical studies and reviews of the literature have found that there was a small but discernible 'sex effect'. 'Generally, female defendants fare better than males' (Nagel *et al.*, 1980, p. i). This applied particularly to sentencing where women were less likely to receive more severe sentences or to be sent to prison. However, Nagel and her colleagues did find:

> Females whose offence pattern is more consistent with sex role expectations seem to experience less harsh outcomes than females whose offence pattern is less traditional (Nagel *et al.*, 1980, p. 20).

This finding is supported by Pearson's work on three British magistrates' courts in which she discovered that single mothers were more likely than other categories of female offenders to be remanded for psychiatric reports even though their crimes were mainly trivial thefts and forgeries (Pearson, 1976).

A British study of Cambridge City magistrates' court does not, however, provide support for the 'chivalry' hypothesis. In a very carefully controlled empirical study, Farrington and Morris found that 36.9 per cent of their sample of men but only 15.7 per cent of their sample of women received severe sentences. Yet when they controlled for variables such as seriousness of offence and previous convictions, the differences disappeared:

> The sex of the defendant did not have any direct influence on the severity of the sentence . . . women appear to receive more lenient sentences and to have a lower likelihood of reconviction only because they had committed less serious offences and were less likely to have been convicted previously . . . we could not detect any leniency towards women (Farrington and Morris, 1983, pp. 245–6).

At the same time the 'evil' or deviant woman theory received some support from this study:

Women who were in the 'other' category on marital status (predominantly divorced or separated rather than widowed) received relatively severe sentences, as did women from a deviant family background (coming from a broken home usually). *It could be that the magistrates disapproved of these categories of women offenders* (Farrington and Morris, 1983, p. 245, emphasis added).

It is likely that the offence-related factors which Farrington and Morris found explained the apparent differences in sentencing of men and women, also explained the 'leniency' towards women cited by Gibbens and Prince (1962). A rather different aspect of the chivalry – leniency question was discussed by Thomas in his study of decisions in the Court of Appeal (which sees few cases, but whose decisions frame sentencing policies for the lower courts). Thomas suggests that while the effects of imprisonment on a man's family is not an appropriate plea in mitigation, it can be so for a woman 'for the sake of the children' (Thomas, 1970, p. 190). He further suggests that, to some extent the ancient doctrine of marital coercion may still be acceptable to the Appeal Court, with some women getting lighter sentences because they were dominated by their male partners in crime (Thomas, 1970, p. 65).

There are virtually no systematic studies based on views which JPs or judges hold of women offenders. Carlen's study in which she interviewed fifteen Scottish sheriffs is therefore particularly important for the insights it gives into the multi-layered images of deviant women which these men held and tried to work with. [She has already stressed the profoundly mysogynistic nature of Scottish society with its emphasis on male drinking and violence (Carlen, 1983, Ch. 2)]. All her subjects 'claimed that they particularly hated sending a woman (to prison)' (Carlen, 1983, p. 60).

However, when faced with women in the dock who were not financially competent and most were not, since they depended on the tempers and whims of their husbands, the sheriffs could end up imprisoning them *faute de mieux:* 'Women normally can't pay a fine ... and if the offence is serious enough for a large fine then they have to go to prison if they can't pay' (Carlen, 1983, p. 66).

Several sheriffs subscribed to the view that women were more 'mad than bad', but when pressed by Carlen on this issue proffered explanations 'more related to social than psychological factors' (Carlen, 1983, p. 65). Carlen observed the considerable degree of 'embarrassment' in the 'sheriffs' feelings when a woman appears in court as accused' (Carlen, 1983, p. 65). They seemed to feel uneasy first because they knew that the women were being dealt with in a highly inappropriate penal tariff system to which they could not respond and second because of the women's role as mothers. The conflict was resolved by the sheriffs differentiating between 'good' and 'bad' mothers:

A high proportion of the women who eventually are [imprisoned] ... are those who in the eyes of the sheriffs have failed as mothers (Carlen, 1983, p. 66).

The sheriffs then redefine Cornton Vale (the prison to which the women are sent, which is in fact a closed prison) with all the appropriate paraphernalia of security and discipline, as a comfortable place, suitable for a spot of kindly paternal discipline (Carlen, 1983, p. 69). Carlen suggests that this is because the sheriffs have isolated and reinforced their image of the bad women/wife/mother from their knowledge of the awful social and economic conditions in which these women live.

The notion that protectiveness can lead to punishment has been emphasised by other writers. Dell noted that many of the women in her sample appeared to have been remanded into custody for medical reports, arising from concern about their mental or physical states (Dell, 1971, p. 18). Yet the custodial remand clearly was, and was perceived to be, a punishment. Of even more concern were a few cases which raised issues of civil liberties because women were imprisoned 'for their own good'. 'The courts and doctors were acting in what they believed to be the best interests of the women's health' (Dell, 1971, p. 30). Dr Bull, a former governor of Holloway Prison, commented on these benign remands with punitive effect to the Expenditure Committee and noted that many women, remanded in custody for reports were not in fact later sentenced to terms of imprisonment.

Contentions about the excessive harshness of the courts to women offenders really have two aspects. On the one hand there is the 'doubly deviant' argument; women offenders are such relatively rare phenomena not just in terms of their recorded crime rates, which are low and relate to trivial offences, but especially because of their rarity in court, more of them are likely to be cautioned for their offences. Women defendants therefore seem stranger and thus less comprehensible than men: they offend both against society's behavioural rules about property, drinking, or violence and also against the more fundamental norms which govern sex-role behaviour (Heidensohn, 1970, p. 134). Parker and his colleagues, for example found not only the instances of shame and embarrassment amongst girls in the juvenile court already noted, but also that they and their parents were more reluctant to participate in the study than boys because they already felt excessively stigmatised and wished to put it all behind them (Parker *et al.*, 1981, p. 11). The tendency to 'deviancy disavowal' amongst women involved in crime was observed in Chapter 2. Casburn found magistrates in the London borough which she studied well aware of this problem with the result that:

> On the whole, the three magistrates took longer to dispense with the girls before them, commonly sanctioning lengthy *adjournments or remands in care,* the latter ostensibly to obtain psychiatrists' and psychologists' reports (Casburn 1979, p. 13, emphasis added).

Obviously the magistrates were trying to take more care with the girls before them whom they saw as doubly problematic. The result was to 'label' the girls more effectively as deviant, even when they were not actually 'delinquent' at all but before the court for truancy or 'at risk' sexually (Casburn, 1979, p. 14). Boys, on the other hand, were treated both more cavalierly and (sometimes) more leniently:

> The differentiation between the sexes is scaled to protect girls from themselves, but it allows boys to be boys (Casburn, 1979, p. 21).

The second aspect of the supposed harshness of the courts to women, and to young girls especially relates to the way in which deviant sexuality and deviant sex roles are punished by the courts. There are several components of the argument, not all of which are common to everyone who has written on it. Four fairly central assertions are:

1. the courts operate a 'double standard' with respect to sexual behaviour, controlling and punishing girls, but not boys, for premature and for promiscuous sexual activities;
2. the courts – and probation officers and social workers – 'sexualise' normal female delinquency and thus over-dramatise the offence and the risk;
3. 'wayward' girls can come into care and thence into stigmatising institutions without ever having committed an actual offence;
4. deviant women who deviate *as women*, that is, women who do not conform to accepted standards of monogamous, heterosexual stability with children are over-represented amongst women in prison because the courts are excessively punitive to them.

Evidence, most of it from North America, lends support to the first proposition. Terry (1970) found that girls were treated more severely than boys in the juvenile court and were far more likely to be institutionalised. This seemed to be because courts were shocked both at seeing girls before them and by the fact that they were referred there for incorrigibility and sexual misdemeanours. Chesney-Lind (1973) studied a Honolulu juvenile court and also found that sexual misbehaviour by girls was seen as morally outrageous and therefore dealt with more punitively. Chesney-Lind goes on to develop the concept described in the second proposition, namely that courts accept or redefine female deviance in such a way as to sexualise it. Non-criminal, non-statutory status offences are 'created' such as 'waywardness' or 'in need of protection'. Once again, Chesney-Lind found that this led to punitive pretrial remands. Shelden (1981) described a similar pattern in Tennessee in the early part of this century:

> The juvenile justice system in Memphis reinforced the sexual double standard punished behaviour that violated sex role expectations and supported the myth of male superiority and female subordination (e.g. by charging females with 'immorality' but ignoring similar or identical behaviour committed by males) (Shelden, 1981, p. 70).

Like Chesney-Lind, Shelden noted the widespread use of medical examinations of girls through which 'young women were given the message that their bodies were not their own' to do with as they chose. Biron, in her investigation in Montreal, also found a similar pattern: 'the girls residing in institutions are still supposedly there for their own protection' (Biron, 1981, p. 14). There were as many girls as boys in the Montreal institutions, despite the girls' less frequent and less serious offending pattern. Biron also noticed the 'redefinition' problem cited by Chesney-Lind:

> Official agencies redefined and interpret girls' behaviour in such a way that they are perceived as being in need of protection rather than as delinquent (Biron, 1981, p. 14).

But do these findings hold true in other parts of the world? In the State of Victoria, Australia, Hiller and Hancock certainly found that:

> The protectionist stance adopted by children's court reformers and unequal implementation of vague juvenile – morals statutes has led to more frequent intervention of the state into the lives of females whose behaviour has contravened moral rather than criminal rules (Hiller and Hancock, 1981, p. 121).

Davies' study of girls appearing before Greenwich juvenile court in London was not comparative, nor did she explore the sexualisation hypothesis, but examination of the tables in her study show that thirty (out of fifty-five) girls were 'non-offenders' and far more of these (seventeen as against four 'offenders') were remanded in custody for reports. In May's Aberdeen study (1977) of the very few girls before the courts for 'status' offences, more than half were put under supervision or institutionalised. Shacklady Smith's work is very interesting in this context in that she too found a high proportion (58.8 per cent) committed to approved schools were in need of 'care, protection and control' and not delinquent offenders (Shacklady Smith, 1978, p. 80). She also observed a tendency for probation officers to 'sexualize' and reinterpret the 'normal' delinquencies of their female clients and she found that the girls themselves suffered from the double standard of morality (although this made them defiant rather than submissive) (Shacklady Smith, 1978, p. 84). Campbell found the evidence conclusive 'with juveniles at least, a clear discrimination can be seen' (Campbell, 1981, p. 206), and Webb (1984), reported one of the first comparative British surveys on a national level and concluded:

> The data here shows that girls recommended for, and subject to, supervision orders include a higher proportion of offenders committing trivial offences and with no criminal history behind them (Webb, 1984, p. 18).

There is no direct evidence here of sexualisation, rather it is the 'tutelary complex' – the need to intervene more closely in the lives of girls than boys – that is at work.

On the third proposition listed above, that wayward girls can slip through a series of agencies and end up in prision or other form of custody, there is less direct evidence. Chesney-Lind suggests that this occurs in the USA (1977), but as we have seen from several other reports of research, many girls adjudged in need of protection by courts in fact have delinquent pasts which this approach masks (Cowie *et al.*, 1965). However, there have been examples of whom 'Millie' in Parker's *Five Women* (1965, pp. 171–89) was one, of girls who, through constant running away from children's homes or from relatives, have found themselves in custody without ever being an official delinquent.

As to women and girls who are harshly punished it does seem that failure to comply with conventional feminine stereotypes may lead to greater chances of imprisonment. Carlen's sheriffs stressed 'If she's a good mother, we don't want to take her away. If she's not a good mother it doesn't really matter' (Carlen, 1983, p. 67), while Morris and Farrington report a similar direct effect on sentencing policy. Simon (1975) and Chesney-Lind (1980) have suggested that women are now being more generally harshly treated by the law and the courts, because of the myth of the new female criminal which has provoked an over-reactive response from the courts. In the sentencing of women who have beaten or injured their children one can see judges actually having to juggle with the two distinct and apparently contradictory images of women: as vicious assailant and loving mother. Thus the Recorder at Leicester Crown Court 'felt too angry to sentence a baby-battering mother yesterday' (*Guardian*, 4 February 1978). Next day he gave the woman a suspended sentence remarking 'The only reason you are not going to prison is because I don't want to deprive the other child of its mother's love (*Daily Mail*, 5 February 1978). Or again from Stafford, under the headline:

Judge frees 'inhuman' mum

A mother who flogged her eight-year old son with a belt, gave him cold baths and forced him to stand naked for hours at night, was called 'inhuman' by a judge yesterday. But the mother Maureen B--- was saved from prison because she has another child to care for (*Daily Mirror*, 24 January 1978).

Two apparently benevolent aspects of sentencing policy can have a harsh impact on women. The individualisation approach, which tends to locate the causes of crime within each offender and then 'treat' them or 'cure' them for their own good, seem more likely to be applied to women than men. This is because women are deemed to be twice deviant, having flouted two sets of social rules, and thus peculiarly suitable and susceptible to such approaches. The concept of proper feminity is in any case fairly narrowly-defined in our society, especially for working-class women and once it has been breached, even though that may be the solution to her problems, a woman may find herself subject to what Carlen has called the 'snowballing effects' of increasing sanctions (Carlen, 1983, p. 70).

Second, for teenage girls, some of the problems lie in the enormous complexities of the justice versus welfare debate being fought over the care of juveniles. With a 'welfare' approach generally dominant, girls are more likely to be dealt with under this mode and to have more of their private lives invaded. But while sentencing philosophies and their unintended impact underpin some of what happens to women in the courts, there is also documentation of some repressiveness and a very little for the concept of a gallant, legal chivalry.

The police

A much more fragmentary picture of women's experiences with the police emerges than for the other two areas presented in this chapter. Encounters between police and public are largely informal and unscripted. Where formal accounts are rendered, they are generally given in court-rooms as evidence, often long after the event. We have some accounts from women themselves, a series of comparative surveys of police cautioning of male and female juveniles as well as the evidence of attitudes and procedures given to the Expenditure Sub-committee. In order to explore further police attitudes to women, I have drawn as several others have done on various studies of women as victims. In cases of rape and of domestic violence, police views about women, about their behaviour, morals and roles are made explicit. It is of course, impossible to prove that the *same* attitudes will inform police behaviour towards women as victims as well as women as criminals, but it can be argued that they are suggestive of a particular and significant view of the world.

As far as teenage girls are concerned, the pattern of shame and double rejection with regard to delinquency starts with their anger and confusion at the role of the police. 'Most girls . . . were perturbed by the extent to which the police themselves can apparently bend procedural rules . . . (they felt) . . . picked on and picked out'. While the boys seemed to accept police behaviour with resignation:

> For the girls on the other hand rough police treatment seemed more frightening, an altogether less expected and accepted experience (Parker *et al.*, p. 98).

In Campbell's sample of girls although many had been involved in fights only 6 per cent had known the police to be brought in and, far from seeing the police as the safe embodiment of law and order 'The girls believed that minor personal disputes that erupted in fights were none of the police's business' (Campbell, 1981, p. 151).

Of adult women involved with the police, prostitutes who ply the streets come most into contact with them. McLeod found that her informants, despite many allegations to the contrary, did not report much police corruption in relation to prostitution (McLeod, 1982, p. 105), but they did report some degree of harassment and entrapment. On the whole, however, there was mutual accommodation: 'You treat them [the police] right and they treat you right' (McLeod, 1982, p. 106). Street prostitutes are probably very unusual in being a group of women who have regular, if unwanted contact with the police in their policing role. Prostitutes themselves appear cynical and resigned [though Mrs Payne is a supporter and claims them among her clients (Bailey, 1983)]. One can only guess at the reverse effect on the police themselves.

More sheltered women unused to the police in their policing role can feel:

> Very frightened and horrified that we were going to travel all that distance in such a confined space, locked in, with our hands handcuffed like that. All of a sudden I realized how barbaric it was and that I didn't have to do it . . . They kept telling me not to argue. I thought that sooner or later I'd have to give in to their authority, but then *I thought, just because they're police in uniforms I don't have to do it* (Cook and Kirk, 1983, pp. 57–8, emphasis added).

In Dell's group of 'inconsistent pleaders' – women who pleaded guilty in court, but denied their guilt, 'police persuasion was cited in a third of the cases as a key factor' (Dell, 1971, p. 36). She was cautious about her respondents' views, but noted that this was a considerable problem. All we can say with certainty at this stage is that prostitutes are the only group of women likely to have regular contact with the police in their policing role and that this is a very fraught situation, given that an officer can caution a prostitute for soliciting and begin the process which leads to her stigmatisation.

On the police cautioning of juveniles there have been a plethora of empirical studies which do not tell us anything very exciting about the importance of sex as a variable in the police use of discretion in cautioning decisions. A much higher proportion of girls than boys are cautioned:

> Since 1976 . . . consistently around 45 per cent of boys and 70 per cent of girls dealt with for indictable . . . offences have been cautioned. The proportion of younger boys (ten to fourteen) has been consistently around 63 per cent compared with 33 per cent of older boys (fourteen to seventeen) with comparable proportions for girls being 83 to 56 per cent (Mott, 1983, p. 249).

It does not seem to be the case that sex plays a part here. Two studies by Landau and Nathan (1981 and 1983) showed that:

The juvenile's sex has no effect on police decision in either of the two stages in which they are involved with juveniles in the Metropolitan area (Landau and Nathan 1983, p. 139).

The factors which were influential in police decision-making in Landau and Nathan were 'legal' variables such as previous records, and 'non-legal' variables such as degree of parental control and ethnic group. Landau and Nathan found a positive relationship with the latter and suggested steps should be taken to eradicate bias in the selection of black youngsters sent to court. Fisher and Mawby in research carried out in Bradford found:

There was no evidence that sex, race or whether the juvenile was at school or not were related to cautioning

and they concluded:

There is no evidence to support the notion that girls are *per se* treated more favourably than boys (Fisher and Mawby, 1982, p. 70).

Using these studies tells us little about police encounters with girl juveniles. This is not surprising, since they follow the traditional criminological path and put male delinquents centre stage (see Chapter 7). This is partly because of the inevitably small numbers of girls involved – 13.2 per cent of Landau's sample (Landau and Nathan, 1983, p. 133) and one-sixth of Fisher and Mawby's sample (1982, p. 65). These methods are not generally helpful with female offenders because their small numbers do not lend themselves to complex statistical analysis nor elaborate cross-tabulation. Criminology, like crime control, tends to focus on males and marginalise females or render them invisible.

This observation is not merely relevant to studies of police behaviour; it is also important to the whole area of legal implementation. As we can see in Chapter 6, criminologists have played their part in refining and perpetuating folk myths about female crime and even creating some new ones. Thus Lombroso and Ferrero and Pollak all stressed the 'evil woman hypothesis' and modern sociologists such as Cohen and Lemert claimed female delinquency was 'sexual' in character. Given their wide presentation in social science textbooks these intellectual rationalisations of stereotypes are bound to have penetrated the minds of some policemen.

In their evidence to the sub-committee of the Expenditure Committee, several police representatives presented their views and perceptions of women offenders. Given the discussion by Rowbotham (1973), McRobbie and Garber (1976) and Campbell (1981) of the power of 'labels' on female sexuality and the damage they can do as well as the control they effect, it is very interesting to examine the exchanges between Leslie Curtis from the Police Federation and members of the Sub-committee. 'Funnily enough, we did discuss the term "common prostitute" and looked at this as being the lowest form of sex, so we were quite happy with the term "common prostitute".' (Expenditure Committee, 1978–9, 61, xii, p. 260). In their letter submitted to the Sub-committee the Federation stressed their perception of 'female prostitutes – the majority of such women are inadequates' (Expenditure Committee, 1978–9, 61, xii, p. 234). They shared the view of almost all those who gave evidence to this parliamentary body in arguing against the imprisonment of prostitutes for soliciting. Rather, they thought prostitutes need medical help.

The Association of Chief Police Officers however, took a rather different line in their memorandum. They wanted it made *easier* for the police to caution prostitutes for soliciting (Expenditure Committee, 1978–9, 61, xii, p. 242) and their representative urged the retention of imprisonment for soliciting:

> In the end if you take away what one likes to describe as the ultimate deterrent, that is, imprisonment, the rest of the procedure will just be taken in their stride (Expenditure Committee, 1978–9, 61, xii, p. 248).

Curiously, the memorandum from the Association appeared to suggest that prostitution itself was a crime (Expenditure Committee, 1978–9, xii, pp. 242 and 244). There were also some interesting sidelights on senior officers' views of prostitutes:

> I think society does want to keep them off the streets completely ... I do not know whether the young ladies would want to do community service or anything like that. The mind boggles, with the supervision of community service, if these were the people

who came to be looked after (Expenditure Committee, 1978–9, 61, xii, p. 248).

The volume of evidence from the Metropolitan Police is particularly valuable because it contains an account of how the Metropolitan Police responded to public outrage at the nuisance of street-soliciting in the Shepherd's Market district of Mayfair, using a squad of *women* officers to patrol, observe and caution girls. They suggest that controlling prostitution helps to control crime in general (Expenditure Committee, 1978–9, 61, xiii, p. 267), and that soliciting is a routine economic activity for prostitutes, while controlling it is like being a traffic warden (Expenditure Committee, 1978–9, xiii, p. 268). No evidence of police 'chivalry' towards women offenders comes through these pages, rather a matter-of-fact stereotyping of prostitutes. This is borne out by Carey's unpublished study which found no evidence of chivalry (and little sisterly sympathy from women officers) in analysis of police procedures in Leeds (Carey, 1977).

Relatively few observers have been concerned to comment on police attitudes to and treatment of women offenders. There are however, two indirect sources on what may be called 'police culture'. These are studies of the police themselves, and reports of their reaction to women victims. For the former there has recently been extensive documentation, at least for the Metropolitan force on whom the Policy Studies Institute conducted four surveys. If anything, these surveys were focused on *racial* rather than sexual discrimination, but they found in fact evidence of a cohesive, macho-culture with an emphasis on drinking with peers as a means of achieving group solidarity (Policy Studies Institute, 1984):

> Ideas about sex, drinking and violence are linked together in a cult of masculinity which is thought to provide the key to the criminal world (Banton, 1984, p. 13).

The Policy Studies Institute team found evidence too of sexual discrimination and harassment of women officers. They do caution against equating *attitudes* with *actions* and instance cases of officers with racist views being meticulously fair in dealing with black people.

A second source suggesting sexism rather than chivalry as the key attitude of the police to women can be found in the considerable volume of material relating to police practices in cases of domestic violence and of rape. If a man assaults his wife he is committing an offence, but as Dobash and Dobash remark:

Research relating to the use of discretion among police officers has revealed that officers are *very unlikely* to make an arrest when the offender has used violence against his wife (Dobash and Dobash, 1980, p. 207, emphasis added),

and they quote a Metropolitan Police memorandum to the Parliamentary Committee on violence in marriage:

It is a general principle of police practice not to intervene in a situation which existed or had existed between husband and wife in the course of which the wife had suffered some personal attack (Dobash and Dobash, 1979, p. 210).

In two British studies Pahl (1978) and Binney and her colleagues (1981) found that many battered women in refuges had found the police unhelpful to them in their plight and very reluctant to intervene. Various rationalisations tend to be offered by the police – that wives withdraw their complaints is the most characteristic, but what seems clearly to be at work is the acceptance of the family as a private place where men have certain legitimate powers and physical punishment is an acceptable hazard for women. The police culture discussed above would no doubt support such a view of women and their role. Translated to criminal women it can hardly be said to be a view conducive to chivalry.

Smart has pointed out that in rape trials it has often seemed to be the victim rather than the alleged rapist who is on trial (Smart, 1977, p. 120). Her character may be questioned and her evidence challenged. Since rape is likely to be an unobserved crime, victims may not have corroborative evidence and therefore, the police argue they must establish the facts of the case reliably before proceeding.

You have to give the girl reporting a rape a hard time . . . you have to push the victim of a rape as hard as you do a suspect to get all the facts (Toner, 1982, p. 158).

Such practices were demonstrated in a BBC television programme on the Thames Valley police (BBC TV, January 1982) which showed police interrogating a woman who had made an allegation of rape. There was considerable public concern over the tactics revealed. Of more concern to us here, however, are the assumptions that underlie the tactics: that women are inveterate liars, that they make false accusations, that they 'ask for it'. These assumptions reveal a whole view of the world which sees women with contempt.

Do women criminals get justice from the present system? I do not think we can answer that question adequately yet, though partial answers can be proffered. At a formal level there is effectively equality with men, save for the treatment of prostitutes, but the values which permeate the whole legal system are drawn from the society around it and largely from those parts of society in which traditional and conventional views of women's role and women's place flourish. The courts and the police process relatively few women as offenders, nevertheless they still seem to have to stereotype them into a narrow range of feminine roles such as 'wife' or 'whore'. Chivalry is an old-fashioned virtue and one that has often been claimed as an attribute of the law, but there is not a great deal of evidence that women are better treated than men, and some that their categorising as sexually deviant harms them. In any case, this begs the question of what 'better' means. The standard as always is how males are treated. We cannot say what a 'best' treatment for women offenders would be like; there has never, so far, been a judicial system which was based on women's behaviour or took them as a norm.

4

Women and the penal system

Prison is still central to our system for dealing with offenders. Imprisonment has historically functioned in three ways: custodially to hold prisoners (and some witnesses) awaiting trial, coercively – for example, to secure repayment of a debt – and penally as a punishment. Historians disagree as to when the last function, which is currently the most important, developed (McConville, 1981, p. 1). What is not in doubt is that the centralised, State-run prison system to which offenders are sentenced as a punishment is a product of modern capitalist society and is less than two centuries old.

Ignatieff (1978) has described in a very interesting analysis the coming of the penitentiary in the early nineteenth century and linked it to the whole social crisis of the period as part of a larger strategy of political, social and 'legal reform designed to reestablishing order on a new foundation'. He finds it 'easier to explain the coming of the penitentiary than to decide how that history continues to constrain the present and define the future' (Ignatieff, 1978, p. 215). He notes that most of the other punitive Victorian institutions for controlling the 'dangerous classes'; 'the asylums, workhouses, monitorial schools, night refuges and reformations' (ibid, p. 214) have been replaced or enormously changed, yet prisons remain.

Only a very small proportion of female offenders are given a custodial sentence in Britain. From 1978 to 1981 8 per cent of the average proportion of the 17–21 age group were so sentenced with half having their sentences suspended. This compares with about 23 per cent for males in the same age group for this period. Among

59

offenders aged 21 or over, 30 per cent of males but 12 per cent of females were given sentences of imprisonment while 18 per cent of males and 5 per cent females received immediate imprisonment. Since, as we already have seen, the numbers of male and female offenders differ considerably, far more men than women are sent to prison. In 1981, 49 000 males and 2500 females were sentenced to immediate imprisonment (Home Office 1982b).

Two immediate sets of questions present themselves about this tiny, unhappy minority of women who are imprisoned. First, who are they and why are they there? Second, what kind of system and regime do they confront when they are inside? We can find some answers to these questions in standard official publications and in a number of studies of womens' prisons which have been published as well as a few reports by former inmates themselves. This account will lead us to consider some important issues concerning the imprisonment of women.

The women in prison

The figures already given show something of the ratio of male to female prisoners in England and Wales at present. But they do not tell the whole story. By no means all prison inmates are convicted *sentenced* prisoners. Of the average daily population of 1407 women in 1981, some 800 were prisoners under sentence while 170 were untried prisoners and 143 were convicted but unsentenced and 190 sentenced to Borstal training. 'Receptions' – that is, the numbers of women received into prison under sentence – have grown fairly steadily in the past decade: they doubled between 1974 and 1981 (Home Office, 1982b, p. 73). In recent years the female prison population has risen at a *faster* rate than the male (Heidensohn, 1981, p. 126) although this trend has recently levelled off (Home Office, 1982a, p. 27).

This is a recent development; there was a long decline in the annual population for most of the twentieth century, from 50 000 in 1895, to 33 000 in 1913 and 11 000 in 1921 (Heidensohn, 1975, p. 44). After the Second World War, the numbers received annually kept fairly stable, unlike the parallel figures for men. In part this decline reflects alternative sentences, new bail and other legal changes, but there was also some diminution of certain deviant female activities as against a rise amongst men. Thus in 1908 32 439 women were convicted of drunkenness offences while in 1938 only 7686 were so convicted and by 1962 the figure was 4793 and the rate per 10 000 of population had fallen from 4.50 to 2.54 compared with a *rise* for males from 30.51 to 45.95 in the same period (Heidensohn, 1968, p. 173).

Until the 1970s the typical daily numbers in women's prisons (between 800 and 1000) were often below those who could be accommodated, in contrast to men's prisons which experienced considerable overcrowding in closed institutions. As recently as 1970, the low and stable numbers of women in prison led the Home Office to suggest that 'as the end of the century draws nearer, penological progress will result in even fewer or *no women at all* being given prison sentences' (Home Office 1970, added emphasis). Within the decade a very different approach was being emphasised: 'an increasing number of women are now being received ... (who) ... need .... training prison facilities .... and discipline staff' (Home Office, 1980, para. 81) and the reasons were clear – 'the female sentenced population rose mainly because of substantially increased numbers serving sentences for violence against the person and in contrast to the male sentenced population for offences of theft; handling, fraud and forgery'. (Home Office, 1980, para. 5).

More women were going to prison than had been the case for some years and, for some time, the rate of increase was higher than for men. Of what crimes were these women convicted, for how long were they sentenced and how did this differ from their male counterparts? The commonest group of offences for which women were (and are) imprisoned are those of dishonesty: 'theft, handling, fraud and forgery' which have remained between about 450 and 500 of the 1000 or so daily prison inmates since 1970. Violence against the person was next commonest, remaining close to 190 from 1978 to 1981, followed by burglary which has declined a little and is the offence of about 10 per cent of the average prison population. Amongst males, on the other hand, burglary was the 'typical' offence for over 11 000 of the 35 500 under sentence, followed by the theft group which covers 25 per cent and then by violence for which 1500 men were serving sentences, although receptions for burglary and violence have increased. The Home Office itself suggested that 'most of the male population under sentence at 30

June 1981 had considerable criminal histories ... Although the availability of information on previous convictions is poor for females' [they do not explain why] 'there is evidence that the population of females under sentence had fewer previous convictions than their male counterparts' (Home Office, 1982a, p. 15, § 10).

Perhaps because of the comparative lack of form, but also possibly because of certain legal developments (Home Office, 1982b, p. 66, § 5) a higher proportion of women offenders were sentenced to three months or less – the percentage had grown from 20 per cent in 1973 to 42 per cent in 1981 (as compared with over 25 per cent males). Another 25 per cent were sentenced for between three and six months and the *proportion* received and sentenced to more than eighteen months had declined (ibid, Table 5 (a)) although the *numbers* have increased since 1971.

In a report published in 1972, the group 'Radical Alternatives to Prison' heavily criticised the plans for the new Holloway Prison on the grounds that they were quite inappropriate for the inmates' needs. In particular the pamphlet emphasised the high proportion of remand prisoners received into Holloway and the significant number who were not subsequently given custodial sentences. This group who experienced custody without sentence at that time amounted to 60 per cent of Holloway's yearly turnover (Radical Alternatives to Prison 1972, p. 19).

Numbers of very young female offenders remanded in custody had fallen away almost completely since 1975 (Home Office 1982b), Table 2 (b)) probably because of the operation of the Children and Young Persons Act 1969, but for all women there have been recent increases in the numbers of untried who were not subsequently convicted. 'Females remanded in custody' observes the official account 'were (1975–81) less likely to receive a custodial sentence' (Home Office, 1982b, p. 39, § 10). As we have seen, this observation raises key points about equality of treatment, 'chivalry' in the courts and punitive remands.

Official figures give us a brief picture of who goes to prison and for how long, but printed tables are stark and to some extent, secretive. They do not tell us, for example, how many women take their children to gaol with them, not how many children are in prison with their mothers on any given day. To clothe these bare bones we have to find other material. Sources on women's prison experiences are at once richer and more problematic than for most of the other topics with which we shall deal.

Prisons have always attracted writers and researchers. Dickens made use of aspects of prison life in *Little Dorrit* and *A Tale of Two Cities*. Incarcerated inmates were readily available as research subjects for the prison doctors and others who first began 'scientific' analysis of their charges. Lombroso and Ferrero in Italy in 1893 (Lombroso and Ferrero, 1895 and the Gluecks in the USA in the 1930s (S. and E. Glueck, 1934) were two of the very few studies of women offenders in their day, both based on captive populations.

However, it was only in the 1960s that, as we shall later see elswhere, interest in women offenders became serious and the first major studies of women's prisons appeared. While women offenders in general might have been rendered invisible or marginal until then as their offences might have seemed trivial compared with those of men and much less publicly threatening, it is harder to understand the comparative neglect of women in prison. They were incontrovertibly there, provision had to be made for them, the prisons staffed and run, and the problems that arose were, as we shall see, considerable. What characteristics, then, does the regime have which women meet when they enter prison? Are special provisions made for them or do they experience the same 'pain of imprisonment' as men? In what ways has the system developed during its history?

A *Brief History of Female Imprisonment* in the USA is Feinman's (1980) account which is both full and succinct. For the UK Ann. Smith's *Women in Prison* (Smith, 1962) is the standard historical account and I cannot compress her immensely detailed and careful work here. She did not herself theorise nor present a social analysis of developments but we can find certain fundamental themes from her history which still have relevance today. First she noted the lower participation rates of women in officially recorded deviance and related this to male dominance and control 'men have largely prescribed the social code for their women folk and male standards have determined how and for what offences they should receive punishment' (Smith, 1962, p. 55). Second, she suggests that the penal system had always been male-oriented and male-dominated and that this had very significant consequences for women.

Smith showed that in pre-industrial times women and men were subject to the same penalties, most of which were non-custodial

(Smith, pp. 65–8). Thus women could be burnt at the stake, mutilated or hanged, although 'modesty' and 'decency' forbade their bodies being exposed after their death. As Bridewells and penal custody developed women were equally liable with men and young children to be imprisoned. An undifferentiated sea of humanity, many poor and starving, others insane or disabled, seethed in these places. In 1729 in the Marshalsea there were both men and women lying at the point of death on the bare filthy rags (Heidensohn, 1975). Howard's initial reforms led to the sexual segregation of men and women, but it was only with the arrival of Elizabeth Fry and her committee of Quaker women at Newgate in 1816 that a distinctive regime for women began. [There had been attempts to run a penitentiary for women at Millbank, but there were continuous problems: the matron was dismissed for corruption, the prisoners had to be dispersed to hulks off Woolwich because damp and disease in Millbank were threatening their lives (Smith, 1962, p. 87)].

Fry was the first person to consider 'that the needs of women prisoners might be different from those of men'. She established an ordered and disciplined system on the women's side in Newgate, apparently with the women's agreement, and organised schooling, work and regular religious observance. Fry became a celebrity and her readings in Newgate were visited by fashionable London (Ignatieff, 1978, p. 144). Fry opposed the penal reformers' prevailing orthodoxy of solitary confinement. She believed that women staff should care for women and that paid work should be provided in prison as well as a shop where prisoners could buy goods, but, apart from the recruitment of female staff or matrons, her ideas had become unfashionable before her death in 1845 and it was a long time before they were introduced.

During the nineteenth century women 'enjoyed' the same regime as men in prison, except that its harshness was softened a little. Women were allowed iron beds instead of planks, better uniforms and tea three times a week (Prison Matron, pp. 121–2). More crucially, women were able to gain remission more easily than men after 1853 and more lenient conditions attached to their release on licence. These differences lead McConville to declare in his definitive study of prison administration:

The contrast between male and female convict management in these decades is pronounced: on the one hand harsh regimentation, on the other a strict regime, but with considerable toleration of refractory episodes and even a degree of individualisation (McConville, 1981, p. 427).

But this lofty and detached comment misses the central issues of comparison and equality in penal treatment.

The purpose of penal systems was clearly to deal with *male* delinquency and crime. Thus the various harsh punishments, the stage systems and marks were inappropriate for women who were far less frequently convicted and whose numbers were declining. Already in 1866 there were 'decreasing numbers' (Smith, p. 125) and in 1887 'the Directors of Convict Prisons announced that the number of convict women in custody had fallen from 1477 to 706 in the preceding ten years' (Smith, 1962, p. 128). A characteristic consequence of this trend, and one that has lingered, was that 'the history of women's prisons ... between 1865 and 1898 (was) concerned ... with the continual shifting round of the convict population from prison to prison' (Smith, 1962, p. 125). The small, disparate and hard-to-handle group of women did not fit easily into the centralised, national system which aimed to standardise conditions in local prisons.

Most women were imprisoned at this time for offences of drunkenness or prostitution. They received very short sentences and as the Webbs pointed out these left 'no room for the beneficial influences of the much vaunted "System of Progressive Stages"'. (Webb, S. and B., 1928, p. 204) which had, of course, been devised to deal with male prisoners.

Further proof of the almost exclusively male concerns of the penal system are provided by early twentieth-century developments. In 1908 preventive detention was introduced to deal with 'habitual criminals' who were dangerous to society. The sentence could be applied to women and men and a few women were so sentenced even though few habitual women criminals were more than social nuisances. In the same year the system of Borstal training was introduced after a series of experiments, under Sir Evelyn Ruggles-Brise's direction, in training for young *men*. Girls, too, could now be sentenced to Borstal institutions which, with their emphasis on grades, houses and monitors were clearly based on the English public school system.

I do not wish simply to suggest that it was in some way 'unfair' that women offenders were neglected by successive administrations and then subjected to regimes designed to deal with the larger and more pressing problems of men. The issue is more complex. First there is the obvious question: how could these women who were actually sentenced to imprisonment remain so 'invisible'? In an age when politicians and indeed most male members of the establishment resisted equal rights for women in other areas of the law, why was penal treatment exceptional, save for a few sops to mitigate its harshness? It cannot be argued that prisons for women were easier to run; on the contrary, McConville remarks 'female convicts were a source of well-nigh intractable disciplinary problems' (McConville, 1981, p. 414). The account given by 'a Prison Matron' describes smash-up and hysterical outbursts in very similar terms to events in modern establishments for women. In their report for 1855 the Directors of Convict Prisons discussed the problems of 'reckless' women and their 'violence and passion'. Apart from noting that women could not be beaten or starved, these mid-Victorian gentlemen are puzzled by the situation which leads to 'the subversion of wholesome discipline throughout the prison' (McConville, 1981, p. 414). Nearly seventy years later the 1923 Report of the Prison Commissioners commented on 'smashings-up' at Aylesbury Borstal wing and in similar fashion noting 'Punishment alone will not suffice'.

There are two probable explanations for the comparative lack of interest in women convicts and the failure to develop means to deal with them in any other way than the standard procedures for men. First, women were probably regarded as more hopelessly incorrigible, more totally irredeemable when fallen. Elizabath Fry had to struggle hard to prove that women could be rehabilitated, hence the wonder at her achievements in Newgate. Harriet Martineau, in an article in 1865 accepted that women were harder to reclaim but only because it was considered pointless to try and improve them. She challenged the accepted view 'that women when criminal are worse than men' and blamed their situation on poverty and betrayal and the lack of programmes for rehabilitation for them (Martineau, 1865).

Elizabeth Windschuttle developd this argument in a paper on the history of women, crime and punishment (Windschuttle, 1981, pp. 32–3). She suggested that the double standard of nineteenth-century morality did not merely refer to 'adultery and promiscuity [which] were approved for men but ... considered to destroy the value of women as the property of husbands or fathers [and] corrupt family stability', but also related to the market place and economic activity. This liberal individualism led to the view that people (meaning, of course, men) chose their social roles and chose to commit crimes. Hence their punishment was to be achieved through persuading them to repentance and guilt. But, women, or at least middle-class women of the governing classes were different:

> While middle class men immersed themselves each day in the competitive, avaricious world of commerce where the only morals or values were those of the 'cash nexus', their women were to be kept out of the market place ... Translated to criminality, the double standard prescribed different attitudes toward male and female criminals. Men could commit crime, but be reformed. If women committed crime, they were destroyed utterly. They were irredeemable (Windschuttle, p. 33).

In short, the notion of the hopelessly fallen woman was based on two concepts; the separation of spheres of activity for men and women and the sexualising of female behaviour to stress its difference from male and even its pathological quality. These are key ideas in the dominant ideology of patriarchy which have much wider currency and impact than in penology.

Middle-class women were largely barred from public office during the nineteenth century but they did participate in public life in great numbers, involving themselves in religious and charitable works and providing leadership and change in fields as diverse as nursing and housing, the temperance movement and education for girls. By no means all were feminists but as Banks has pointed out (Banks, 1981) there were very close links between social reform movements and feminism. She traced particularly the way in which women in the USA, Britain and elsewhere, drawn to a cause such as anti-slavery, were radicalised into some degree of feminism either through what they saw of their suffering sisters or because, like a much later generation, they were frustrated by the social and political constraints on their activities. Fry herself, while no feminist, was criticised for neglecting her home and family and replied by urging women to aid the 'helpless, the ignorant, the afflicted and the depraved of their own sex' (Banks, 1981, p. 25).

While, of course, it was not only women who cared for the welfare of other women, there are clear links to campaigns for the improvement of social conditions for women and their participation in social movements. Without decisive female leadership such projects foundered. Thus part of the reason for the neglect of women in prison at this period was probably that they lacked champions. Josephine Butler's work on the repeal of the Contagious Diseases Acts is a notable example of what could happen (Petrie, 1971). In surveying from retirement the previous history of imprisonment for women, Ruggles-Brise himself noted the failure to recognise the needs of women and that it could not be shown

> that at any time the method of dealing with criminal women has engaged that close attention which might have been expected from the nature and difficulty and importance of the problem. The law strikes men and women indifferently with the same penalties of penal servitude and imprisonment (Ruggles-Brise, 1921, p. 16).

As I have already suggested, it would be unwise to regret too deeply the tempered indifference of the penal system at this time. None would have gained had women been flogged or even placed on restricted diets as were men. However, a more fundamental question is raised about fair and equal treatment of the sexes: if men and women are treated in the same way, given the same opportunities or punishments, are the end-effects justice and fairness? In recent times these questions have been raised most fully in relation to education and employment. They have relevance too in relation to punishment and this has become an important issue in debates about the modern penal system (Heidensohn, 1969) to which we now turn.

Prisons for women today

Despite the long period of relative stability in women's prisons in the middle of this century few positive developments occurred. A cosmetic approach was in order: 'gallons of pastel paint on old prison walls, cretonne flowery curtains over windows' did not, I noted in researching in women's prisons in the 1960s, disguise the old system (Heidensohn, 1975). Smith was more devastating still:

Whatever the efforts of the Prison Commissioners and the staff, there can be no real progress in the surroundings of a sepulchre, whether whitened or painted in pastel shades (Smith, 1962).

But in the late 1960s and early 1970s several developments occurred which influenced at least our thinking about the imprisonment of women. The rise of modern feminism brought about a reappraisal of women's role in society as a whole and, in relation to crime, women's role as deviants and victims. Crime rates among women began to rise (and apparently) at a faster rate than for men (Chapter 1). More women were therefore being imprisoned. Finally an initiative was proposed in 1968 in Britain which for the first time would treat women in a unique and special way in accordance with their alleged needs and problems. A rebuilt Holloway prison was to cater for the physical and psychological problems of women offenders.

It is typical of the second-class status to which women are relegated within the penal system that they are still housed in second-hand accommodation, often designed for quite other purposes. In Britain for instance Styal is a former children's home, East Sutton Park and Askham former country mansions; Holloway was once a debtors' prison. In the USA, women are often imprisoned in poor conditions in local gaols intended for males.

Since 1960, more has probably been written and discussed in relation to women in prison than at any previous time. Several major American studies of women's institutions have made important contributions to sociological understanding (Ward and Kassebaum, 1965; Giallombardo, 1966 and 1974). A few, smaller scale British studies have also appeared (Ward, 1982; Mawby, 1981; Goodman and Price, 1972) as well as various personal accounts from former inmates (Buxton and Turner, 1962; and Arrowsmith, 1970) and a former governor (Kelley, 1967). Concern over plans for the new Holloway led to considerable public debate and interest, unprecedented for a women's prison since Fry's days at Newgate (Faulkner, 1971; Radical Alternatives to Prison, 1972). The proposals were the main lead story on Independent Television's news on the night of 16 December 1968!

While in some political and official quarters little has changed since Du Cane's day, in others there are interesting signs of the times. Thus the May Committee Report says virtually nothing about staff or inmates in women's prisons, and the 15th Report of the House of Commons Expenditure Committee (Education, Arts and Home Office Sub-Committee) on reducing pressure on the prison system had very little to say either. However, the Sub-Committee were well-aware of the omission and took steps to remedy it by starting up a new enquiry on 'Women and the Penal System'. To that end, they began an extensive review, examining administrators and prison staff, representatives from staff bodies and the police, academics and pressure groups and, most fascinatingly, women and girls in prison and prostitutes who had been in gaol. The fourteen volumes of published evidence (Expenditure Committee, 1978/9) provided more detail and more frank comment than has ever been available before. Perhaps it is carrying the 'Cinderella complex' view of women's penal treatment too far to note that, poised to produce a report and recommendations on their findings, the Sub-Committee was foiled by the calling of a general election in April 1979 and the report and recommendation have never subsequently appeared. In looking at the present-day prison system, I shall draw on all these published sources.

Another, more ephemeral, source of note has been the growing treatment of this topic in the mass media. A commercial-television series in the 1970s '*Within these Walls*' concerned a women's prison in many ways like Holloway. With Googie Withers in the chief role of the Governor and some rather sentimental story lines, the series was obviously for the mass entertainment market. Nevertheless, professional advice was credited and several episodes were clearly based on real incidents: in one the problem of a hunger strike was raised, in another a clear reference was intended to the much-discussed 'walk on the heath' taken by Myra Hindley and the then governor of Holloway. Several documentaries have also been made about women's prisons – on Holloway, Bullwood and Styal – with official blessing and some, for example, Broadside's, without.

We have already seen that far fewer women than men are sent to prison. The current British ratio is about 1 : 27. A significant proportion are imprisoned on remand awaiting trial or sentence. Of the convicted sentenced prisoners most receive short sentences and the majority are incarcerated for property offences. What are the effects of these features on prison life for women?

First, and paradoxically, women's under-achievement in offending does not bring them benefits in the penal system. The very low numbers of women inside pose problems: there are few establishments, they are scattered haphazardly and inmates may be many miles from home:

> Many women have to serve their sentences at long distances from their home areas making visiting difficult or impossible and causing hardship for them and their families (Home Office, 1979, p. 124).

There can be little specialisation of treatment or careful segregation of offenders with such small numbers (Expenditure Committee, 61–vi, p. 112, § 1.1). When exceptional prisoners have to be housed, under secure conditions, for example, they have to go to specially created units within male prisons, as with Mary Bell who had murdered two small boys, and the Price sisters, convicted in the Old Bailey bomb case. Training and employment opportunities are also poor in women's institutions, partly at least because of numbers and geography. Even in the 1980s, the main work at Bullwood was making cardboard cartons (National Association for the Care and Resettlement of Offenders, 1982) and of course it would be quite impracticable to have a full-scale industrial prison such as Coldingley. Although there were once plans to provide specialised psychiatric facilities for women, such as exist at Grendon Underwood for men, these have never materialised.

The high turnover of short-term prisoners and the numbers of remand prisoners (who may need to be regularly escorted to court) lead to a 'transit camp' effect; 'the main thing that strikes one about Holloway is the enormous number of people flowing through on remand for various purposes . . . it is like Victoria Station . . . many are just milling around' (Expenditure Committee, 61–vi, p. 148, § 568). The Deputy Governor of Bullwood provided a comprehensive analysis of the system's ills before the Sub-Committee. Inmates were far too diverse in age, criminality, culture and psychiatric needs to be treated altogether:

> Again one of the implications of having a national intake is that there are few visits from families and therefore dependence . . . is greater than normal. The strength of the subculture within Bullwood is very great and girls do become involved very quickly in Bullwood's subculture (Executive Committee, 61–xi, pp. 215–6, § 935).

She went on to add that distance from home and family precluded the use of rehabilitative measures available to boys and that the lack of any alternative facilities for girl offenders added to the strain of the institution. [She had already categorised the buildings as 'significantly oppressive and unsuitable for the training of young adolescent girls'.] Most of the prisoners interviewed – from Styal, Holloway and Bullwood – complained about the difficulties of maintaining family contacts (Expenditure Committee, 61–v, 62–ix and 61–xi).

In one distinctive way not found in all penal systems, British women prisoners are helped to maintain some family links. Prison rules stipulate that 'the Secretary of State may, subject to any conditions he thinks fit, permit a woman prisoner to have her baby with her in prison and everything necessary for the baby's maintenance and care may be provided there'.

Some thirty-four mother-and-baby places are provided in the system at present and a further forty for pregnant women (National Association for the Care and Resettlement of Offenders, 1982). In 1980, seventy-five women prisoners were confined in NHS hospitals and in 1981 the number was seventy-four. The practice has been that babies should not remain with their mothers in Holloway beyond the age of 9 months. They can stay longer at the open prison at Askham Grange – up to the age of $2\frac{1}{2}$ years. Babies are sometimes refused entry to Holloway because there is no room or they will be too old before their mother leaves. There were five such instances in 1981 (National Association for the Care and Resettlement of Offenders, 1982). Some mothers and babies were also turned down by Askham, but there are no figures for this. Styal takes Borstal trainees who are mothers and several of their babies are adopted or go into care.

The topic of babies in prison – 'incarcerated innocents' – is obviously a deeply emotive one, for the women themselves and for everyone else who considers it. The Expenditure Sub-Committee put it on their agenda and questioned witnesses at length as to their views. Almost all the witnesses agreed with two fundamentally contradictory points. One, prison is the least suitable place to rear young children: it is isolated from the real world so that the infants see neither men nor traffic and do not mix with outsiders. The institutional atmosphere is inappropriate. On the other hand, if mothers wish their children to come to prison with them then they should be able to have them there. Even the Prison Officers' Association – otherwise implacably opposed to extended family visits and women wearing their own clothing – agree to this (Expenditure Committee, 61–vi, §s 540 and 545, pp. 140–1). There are obviously deep dilemmas here. On the one hand there is the stereotype of woman-as-mother being used to give women what are, in effect, special privileges; on the other there is the question of the welfare of the child.

At least one Prison Governor sees imprisonment as benefiting women offenders. At the Cropwood Conference (Morris and Gelsthorpe, 1981) she suggested that many women, mothers with their babies in particular, were actually better-off in prison. Well-housed and fed with no money worries and a properly clean and organised environment for their infants, away from men who battered or abused them, they and their children could flourish. Many were bad mothers, she suggested, and might improve their mothering skills in prison.

The plans for the new departure in penal treatment for women were first announced in 1968 and then later elaborated with a spate of articles and carefully encouraged publicity (Faulkner, 1971; Blythe, 1971). Women offenders were, it was argued, mentally and physically sick, or possibly both. Few (and declining) in numbers, they were to be offered therapeutic regimes ranging from psychotropic drugs to deep analyses and counselling (Heidensohn, 1975, p. 52). Legal and justice models were to be abandoned for treatment: 'patients can be located in therapeutic groups instead of legal or imprisonment groups' (Blythe, 1971). However, even at the start these plans were studded with ambiguities. Although the new prison has still not been completed (1984), it is clear that events, notably the overcrowding and increased numbers of recent years have forced modifications.

At a deeper level, however, the concept of the mentally abnormal female offender has come under scrutiny. Women's prisons have always been very difficult to run. By far the highest rates of offences against prison discipline occur in female establishments – in 1981 the rate was 144 per 100 population for all males and 310 for females. 'Smash-ins', 'bang-ins', self-mutilation have all long been acknowledged to be more widespread and to pose greater problems in women's prison. Here are reactions from staff members to the tensions and hysteria of Bullwood:

We get a quite high incidence of self-mutilation here, mainly self-inflicted cuts and abrasions, ear-piercing, inserting needles into their bodies (self) tattooing ... and even self-strangulation (Expenditure Committee, 61–xi, § 888, p. 211).
I have worked at ... the psychiatric Borstal for boys, for four years prior to coming here last week and in my experience this population must be one of the most – if not the most – collectively disturbed and unstable (Expenditure Committee, 61–xi, § 976, p. 224). I was absolutely amazed and astonished that during the two hours I sat with the branch committee (at Bullwood) to get their views they had to leave me on four occasions to answer the alarm bell. On the last occasion one of the officers was seriously assaulted. This was not something specially set up for me; it was a fairly regular occurence. (Expenditure Committee, 61–vi, § 521, p. 133).

But do these stresses and tensions and their expression in sex-role-reversed levels of violence mean that women in prison are more likely to be mentally abnormal than men? If so, is this because women sent to prison are already disturbed or because prison, being a more traumatic experience for women causes their mental disintegration? In support of the first proposition are two widely-held views about female offenders: (i) that they must be abnormal or pathological, and (ii) that those who end up in prison are especially likely to be mentally ill or in other ways highly deviant since so few women commit offences and so very few of those are sent to prison (Smith, 1962, p. 194). In this argument we can recognise certain familiar aspects: the implicit assumtpion that female offenders are less reclaimable, more vile, more 'unnatural' than male, which we noted earlier.

There is no evidence that the Home Office had conducted large-scale studies of female prisoners before deciding on their therapeutic approach to them. There had been two smaller surveys whose results indicated some degree of disturbance in the population. Gibbens in his 'gate' sample of prisoners found mental health to be a problem for over one-fifth and physical health a problem in one-sixth (Gibbens, 1971). Davies and Goodman were also anxious to stress that disturbed inmates were a minority:

While it is generally agreed that a larger proportion of girls than boys in penal institutions are psychiatrically disturbed, these are likely to form at the most about a quarter to a third of receptions into custody. (Davies and Goodman, 1972, p. 13).

They were well aware of the dangers of implicit sexism in this issue:

This raises many questions ... the anxiety of authorities was aroused in some cases through the girls' unconventional or promiscuous sex behaviour or their inability to form 'satisfactory' relationships with men ... How much is the mental disturbance shown by these girls an initial reaction to their incarceration? (Davies and Goodman, 1972, p. 13).

There was then, as there still is today, some evidence of significant mental and physical illness among women in prison. The number of (medical) treatments given per person per day was much higher for females than for males. (Home Office 1982b). Prescribing psychotropic drugs is also much commoner: in 1981, 36 875 such doses were dispensed in *eighteen* boys' Borstals and 11 900 to *two* girls' Borstals.

Yet as both the studies quoted suggest, this has only been true for a minority of prisoners and doubts have been raised as to the efficacy of treatment in closed institutional settings (Davies and Goodman, 1972) and also to the origins of the disorder. Professor Gibbens made his views clear to the Parliamentary Sub-Committee

All the sorts of mental illnesses are distorted by imprisonment, especially the artificial psychoses that really are hysterical. *They look as mad as can be but they are really reacting to prison life* (Expenditure Committee, 61–viii, p. 154, § 594) [emphasis added].

Most women in prison are not therefore disturbed and the provision of a treatment regime for them seems inappropriate for the majority at least some of whom will be 'normal' criminals. The argument that women find prison harder to take and that its effects are more traumatic for them than for men has quite widespread support both from the continued evidence of their behavioural reactions and also from a series of studies which have looked at inmate sub-cultures.

The sociology of women's prisons

Women's criminality has generally been neglected by academic social researchers but their experience in penal institutions has received rather more attention and there is even a reasonably flourishing scholarly debate on certain crucial issues. Sociological studies of institutions began in post-war America. Sykes (1958) studied the inmate social code of a maximum-security prison and showed that this developed in response to what he called the 'five pains of imprisonment': loss of liberty, goods and services, heterosexual contacts, autonomy and security. Clemmer (1958) proposed the concept of 'prisonerisation': inmates became socialised into a subsidiary sub-culture negatively opposed to staff and institution goals. Cressly (1961) suggested that it was *external* values and roles which determine response to prison.

These themes were picked up in the first US studies of women's prisons which began to appear in the 1960s. Ward and Kassebaum studied the Californian State Penitentiary at Alderson and Giallombardo the Federal Penitentiary, and later three state institutions for delinquent girls (Giallombardo, 1966, 1974). They all suggested that the responses of the women and girls they studied were strikingly different from men's. In all institutions complex social systems flourished, based on close emotional, homosexual relationships. Ward and Kassebaum focused only on the 'homosexual dyad' and the importance this had for penitentiary life. This was the response to an interview with an inmate:

Q. 'Do the women talk about homosexuality much?'
A. 'That's all they talk about'. 'Guess who's going with who?' and 'They had a fight'. 'O Jesus, that's all they talk about … because really, that's all that's happening here' (Ward and Kassebaum, 1966, Ch. 4).

They suggested that women find prison life harder than men, crave affection and hence participate in sexual relationships. Giallombardo – is critical of the limitations of their research:

Unfortunately, most of their research is devoted to detailed and repetitious descriptions of homosexual practice (Giallombardo, 1974, pp. 6–7).

She herself found in both studies that:

homosexual alliances took the form of marriages; together with the family and other kinship ties, these structures integrate female inmates into a social system and represent an attempt to create a substitute universe within the prison.

Giallombardo suggested that both:

male and female inmate cultures *are* a response to the deprivations of prison life but the *nature* of the response in both prison communities is influenced by the differential participation of males and females in the external culture (Giallombardo, 1974, p. 3).

In particular:

the family group in female prisons is singularly suited to meet the inmates' internalised expectations of the female role (Giallombardo, 1974, p. 3).

Undoubtedly homosexuality plays a part in life in British women's prisons. Indeed, so concerned were members of the Prison Officers' Association about the issue that they made a plea to the Sub-Committee for a return to uniforms for women prisoners to combat 'masculine dress': 'homosexual activity ... is one of the more dominant features of women prisoners subculture'. (Expenditure Committee, 61–vi, p. 130). Gibbens too suggested that 'homosexuality ... runs through the whole female criminal population in a much more subtle way' (Expenditure Committee, 61–vii, p. 154, § 591). Researchers in Britain however, have not, found homosexual relationships to have the same importance as the basis of a subculture. Both Mawby at Askham Grange and Ward at Styal found far less evidence of inmate dependence on lesbian or pseudo-family structures. Mawby shows that other factors such as previous educational experience are more important (Mawby, 1980). Ward found that there was a 'lack of solidarity' amongst inmates and that what subculture there was was based on 'telling tales' or grassing. She suggests that the prison organisation itself and the uncertainties of its decision-making determine the inmates' response (Ward,

1982). She emphasises that this response 'is not a direct result of the prisoners being women but . . . a diversity of pre-prison careers and the structure and organisation which exacerbate the differences'.

More recent American research has also questioned the simple assumption of a single response to prison conditions. In a Minnesota study a combination of aspects of the institutional environment and pre-prison experiences determined whether prisoners edorsed an 'inmate code' and/or opposed the staff (Kruttschnitt, 1981). The author does conclude that there are significant attitude differences between male and female inmates and that women do not have a 'normative system guiding inmates' behavioural repertoire, as exhibited in male facilities'. In short 'women's prisons' contain 'a subculture of inmates rather than an inmate subculture' (Kruttschnitt).

When penitentiary reform began in the eighteenth century, men and women, as we have seen, were usually imprisoned together. Segregation of the sexes was one of the first aims of the reformers and this has remained so on the whole ever since. Indeed in Britain a consistent policy of closing down female wings in men's prisons was pursued until the 1970s when problems of security led to units being provided for women at Brixton and then Durham gaol. However, in some penal systems experiments in 'co-educational' prisons have been made and these provide some further information on reactions to imprisonment. In a USA study, Tittle found that women associated with a best friend or in a small group (Tittle, 1969) while men in the same institution participated in an overall inmate code and grouping. However the experimental Danish Ringe Prison near Odense has a much more radical approach with four mixed blocks of cells where young offenders can meet freely during the day and sexual relations are permitted. The experimental prison has been claimed by its governor to be successful and staff attitudes have grown very positive (Follett, 1981). Most of the few reports we have suggest that it is male prisoners who are most helped in co-educational institutions, yet it is women who seem to show the more extreme and distressed reaction to prison.

Prison staff

It was a central tenet of Fry's reformed regime for women prisoners that they should be looked after by other women. In 1823 an Act was passed requiring the appointment of prison Matrons to supervise women prisoners. Male officers were always to be accompanied when visiting the women's wing of a prison (Smith, 1962, p. 88). In fact it was a very long time before prisons for women were wholly staffed and run by women. [Indeed institutions for women have generally had some male staff employed.] The first woman Prison Governor was Dr Selina Fox, appointed to Aylesbury in 1916. It has been very difficult too for women to reach the higher levels of penal policy-making and administration. The first 'Lady Inspector' of prisons was Dr Mary Gordon, appointed in 1907, but at present there are no women executive members of the Prisons Board (Home Office, 1982a, p. 72).

We have already looked at the pains of imprisonment suffered by women and how these affect them. The deprivation of family and social ties seem most acute although loss of liberty is also acutely felt. It has often been pointed out that women in our society are much less likely to experience a single-sex institutional environment than are men. Men may live in army barracks or troopships; even in peace-time they may be members of the Royal or Merchant Navies or join monastic orders. There are no female equivalents for any of these bodies and thus women's prisons are more strikingly unusual an experience for women. Of course even those few organisations which are all-female in practice have male chaplains or doctors and, in the case of prisons, men who man the gates, and do technical work, and the overwhelming majority of the policy-makers, political and administrative, are men.

Prison for women is therefore an exceptionally strange experience in our society for the inmates. What of the staff who are employed in the prisons and who are likely to spend more of their lives 'inside' than is the typical prisoner serving only a short sentence? Is the role of prison staff very different in women's than in men's prisons?

Just as women prisoners tend on the whole to suffer because of poorer facilities and lack of flexibility because there are few of them, so do the staff of women's prisons. With so few establishments widely and arbitrarily scattered over the country it is very hard for staff to plan their careers in a nationally run, centrally organised service. Promotion to a higher grade can mean a move from Kent to Durham. As the 1981 Prison Department Report noted:

The comparatively small size of the women's population, and therefore the small number of establishments in which they can be accommodated, causes its own problems.

Prisoners frequently have to be escorted to court or to other prisons. A relatively high proportion of female prison officers are 'temporary', that is, locally recruited staff who work from their homes at a local establishment and are not required to be mobile (Home Office, 1982b, Table 5, p. 16 and Expenditure Committee, 61–i, part 48). Women prison officers have been a remarkably silent group: there have been no modern personal accounts by them and their problems did not rate discussion in the May Committee Report, but from the evidence to the Expenditure Sub-Committee and from a few less formal sources the issues of mobility and stress emerge as central in the lives of prison staff in British women's prisons. There are also concerns over careers, promotion and domestic responsibilities which are fairly similar to those faced by women in other kinds of work in the late twentieth century.

We have already seen that the 'few and far between' distribution of penal institutions creates difficulties for inmates and staff. The relatively high proportion of temporary staff leads to high turnover and an unwillingness to seek promotion, hence a shortage of middle management. Thus on the female side where there may be relatively more disturbed people to deal with 'it is the recently-joined and relatively-inexperienced officers who have to face these problems without ... support' (Expenditure Committee, 61–iv, p. 83, para. 260).

Recent changes in approaches to women offenders and the rise in their numbers in prison have obviously increased the problems faced by prison staff. The emphasis on 'therapy' which marked the plans for the new Holloway did not fit with a more benign and caring role which some female prison staff saw themselves as taking (Heidensohn, 1969 and 1975), but there were always unresolved ambiguities in this treatment approach and there are clear signs of its being abandoned long before the new Holloway was near completion (Expenditure Committee, 61–i, p. 17, para 89).

Working in prisons, with the need for round-the-clock supervision poses particular problems for women who also carry traditional domestic responsibilities. Women prisoners are often faced with crises at home when they are sent to gaol; women prison officers too confront dilemmas about their roles and responsibilities. Since demands of the job are harder to combine with family life, fewer female than male officers are married, yet this is regretted by the Home Office and senior staff. Women officers find it difficult to get to training courses, feel themselves disadvantaged and lack self-confidence (Expenditure Committee, 61–iv, pp. 79ff.). These are familiar complaints from many women working in an environment designed for men who may have domestic support while the women have domestic responsibilities.

One solution which has been rather tentatively tried is to have greater mixing of prison staff. There are now once again male governors and officers in women's prisons and some women governors in men's prisons. The first woman governor of a men's prison was appointed in 1982 to Kingston Prison in Britain. The Prison Officers' Association remain opposed to cross-staffing, while the Governors favour it.

In the US Equal Rights provisions have been used to ensure fairer treatment of both inmates and staff. Under the Fourteenth Amendment to the Constitution 'equal protection of the law' clause women prisoners have sought and obtained greater equality with them. They have asked for better job training and education, for better access to their lawyers and improved post-release facilities (Crisman, 1976). The American Civil Liberties Union was active in supporting prisoners' rights. Sex segregation came much later to the US system than to the British: the Indiana Reformatory for women and Girls was opened in 1873. Moreover, segregation has never been complete, with many states housing women prisoners in gaols for men, sometimes in very poor conditions.

The women's movement has had a direct impact on women's employment in the US penal system. Until the 1970s men could be wardens of female institutions but women were excluded from male institutions; but Title VII of the Civil Rights Act 1964 forbade discrimination on the grounds of sex. In practice, it was only when further legislation gave broader powers to the Equal Employment Opportunity Commission and, crucially, prevented funding to agencies where sex discrimination was found that positive programmes were begun (Feinman, 1980, p. 54). Civil rights provisions have also been used in the US by male inmates against women officers. These prisoners claimed that their constitutional rights to privacy were violated by the presence of women in areas where men might shower or bathe or be stripsearched (Feinman, 1980, p. 57). But mixed staffing has had considerable impact in the US.

Prisons are not only staffed by discipline staff. There are many medical, educational and social workers who work with prisoners. They are, however, much more like their professional colleagues working in other settings. There is a special prison medical service and some prisons have full-time medical staff. Their activities have been the focus of some controversy since rates of sickness and medication are so high amongst women prisoners. On the other hand some institutions are served by GPs working part-time. Clearly there are times when correctional staff and professionals come into conflict over their aims. These problems are not necessarily more acute in women's prisons, although they may be exacerbated by the small, inflexible nature of the provision for women and by the high levels of need for services such as health and education which they have. Recent history at Holloway has highlighted these issues very dramatically (*Guardian*, 25 July, 1983). What these also reveal, of course, especially when comparison is made with the USA, is the enormous secrecy which surrounds British prisons.

Women do not fit neatly into penal systems. Prisons are all too obviously designed to deal with the public delinquency of boys and men. In the nineteenth century 'fallen women' seemed beyond redemption and were ignored or neglected. For most of the twentieth century, as fewer women went to prison, regimes were humanised a little but no serious effort was made to deal with what seemed to be a declining problem. Plans were introduced in the 1960s for one new-style prison for women, but they were soon overtaken by rising numbers and a tougher approach. As this century draws to a close almost all the particular problems of imprisoning women are still unresolved from the early Victorian era. (There are of course also major issues to do with the high level of imprisonment in England and Wales which are common to women and men). Violence and disturbance seem more prevalent in female institutions and because their domestic responsibilities are heavier women find that imprisonment imposes heavy penalties on them and their families. Because women prisoners are so few in number special needs cannot be met and there are added losses of family contact and links with social workers. Staff, too, are penalised having limited opportunities for training and promotion.

Feminist discussions have hardly touched on women in prison, although in the US equal opportunities provisions have been used with some success. Imprisoning women does raise some very difficult issues for feminists. Should women be treated exactly as men are? Is it fairer to recognise their lower levels of criminality and their lesser social threat and their domestic ties? Should babies be imprisoned with their mothers? What are the arguments for and against co-educational prisons? I discuss elsewhere in this work the private nature of the social control of women as compared with the more public control of men. Given this difference, it is, perhaps, not wholly surprising that the official confinement of women has been so marginal and ill-considered. In this, as in so many things, women have lacked voices and have been punished not just for wrongdoing but also for not keeping to their proper places.

5

Images of deviant women

Probably the most important single contribution made by modern sociologists to the study of deviance has been their emphasis on the need to study public descriptions of, and social reactions to, deviant behaviour. Becker's famous definition:

> Deviance is not a quality of the act the person commits, but rather a consequence of the application by others of rules and sanctions to an 'offender'. The deviant is one to whom that label has successfully been applied; deviant behaviour is behaviour that people so label (Becker, 1963, p. 9)

has been much criticised (see, for example, Plummer, 1979, pp. 87–9). Nevertheless, the 'labelling' approach with its emphasis on the reactions of others has had considerable significance in helping to focus research and develop important new understandings well beyond the adherents of that particular approach.

Cohen, for example, has shown how press and television reaction, and the responses of agents of control such as the police and JPs, were in themselves important factors in the development of mods-and-rockers' 'riots' at English seaside towns in the 1960s (Cohen, 1980). Hunter Thompson depicted similar reactions to, and consequences of, Hells Angels' activities in the USA (Thompson, 1966). 'Moral panics' were observed to occur over 'Teddy Boys' or drug abuse, often exaggerating and distorting the original delinquent acts quite disproportionately. Pearson (1983) has argued that there have been 'respectable fears' of urban, working-class male juvenile delinquency for generations, that these fears are always related

back to a supposed earlier crime-free period and that the delinquents are frequently 'labelled' with an alien name 'hooligan',
'street arab', 'mugger' to emphasise distance and distaste.

Exponents of the cultural studies approach have argued that
young males now adopt specific styles of dress and behaviour in
order to rebel or be deviant. They affix their own labels, they resist
social conformity through the stylistic rituals of skinheads, greasers
or punks (Willis, 1978). In short, these writers have shown the
powerful impact that images and stereotypes of deviance can have.

Even a wrong or distorted image can have impact and, given what
we know of the problematic nature of definitions of crime and
deviance, it is very likely that their images will be distorted. Ditton
and Duffy (1983) found that Scottish newspapers over-reported
sexual offences while Roshier (1973) and others have found an
over-emphasis on crimes of violence in the press. Ditton and Duffy
suggest that these distortions increase people's fears of crime and
produce fear-of-crime waves, 'The fear of crime is currently out of
all proportion to its incidence' (Ditton and Duffy, 1983, p. 164).

The importance of both the media and the related public reaction
to patterns of crime and deviance is, therefore, well-established.
What then of deviant women? Are the images presented of them
very different from those of men? Are public reactions different and
if so, what consequences do these differences have? In this chapter I
shall try to demonstrate that there are important differences in the
public presentation of deviant women as opposed to deviant men
and that this has considerable impact on female behaviour.

For at least two reasons it is surprising that no major work has yet
been done on the images of deviant women. First, image: 'form,
semblance, counterpart' (Oxford English Dictionary) is particularly
crucial to the process of defining deviance in women as is the social
reaction to it. The central point at issue in the laws on soliciting is
that public nuisance is caused by prostitutes plying their trade.
Second, the ways in which women in general are portrayed, especially in the mass media such as advertising and popular journalism
have been extensively studied. In what follows I shall draw on some
of these latter works which offer important insights and I shall also
be looking at a selection of portrayals of female deviance and at
some studies, notably of 'famous trials' where women have been
defendants.

Millman, in her essay on the sociology of deviance, pointed to the

very different ways men and women have been studied and described in that literature: 'women have either been largely overlooked in the literature – or else regarded as deviant in only
sex-stereotyped – ways' (Millman, 1982, p. 342). But the modern
sociology of deviance is a rather special case, as I shall show in
Chapter 7. In fact, to a remarkable extent popular media such as the
press, films and television do depict deviant women. There is
considerable stereotyping of them, from a rather narrow range of
stereotypes; that is not, however, the whole story as we shall see.

Women involved in very serious crimes such as murder seem to
provide the media with some of their most compelling images of
crime and deviance. This is how one recent account introduced the
case of Lizzie Borden who was tried for and acquitted of hacking to
death her father and stepmother in Fall River, USA, in 1893.

The American public, swimming as it is in a sea of contemporary
violence, still finds the trial of Lizzie Borden in the early 1890s
the *most continually absorbing case* in the annals of this nation's
homicides. Many sensational murder trials of the twentieth century have received extensive press notice and a few have been
given saturation news coverage. It is unlikely, however, that any
capital crime has held such a firm purchase on public attention
and so completely engrossed the nation's press (Sullivan, 1975,
p. 1, emphasis added).

Sullivan goes on to point out that there have been thousands of
articles, several books and plays, a ballet and films on the case. Even
more striking perhaps was the press reaction before and during the
trial.

For months before the trial Lizzie had been pictured as a frail
woman who had been put upon by the police and prosecutors; she
was portrayed in the press as a proper subject for public sympathy
and public support. This widespread image of Lizzie was calcu-
lated to make it difficult, if not impossible, to find twelve prospec-
tive jurors in Bristol County who were totally unaffected by the
favourable pre-trial publicity she had received (Sullivan, 1975,
p. 185).

One consequence of this was that, when the *Boston Globe* newspaper published an unfavourable story about her, claiming that she

was pregnant, and this then turned out to be a hoax, the *Globe* grovelled in its apology and its continued support thereafter helped Lizzie's acquittal.

Sullivan suggested that part of the public concern over the Borden case was due to the existence of capital punishment and the reluctance to execute a woman. No woman had been put to death in the state since the American Revolution. The last woman hanged there in 1778 had 'pleaded her belly' without success, but when her body was cut down from the gallows and a post-mortem performed, an unborn child was found in her womb. 'The self-guilt of the people of Worcester County was not soon erased' (Sullivan, 1975, p. 193).

The threat of the death penalty cannot, however, explain the 'fascination' which attached to another American murder trial nearly a century later – that of Jean Harris in 1980 for the murder of her lover, Dr Tarnower, in Westchester, in the so-called 'Scarsdale case' after the slimming diet advocated by the doctor. This case, too attracted world-wide publicity. Trilling describes the 'fascination' of the case and also notes how, during the pre-trial build-up, Mrs Harris had become 'a figure in public relations rather than – the woman who had shot Herman Tarnower' (Trilling, 1981, p. 5).

Mrs Harris, like Lizzie Borden and like the thirteen women whose sensational cases are described in Hartman's 'Victorian Murderesses' (1977) came from a highly respectable middle-class background. It can perhaps be argued that this added an extra *frisson* to public interest in these cases. But this was certainly not true, for instance of Mary Ann Cotton, convicted of murdering her stepson in March 1873 and believed to have murdered between fifteen and twenty more of her relatives and close acquaintances. A popular history of crime produced a century later notes that by the time she was hanged, less than three weeks after her conviction:

> She was by then already a legend. What was described as 'a great moral drama', *The Life and Death of Mary Ann Cotton* was in rehearsal for a variety tour which started eight days later. Mothers of children who would not go to sleep or eat their cabbage threatened them with the spectre of 'the monster in human shape' (Donaldson, 1976, p. 58).

Women involved in murder cases have been especially highlighted, but so too have women involved in spying, terrorism and sexual-cum-political scandals.

There are, I think, several reasons why certain categories of female criminal behaviour are either over-represented or over-sensationalised in the popular press. Such cases, particularly of murder, were comparatively rare, as they still are. Hartman observed 'Unsurprisingly, fewer women than men were accused of murder in both England and France' (Hartman, 1977, p. 5). In addition to the statistically low frequency of trials of women, there seems to be an added factor of dissonance in placing women in the dock as publicly arraigned offenders:

With each week of the trial one saw Mrs Harris wearing away. Physically she was a shadow of herself by the end of the trial and always there had hovered over the courtroom the fear that she'd not survive to a verdict. In such cruel circumstances did one send a person to jail? (Trilling, 1981, p. 297).

Prurience, a morbid interest in sexual and other aspects of such cases, seems often too to have been excited by female crime. Hartman reports how Constance Kent was depicted as the victim of pubertal changes and how outrage was expressed at this, and yet the whole question was endlessly rehearsed and in detail. (Hartman, 1977, p. 126). Indeed the key which such cases give to unlock the private domestic worlds in which women, more than men, live, has clearly been another aspect exciting interest in some of these cases. There was enormous interest, for example, in whether or not Florence Bravo, accused of poisoning her second husband Charles in 1876, did or did not have an affair with Dr Gully, her medical adviser and confidant of longstanding. Florence tried to object to being queried on this topic, 'I think it is a great shame that I should be thus questioned, and I will refuse to answer any further questions with regard to Dr Gully' (Hartman, 1977, p. 146) but *The Times* rebuked her, remarking that she had 'no right to complain of having been asked to explain circumstances of apparent suspicion.' Hartman observed how 'Florence's accusers were so busy looking for the sex outside marriage' (Hartman, 1977, p. 172). An element of sadism was evident in the depiction of some of these cases: lengthy reports dwelled on Lizzie Borden swooning at the verdict, Florence Bravo sobbing and Constance Kent's anguished repentance. But what stands out in all these cases, and comparable ones over many decades, is the way in which they are turned into moral fables about the lives of women involved. Two moral purposes are achieved. First, appropriate gender roles are underlined: Constance Kent's guilt was linked to a past escapade in which she had run away disguised as a boy (Hartman, 1977, p. 109). More generally, such cases were reported with heavy moral underlinings, to act as awful warnings to young women against the dangers of reading or of flirtation or to older women against adultery or 'new ideas'. As Hartman (1977) and Sullivan (1975) show, those women who were acquitted in the nineteenth century trials (and who may well have been guilty, such as Adelaide Bartlett and Lizzie Borden) got off through their (or their advocates') use of conventional stereotypes of femininity. Lizzie's counsel insisted to the (all-male) jury 'it would be morally and physically impossible for (her) to have committed these crimes' (Sullivan, 1975, p. 166). That moral lessons were being learnt is clear both from the immense interest in all these cases and in particular, as Hartman notes, the large numbers of women who attended the trials. However, when, as in the case of Florence Maybrick, women spectators and women generally regarded the verdict as unfair, and petitioned the Home Secretary for her release, the gentlemen moralists of the Press were outraged: the *Spectator*, for example, declared:

In the Maybrick case there has been an element of partisanship which we can hardly be mistaken in referring to something like a claim for women of the right to observe or disregard the obligations of marriage at their own pleasure ... There seems to be at present time a sort of partisanship for unfaithful wives, which has long disappeared, if it ever existed in precisely the same form, for unfaithful husbands. Doubtless there was a time when libertinism was regarded almost as a sort of distinction in a man. But we cannot remember that there was a tide of the sentimental sympathy and admiration for it which seems to have been felt towards Mrs Maybrick (Hartman, 1977, p. 304).

The solution proposed was that women should be excluded from attending such trials! (Hartman, 1977, p. 251).

Women can, then, be found fully depicted in various calendars of villainy and murder. If anything, they appear to attract more interest than do men in such cases, the image created is more powerful and may leave a long-lasting impression. But are they typified differently from men? Their records of official deviance, their chances of being formally arraigned are, as we saw in Chapter 1, lower. How are these differences represented?

Several writers have pointed to the narrow range of typifications of deviant women. Feinman suggested that there is a crude and simple duality:

> In the modern criminal justice system women are viewed according to attitudes that derive in large measure from classical Greece and Rome and medieval Europe. Both pagan mythology and Judeo-Christian theology present women with a dual nature, either as madonnas or as whores (Feinman, 1980, p. 1).

Smart, too, talked of the 'myth of the evil woman whose physiology is the source of her ability to deceive and manipulate' (Smart, 1977, p. 176) while Omodei asserted

> Myths about women and their innate capacities have pervaded every aspect of society; they have affected and been perpetuated by many specific elements of our social organization ... One of the most pervasive of myths relating to female crime (is) that female delinquency is predominantly sexual delinquency (Omodei, 1981, p. 51).

Edwards adds an important exception to 'The chaste/unchaste, good/bad, virgin/whore and madonna/magdalene distinction ... well understood in nineteenth and twentieth century accounts of femininity' (Edwards, 1981, p. 49) that is, that women can be perceived as provocative temptresses who bring about their own downfall in cases of rape or sexual assault.

Let us look at a range of portrayals of deviant women and see how narrow (or broad) they are and whether they link female deviance with evil and sexuality.

In the Judaeo-Christian tradition, a woman was the world's first sinner since it was Eve, tempted by the serpent to try forbidden apples in the garden of Eden who 'took of the fruit thereof, and did eat, and gave also unto her husband with her; and he did eat' (Genesis, 3:6, AV). It is interesting to observe how much in pictures, poetry and literature, Eve's role as temptress is highlighted and stressed. It is rarely remarked that what she sought to gain from eating the apples was *Knowledge*.

Shakespeare's Lady Macbeth fulfilled almost all the requirements of a criminal woman imbued with evil. She was ruthlessly
ambitious for her husband and commanded him to murder and to
dissemble

> To beguile the time,
> look like the time...
> ...and you shall put
> this night's great business into my dispatch
> (*Macbeth*, Act I, sc. V, 60–69).

She recognised the clash of 'natural' femininity with her ambitious
plans and conjures demons to

> Unsex me here,
> And fill me, from the crown to the toe, top-full
> Of direst cruelty!
> (*Macbeth*, Act I, sc, V, 38–40).

She is linked in imagery, in a play full of witchcraft and dark images,
with ravens, blood, smoke, illness, demons and infanticide. Her end
was horrible; tormented by her complicity in number she went mad,
sleepwalked and died.

Shakespeare's witches were women too – 'evil hags' – and he was
reflecting both popular and élite concerns because his monarch,
James I (of England and VI of Scotland) was particularly interested
in witches, publishing a pamphlet, *Daemonologie* in 1593 himself
on the subject. Later in the seventeenth century there were, of
course, major witch-hunts in Scotland which resulted in the execu-
tion of several hundred witches, most of them women. Larner has
analysed the witch–evil-woman image and its relation to the Scottish witch-hunts in fascinating detail:

> Witch-hunting was the most public form of social control ever
> devised because the identification of the witch was dependent on
> the public status (ill-fame) of the accused, and conviction was
> normally dependent on the reinforcement of her confession by
> witnesses to her malefices (Larner, 1981, p. 64).

Larner observed that 'Witchcraft was... in Scotland almost the only
woman's crime in this period' (Larner, 1981, p. 91). Further, although some 20 per cent of suspects were male:

It is argued here that the relationship between women and the stereotype of witchcraft is quite direct: witches are women; all women are potential witches (Larner, 1981, p. 92).

She suggested that 'Women are feared as a source of disorder in patriarchal society' (Larner, 1981, p. 93). This fear was based on the sinful/corrupt view of womankind as the source of evil and the fall of man and also because of the powerful mysteries of female sexuality and reproductive powers (Larner, 1981, p. 93). Because women were closer to the stereotype of the witch they were more likely to be persecuted for witchcraft:

Witch-hunting was directed for ideological reasons against the enemies of God and the fact that eighty per cent or more of these were women was, though not accidental, one degree removed from an attack on women as such (Larner, 1981, p. 92).

The witch is one very powerful image of the deviant woman which was used in 'control waves' of witch-hunting in various periods of history. As Larner pointed out, some of the women accused either did accept and use their reputation, others grew to accept it during trial, some did deny the charge up to the end. In the end, this would make little difference, since the whole emphasis on the charge was based on the reputation, the *mala fama* of a witch, in other words, the reaction of her own community to her (Larner, 1981, p. 103).

Women are no longer hunted as witches in Scotland, nor indeed anywhere in the British Isles. The witch image, however, does, remain, at least as a folk memory. It sits on top of a pyramid of related images of deviant women as especially evil, depraved and monstrous. Consider for example, the treatment of the case of Carole Compton who was convicted in Italy in 1983 of one charge of arson and two of attempted arson and acquitted of attempted murder. Because of certain allegedly bizarre aspects of the case, the Italian press began to suggest that the paranormal was involved and soon she was being labelled *strega* – a witch. This was taken up by British television and press and by media from other countries. With considerable hypocrisy, the non-Italian media scorned Italian superstition for the belief in witchcraft, while at the same time branding Compton as 'witch' or 'girl in the witchcraft case' at every opportunity. Even months after her return from Italy to Aberdeen:

Carole carefully avoids using the word witch. But no one else did
... she went to a disco. But even in the darkened room, even
sitting in the shadow, notoriety sought her out. 'Aren't you
frightened what might happen with *her* sitting next to you?' a
young punk asked one of her friends. 'It wasn't the first time' says
Carole. 'I had to move home because of the gossip. I even thought
of changing my name' (Pearce, 1984, p. 14).

The image of the witch then remains a potent symbol which can
be easily conjured up – sometimes almost subliminally – as in the
report of the release of two politically-motivated, highly organised
women convicted of causing explosions and conspiracy to cause
arson. It was headlined 'IRA's *Evil Sisters* Free' (Evening Standard
30 August 1983). A reappraisal of the Moors murder case, suggesting that Myra Hindley's role was much more dominant than had
previously been suggested concluded, 'It should therefore no longer
be surprising that epithets like *evil* and *wicked* should be applied to
Myra Hindley (Melvern and Gillman, 1982, p. 34).

In Chapter 6 I discuss how the notion of the extraordinarily evil
woman, the witch, was taken from folklore and popular accounts
and used by 'scientific' criminologists like Lombroso and Pollak as
the basis of their theories, theories which, as we shall see, have not
only had a stigmatising effect, but have also had unfortunate
consequences for the treatment of women offenders.

Alongside the witch, the whore is the most potent image of
female deviance. It is in fact quite a complex and distorting image or
set of images. In particular its use leads to the sexualising of many
other, sometimes all, types of non-conforming female behaviour.
Prostitutes themselves tend to be depicted as *sexual* deviants,
vicious, depraved and beyond redemption, as a Victorian author of
a popular account of 'Magdalenism' put it: 'Once a woman has
descended from the pedestal of innocence ... she is prepared to
perpetrate every crime' (Walkowitz, 1980, p. 39). We can recognise
in this telling image the sad histories of an army of fallen women,
forever damaged by their sins, the Nancies, Little Emilies and other
lost girls of the Victorian novel. Roberts has analysed mid-
Victorian paintings of 'Fallen Women' pointing out how the abject
position of the 'Outcast' is stressed and a moral point is made.
Ruskin in a famous critique of Holman Hunt's *The Awakening
Conscience* saw morality being imprinted with every brushstroke:

The very hem of the girl's dress, which the painter has laboured so closely, thread by thread, has a story in it, if we think how soon its pure whiteness may be soiled with the dust and rain, her outcast feet failing in the street (Ruskin, quoted in Roberts, 1973, p. 67).

These images of kept and fallen women are of course, largely fanciful; they have very little to do with the real histories of prostitute women, then or now, which are being increasingly well-documented (see for instance Vicinus, 1973; Walkowitz, 1980; Finnegan, 1979; McLeod, 1982; etc.). These modern accounts stress what Victorian feminists had already recognised, that prostitution was an illicit profession, and involved *economic* rather than *sexual* deviance. It was of course the social reaction to prostitution, the various attempts to control and regulate prostitution which caused its stigmatisation and, as Walkowitz and others suggested, changed the character of prostitution and its recruitment patterns (Walkowitz, 1980, ch. 10). Prostitutes today present a very interesting example of a group of women who have quite consciously determined to rid themselves of their traditional image and its associated stigma by manipulating the media themselves (see McLeod, 1982, and Chapter 2). They have been involved in making a feature film, in TV programmes, representations to parliament and in publishing their own newspapers and handouts. McLeod reports that some of the prostitutes who saw Garnett's film *Prostitute* at a pre-release showing were worried that it was pornographic and would give the wrong impression (1982, p. 141).

The 'contaminating sexuality' associated with prostitution tends to leak into the portrayal of other forms of female deviance. I discussed in Chapter 3 the sexualising of female teenage delinquency. Offences which have apparently nothing to do with sexuality are – when committed by women – transformed into expressions of female sexuality or the lack of it. Thus are created the images of the kleptomaniac – the compulsive, menopausal woman shoplifter – or the pre-menstrual violent women and an associated range of feminine stereotypes in which deviant behaviour, sexuality and sickness are all enmeshed. What distinguishes this group of images of deviance from those discussed earlier, despite the common link of sexuality, is that they tend to be built on 'scientific' bases, chiefly of a medical kind, but they have long since slipped into popular currency.

Ehrenreich and English have described 'the sexual politics of sickness' through which the medical profession came to view the entire female reproductive system and its generative cycles as pathological, dangerous and liable to induce disturbances of behaviour and personality. Although this was primarily a nineteenth-century phenomenon:

For decades into the twentieth century doctors would continue to view menstruation, pregnancy and menopause as physical diseases and intellectual liabilities (Ehrenreich and English, 1979, p. 126).

Cameron traced the creation of the image of the woman kleptomaniac from the conjectures of psychiatrists (Cameron, 1964, p. 155) and noted that she could find no examples of compulsive, hysterical thieves among her sample. Nevertheless this is a frequently-invoked image for certain women convicted of shoplifting.

Pre-menstrual tension, undoubtedly a clinically real experience for some women, has been linked to crime (Dalton, 1969). In fact the thesis that 'disturbed hormones equal offensive behaviour' is not a new one. It is obviously a premise that underpins the definition of infanticide. It can also be related to the older images of deviant women as inherently evil, which in turn depended on the assumption *either* that all women were evil, *or* that femininity consists of a duality, with the sinner always juxtaposed to a saint. What is so striking about all these images of deviant women is how profoundly damaging they are, once attached to any particular woman or group of women. Amongst them all, there is no conception of the 'normal' exuberant delinquency characteristic of males. Any woman would be damaged by being portrayed as a witch or a whore; and while a 'sick' female deviant may be less punitively treated, she will attract other stigma – as the resistance to such labelling by Patricia Hearst and Mrs Harris and the appalling experiences of Frances Farmer testify (Farmer, 1974, p. 215).

Folklore and myth supplied the first set of images of deviant women at which we looked; so-called science, with a heavy ideological bias supplied the second – both have been eagerly taken up by criminologists who have sought to explain female crime. Lombroso and Ferrero, Pollak, Thomas and Freud all used the notion of inherent female pathology to explain the feminine character and behaviour, as we can see in Chapter 6. What none of them – with the possible exception of Pollak – did was to question these images of women, or the assumptions underlying them. Pollak observed the double-standard of morality, but none of the rest seems to have noticed that the images of women they were using had been made by men. The witch-finder was pricking his own thumb.

There is a remaining image, perhaps a set of images, or recurrent themes in the presentation of female behaviour which is very significant, yet not as quite as clearly defined as those already discussed. Paradoxically, it is even more damaging, until treated ironically by some women or groups of women. This is the concept of deviant women as 'not-women' or as masculine, unfeminine women. Joan of Arc was one of the earliest – and best-recorded – cases of a highly exceptional woman whose behaviour was ultimately stigmatised, for political purposes, as unfeminine and as witchcraft and heresy. Joan of course wore men's clothes, led soldiers and indeed won battles. While her celebrated case gave rise to no clearly recognisable stereotype, the link between role-deviance and social deviance for women regularly reappears.

The Roaring Girl by Middleton and Dekker, first played in 1610, is a fascinating, curiously modern play about a real woman criminal – Moll Firth or Mal Cutpurse – who lived and thieved in London in the seventeenth century. The real Moll, as in the play, wore men's clothing, fought skilfully with sword and cudgel 'and in later years she was notorious as a whore, bawd cutpurse and receiver, a female Moriarty keeping a gang of thieves in her service' (Gomme, 1976, p. xiv). The real Moll had a considerable and celebrated criminal career; what is interesting about the play is that, while it shows Moll in her male apparel, gives her a fight scene in which she triumphs over the lascivious rake Laxton, it plays down her criminality. In fact, Moll is given lines to deny her record at least twice in the play:

>   . . . must you have
> A black ill name, because ill things you know?
> Good troth, my lord, I am made Moll Cutpurse so.
> (Act V.i.l. 315).

When her delinquencies are denied, what the playwrights leave of her character are some very interesting and unusual aspects. She is a free and independent spirit; uniquely in such a comedy, she remains as firmly unwed at the final curtain, despite numerous suitors, as at the first. Her attacks on male attitudes are remarkable for the period:

> . . . Th'art one of those
> That thinks each woman thy fond flexible whore:
> If she but cast a liberal eye upon thee.
> (Act III.1. 70).

Again, this particular portrayal of a celebrated woman professional thief did not develop into a permanent typification, any more than did the female pirates, Ann Bonny and Ann Read, in the eighteenth century, who sailed the Caribbean in flamboyant style and masculine dress. Traces clearly do survive (for example, see Donaldson, 1976, p. 59) but these characters have not been assimilated into popular legend. Their male attire and swashbuckling habits do, however, live on in the link often made between female crime and 'masculine' women.

Women involved in politically deviant activities, whether suffragettes, urban guerillas or peace protestors have been particularly subject to this treatment – indeed such disparate groups have been linked in some accounts. For instance, in a popular history of Christabel Pankhurst, Mitchell compares her with Ulrike Meinhof, with lesbians and with 'Samurai' women (Sarah, 1983, pp. 261–2). Much of the media interest in the Patty Hearst case centred on the descriptions of the three women who led the Symbionese Liberation Army and developed its ideology and the way that Patty Hearst was 'brainwashed' into participating in this 'unnatural' way of life (Pascal and Pascal, 1974, p. 92). The modern female terrorists, in particular have been portrayed as unisexed or unfeminine and representing a terrifying new phenomenon (Becker, 1977) summed up in the paranoid headline 'Armed Feminism on Rise in Europe' (Morris and Gelsthorpe, 1981, p. 64). Of course, much of the reporting of the Greenham Peace Camp women has included masterly innuendoes about their 'unattractive' looks, 'unfeminine' ways – which include getting drunk, kissing each other and not keeping their camps tidy.

That deviant women may be inherently masculine, since true femininity precludes improper behaviour, is a theme taken up by some of the classical criminologists, particularly Lombroso, but this concept also surfaces in the modern liberation-causes-crime-in-women argument, with proponents such as Adler arguing that the new female criminal is a free masculine spirit (see Chapter 8.

The range of distinctive images of deviance which depict women is fairly small. There are no male equivalents for the witch and the whore as conventionally portrayed, nor for the notion of crime as doubly-deviant. On the other hand, the gallery of types of male deviance is far more richly furnished. In particular, many deviant and indeed criminal male roles either receive public approval – 'boys will be boys' – or are at least positively portrayed. Otto has shown:

There to be no female equivalent of the 'noble-savage' portrayal of the male homeless alcoholic seen most vividly in the novels of Anderson (1923), Orwell (1933) and Kerouac (1962). Almost no films or books romanticize the female tramp or hobo; such women really do not excite anyone's fantasies or envy (Otto, 1981, p. 163).

Equally, there is no female equivalent of the vein of popular literature which celebrates the brutal rites of organised crime. McVicar aptly describes 'crime [as] a sort of blood sport played for real. *Before anything, the professional criminal wants respect, prestige and the recognition of those who subscribe to his own need of machismo*' (McVicar, 1974, p. 12, emphasis added).

It is quite clear that this want has been achieved by curious alliances of press, and criminals themselves. Pearson, for instance, describes how the Kray twins tried to recruit him to write their official history (Pearson, 1973, p. 11). In Chapter 7 I discuss the romanticising of male urban juvenile delinquency by modern sociologists, but they are not alone. Baden-Powell, for example, the founder of the Scout Movement was a fan of the juvenile delinquents of his day:

Scouting attracts the hooligans ... who really are the fellows of character ... well, the best class of boy ... (quoted in Pearson, 1983, p. 111).

There exists, in other words, a typification of male delinquency as a normal, healthy activity attributable to 'natural' high spirits in boys. There are many other deviant roles whose scripts exclude women. The most striking aspect of several of them is that they can be and in films, novels, etc. often are, positively depicted. In contrast it is difficult to think of a deviant female role which is not perceived as damaging to its protagonist.

The most positive portrayal of criminal women or delinquent girls tends, at best, to stress their helplessness and vulnerability and to minimise any depredations they may have caused. A Granada Television series on women in Styal prison so incensed a group of women who had themselves been in prison that they made a contrasting drama-documentary. Their main criticisms focused on the portrayal of women inmates as mentally ill or handicapped and lacking any control over their own lives. While certain groups of men may be depicted as helpless, it is not a popular image of the criminal man or delinquent boy.

Deviant men and women are represented in markedly different ways. In consequence, social reaction to their deviant behaviour differs: the 'respectable fears' attached to each gender are distinctive. There is, however, an even more remarkable divergence in these portrayals. Feinman and others, as I have already noted, have pointed to the constant duality in images of women – the possibility of good behaviour is displayed beside the bad. I think a further characteristic can be stressed: the good/bad woman is a constant theme in art literature, films and other media and so is the control of female behaviour by a variety of means.

Large sections of our cultural heritage can be reduced to two basic themes of either (i) the bad woman gets her just deserts or (ii) the good woman is put in her proper place. Consider, for instance, the classic European novel. Richardson's first two works, the earliest 'novels of character' in English are *Pamela* and *Clarissa Harlowe*. Pamela is subtitled *Virtue Rewarded* (Richardson, 1740) and tells of a servant girl pursued by a young man who tries to seduce her; she resists, he then marries her and she puts up with his profligate behaviour. *Clarissa* (1747–8) was intended as a 'warning' and describes the downfall and death of the eponymous heroine, ruined by her unscrupulous lover. The same or similar themes – of the abject misery and disgrace (usually followed by death) of women who stray from the strict path of marital or pre-marital chastity – run through novels as diverse in authorship and setting as *Madame Bovary, Nana, Anna Karenina* and *Tess of the Durbervilles*. These are, of course, major works of literature and cannot just be dismissed as 'awful warnings'. Beneath them flourished hundreds of inferior and lesser known works exemplified perhaps by Mrs Henry Wood's *East Lynne* – the tale of a young wife whose adultery leads her to poverty, disfigurement, and the loss of two of her children, her husband and her lover and finally her own death. The moral purpose of all these authors may not always have been as explicit as Richardson's was, but the message to the female reader is clear: wayward women are doomed.

Not all expressions of the theme of controlling women are tragic. Shakespeare's *The Taming of the Shrew* is only one of a whole genre of Elizabethan plays which dealt, usually in a coarse and rumbustious way, with the bridling of scolds and the breaking-in of 'shrewish' wives who finally submit to the 'lawful' authority of their husbands. Sometimes the message has been much more subtle and capable of reinterpretation in a later and more conscious age. The Hollywood *film noir* of the 1940s and 1950s have classic plots which centre on beautiful dangerous women who are literally *femmes fatales*. In *Double Indemnity, The Postman Always Rings Twice*, etc., one or more men are trapped and die in their deadly lures; the women usually meet their doom too, proper punishment for their evil ways. Recently feminist writers have reinterpreted these films to suggest that nowadays the intelligence and power their heroines show is more striking than their unhappy ends (Place, 1978).

Pictorial representations of women can carry all kinds of subtle hints and messages, can indeed convey a whole world-view of meaning. Berger, in a telling essay, has examined the pictures of women, particularly nudes, in European painting. Men and women are depicted quite differently, he argued:

> To be born a woman has been to be born, within an allotted and confined space, into the keeping of men. The social presence of women has developed as a ... result of their ingenuity in living under such tutelage within such a limited space ... A woman must continually watch herself. She is almost continually accompanied by her own image of herself ... From earliest childhood she has been taught and persuaded to survey herself continually ... [to] simplify ...: *Men act* and *women appear* (Berger, 1973, pp. 46–7).

Berger then went on to analyse the European tradition of painting in which women, as nudes, were the principal subject. In fact,

Berger suggested women were the objects of these pictures 'the painters and spectator – owners were usually men and the persons treated as objects, usually women' (Berger, 1973, p. 63). He showed that although the dominant man is not normally depicted in these oils, his presence is implied and the female subject–object looks at him as 'a sign of her submission to the owner's feelings or demands' (Berger, 1973, p. 52), yet

> The principal protagonist is never painted. He is the spectator in front of the picture and he is presumed to be a man. Everything is addressed to him. Everything must appear to be the result of his being there (Berger, 1973, p. 54).

Nude photography and pornography share some of this conventional approach, Berger suggested. In short, male dominance can be strongly suggested in pictorial representation without the patriarchal male being directly represented at all. Again, a clear if subtle message is conveyed. Beauty and femininity are defined in the eye of the (male) beholder. The woman must look to the male spectator for definition and approval.

Now I am not suggesting here that the women painted by Rubens, Tintoretto, etc. were all deviant women whom the artist admonished (although in fact many of the models were mistresses, courtesans and other 'unrespectable' women of their day). Rather it is the broad vision conveyed of how women should behave, to whom they should respond that seems to me significant.

Berger's pictorial analysis has been taken further by Goffman in his decoding of the subtle and not-so-subtle notes struck in *Gender Advertisements* (1976). He anatomised advertisements in great detail and shows how in all kinds of ways visual meanings are conveyed about gender difference and especially male supremacy. Sexual dimorphism is always emphasised so that 'every male participant will (seem) bigger than every female participant' (Goffman, 1976, p. 28). Males too are depicted in dominant roles in what Goffman calls 'function ranking' (Goffman, 1976, p. 32) and in the family (Goffman, 1976, p. 39). He gives a great deal of space to what he calls 'the ritualisation of subordination' of women to men: 'Women frequently, men very infrequently, are posed in a display of the "bashful knee bend"' (Goffman, 1976, p. 45). Goffman follows Durkheim in seeing the portrayal of female behavioural style as not just 'incidental' but 'a political ceremony, in this case affirming the

place that persons of the female sex-class have in the social struc-
ture, in other words, holding them to it' (Goffman, 1976, p. 8).
These and similar analysis are succinctly summarised by the
'Pictures of Women' group who declare

> Modern media continue to portray women in a way which is
> telling us what we are and what can be done to us . . . it is
> important to start to look at and understand the 'pictures of
> women' which are being offered up to us as images of what we
> want or should aspire to . . . we want to show how, in a society
> which is controlled by masculine values, women are regulated,
> manipulated, constructed and defined (Root, 1984, p. 6).

So far I have tried to show that how women should behave, and
the dire consequences for them if they misbehave, are pervasive
themes in our culture. There are of course, dangers in adding
together examples from various media and distinctive epochs, but
the examples I have used are not isolated nor evidence of personal
pathology (as are, I think, the woman-hating plays of Strindberg or
the denigration of women in the novels of Henry Miller (Millett,
1977, p. 294). I think it significant that warning images of non-
conforming women are presented in so many different contexts and
that patriarchal authority is expressed in so many ways. (There are,
of course, many other instances which I could have used in this
analysis: the rites and symbols of the Christian religion or the ritual
observances of Judaism are just two).

It would be wrong to suggest that there are no moral fables, no
cautionary tales for male delinquents or deviant men in our culture.
But they are very different in kind and in presentation. Consider
Shakespeare's only fully-realised portrait of a young delinquent:
Prince Hal. His is a classic case for the juvenile bureau or the
probation service: he drinks too much, sleeps around, leads his gang
in what can only be described as a double-mugging (*Henry IV*, Pt I,
Act II, Sc. ii), neglects his family and his duties. Yet it is not he but
the virtuous Harry Percy who dies and poor old Falstaff who has to
shoulder the opprobrium. Hal goes on to become the patriotic
monarch and leader of men in *Henry V*. Shakespeare of course
merely followed and embellished history. Yet he was using an
archetypal plot reserved almost exclusively for men – the adventure
story in which our hero after numerous experiences often of a

dubious character with deplorable people, emerges, or returns home, unscathed but wiser, to claim his own, marry the heroine and settle down. This is essentially the plot of *Tom Jones* and most of Dickens' novels with eponymous heroes – *David Copperfield, Martin Chuzzlewit, Oliver Twist* and *Nicholas Nickleby*. There are a few such *Bildungsromane* written about women like Defoe's *Moll Flanders* and Cleland's *Fanny Hill*, but they stand out as exceptions, generally the licence granted to heroines to travel and to have adventures is very limited. When Jane Eyre finally married Mr Rochester she was still, after all, a virgin.

The presentation of straying males is, then, much less censorious. Some sowing of wild oats is approved of, indeed positively welcomed in certain circles and settings. There are, too, a range of typifications of male deviance where negative and deplorable aspects are stressed, but in general these are not as potentially stigmatising, as threatening to the identity of a man as are their equivalents to women.

To conclude the arguments in support of this case, let me draw on the huge and distinctive amount of advice, moral uplift and guidance offered to women on how to be good women – that is, good wives and mothers. There is simply no equivalent directed in such substantial quantities to men. Compare and contrast, as we say in examination papers, Giovanni Boccaccio's two most famous works – his *Decameron* (1348–58) and his *Concerning Famous Women* published a decade or so later. While the former set of tales does have some exemplary purpose it is essentially a set of celebratory stories, sometimes bawdy and satirical . . . some of his heroes meet unfortunate ends, like the deceitful Brother Alberto, but others like Masetto the 'mute' who becomes the convent handyman, triumph. Masetto spends the rest of his life bringing 'little monks' into the world. But *Concerning Famous Women* is very different. Through re-telling a series of biographies of women from Eve through classical Greece and Rome up to his own day, he seeks to achieve a positive moral purpose:

I have extolled with praise the deeds deserving of commemoration and have condemned with reproach the crimes, there will sometimes be not only glory for the noble, but opprobrium for the wicked [women] . . . [I] include among these stories some pleasant exhortations to virtue and add inducements to avoid and detest wickedness, so that by adding pleasure to these stories their value would enter the mind by stealth (Boccaccio, ed. by Guarino, 1964, p. xxxviii).

His modern editor notes how much more prescriptive is his work on women than the *Decameron*, how much more censorious the author appears and how idealistic the norms he sets for women (but not for men) even when these appear to clash.

Boccaccio is simply an early example of a vast trend in culture, the promotion of good-womanhood by exhortation and prescription. At least two major streams can be distinguished: the stern and the sweetened. Under the first we can find innumerable tracts urging women how to be good, especially good mothers and wives. Badinter (1982) has analysed advice to mothers from Rousseau on, noting how practical advice – do not swaddle your baby, do breast-feed him – is mingled with exhortations to proper feelings. Ehrenreich and English took the development of what they term 'scientific motherhood' as one of many instances where 'experts' claimed to know:

> What is woman's true nature? . . . and what . . . was she to do? . . . and to prescribe the 'natural' life plan for women . . . experts used their authority to define women's domestic activities down to the smallest details of housework and child raising . . . The experts wooed their female constituency, promising the 'right' and scientific way to live (Ehrenreich and English, 1979, p. 4).

They showed this trend has continued until the very recent past with (mainly male) experts prescribing how women should act out their lives.

Stern and serious moral advice to women on how to behave has a sweeter-natured sister. She lives in the parallel world of women's magazines and romantic fictions for women so neatly apostrophised by Ferguson as *Forever Feminine* (1983b). Ferguson dissected the consistencies and the changes in the subject matter of women's magazines since the war and traced how 'getting and keeping your man' remains a central theme. She concluded by asking:

> But what, finally do women's magazines 'do' for women? The answer to this is complex. It relates to two powerful but implicit

assumptions in the messages of women's magazines. The first is their generalised approach of 'a woman is a woman is a woman' ... The second assumption is that *females require step-by-step instruction and continuing education in the arts and crafts of feminity*. Whereas a more powerful and confident male sex does not require a masculine equivalent ... there is a woman's press where 'how to' is the keynote struck across decades (and centuries) by the high priestesses of women's magazines ... guidelines such as these take on aspects of a sacred cult. They form part of a wider social process that locates women within a feminity which focuses on Him, Home and Looking Good (Ferguson, 1983a, pp. 96–7, emphasis added).

As Ferguson pointed out in the same passage 'there is no men's periodical press in the same generic sense'. It is easy enough to try this simple experiment: ask any teenage boy what he thinks a magazine for his age group called *Jimmy* would be about. He will probably reply 'football' or 'adventure'. Ask an adult male to guess at the contents of new journals with titles like *Man, Man's Own, Man's Realm* and he will probably suggest that they are pornographic – that is, they will contain pictures of *women*. While there are considerable numbers of periodicals which cater for male hobbies and sports such as fishing or motor-racing, there is no equivalent for men to the vast array of periodicals which advise women on how to be good, brave, beautiful, slim, well-organised feminine women. That is not the same thing as saying that men neither need nor want such advice. Indeed many men read women's magazines, especially the advice pages and write to their editors about their problems, but there is no mass socialisation of males into their proper roles by either stern example or sugared didactic.

This gap can even be found in the pulp fictions, mainly thrillers and romantic novels, which are directed at and read by, genderdifferentiated markets. The male heroes of Westerns, cops 'n robbers and other thrillers are *asocial or extra-social*. They embody the supposed virtues of machismo – they are hard and tough, they fight fair – but they are often 'outlaws' either actual criminals or, as in Clint Eastwood-type films, they bend or break laws in order to achieve 'justice'. Romantic heroines, on the other hand, are usually *over-socialised*. They conform to stereotyped notions of feminine virtue and decorum whatever the circumstances. To break frame, to step out of the gender role and play another part invites disaster. A Mills and Boon heroine's goal is marriage, not a Nobel Prize nor a seat on the board, and the message that she will achieve that goal by staying feminine is reinforced continually.

It is my contention that the effect of many aspects of our culture is to produce conformity in women. Conformity, that is, to both their proper place in society and on the whole, to a stricter observance of society's rules, both legal and moral. Only women are instructed every week, in case they should possibly ever forget, in how to *be* women; only women were led to believe that adultery could be a terminal condition. Although men provide more menace to the basis of a society, it is women who are instructed in how to behave. I am not suggesting that there is a conspiracy here. It is much more likely that common concerns over women's reproductive powers and mysterious sexuality, as Larner suggests, may lie behind earlier fears of witchcraft and also later 'expert' attempts to control and isolate them. There are many theories as to the origins of male dominance in human society. None seem to me sufficient. At this stage I want merely to put forward the hypothesis that ensuring female conformity has been a near-universal goal of male-dominated society and that much of the evidence to support this can be found, as any good anthropologist would expect, in the cultural artefacts, the pictures, books, films, plays and programmes in which are expressed the key images and symbols of our own society.

How effective is this pervasive imagery in achieving female conformity? Do women accept and act on the messages they receive? There is of course the evidence of the sex–crime ratio. As we saw in Chapter 1, women commit fewer crimes, less serious crimes and do less often. There is no support from self-report studies for Pollak's thesis that women are actually more criminal than men, but succeed in concealing their deeds.

Women do appear to accept their prescribed roles in life – the overwhelming majority marry and most become mothers. Sharpe (1976) in her study of schoolgirls and Oakley (1974) with both housewives and new mothers, have shown how powerful are the stereotypes of feminine behaviour and how closely women identify with them, even when they resent aspects of their roles, such as the boring routines of housework or the demands of a young baby. As Oakley notes:

Various writers have drawn attention to the domesticated image of women put over in the mass media, in textbooks and reading books for children and in school curricula . . . For girls caught up in this nexus of processes, the effect is that the feminine role, the 'little housewife' role and self-definition are blended together in 'unself-conscious complex of unobstructed behaviour'. Through the integration of feminine role learning with self-definition, housekeeping behaviours tend to be developed as personality functions (Oakley, 1974, p. 114).

Morris found that girls were more inclined than boys to feel shame in admitting delinquent acts. Boys were more likely to boast of their activities (Morris, 1965). Similar observations were made by Parker *et al.*, about young people brought before the juvenile court (see Chapter 3). We saw too the marked trend to disavow deviance amongst the women whose personal histories are discussed in Chapter 2. Women who have been labelled as deviant have tried to 'normalise' their image, as the compaigning prostitutes have done, by stressing their conventional femininity, their conformity to the ideals of motherhood and competence in housework. This provides a considerable contrast to the celebrations of criminal subcultures, the glorification of violence and villainy found in a range of works by or about male gangsters. Women, then, seem to conform, to want to be seen as conforming and to know what their assigned role should be. Friedan was one of the first to point out that when women do feel unhappy in their 'proper' roles, they tended, in the past at least, to blame themselves and to define themselves as having a problem without a name (Friedan, 1963).

Typifications of deviant and conforming women affect women themselves; they also have effects on agencies of control and on the public. In several of the famous murder trials discussed earlier in this chapter the image of innocent femininity was successfully used in pleas for the accused women or girl. This was true of Lizzie Borden and Madeline Smith, who were both probably guilty. Adelaide Bartlett seems to have manipulated those around her by using presumed female innocence/ignorance as cloaks to disguise her real actions. As Hartman points out:

[A] remarkable feature of (these) cases is the illustration of how prevailing images of women not only were internalized and acted upon by the accused murderesses themselves, but also how their judges, both inside and outside the courtrooms, were mesmerized by the popular stereotypes. The new image of the blameless and pure middle class maiden was accessible . . . having mustered the required appearance and demeanour [the young ladies] gained public immunity (Hartman, 1977, p. 261).

Root quotes a bizarre case from Edinburgh in 1811 of two women who won a libel case because the court thought that they were too respectable and too affectionate towards each other to be lesbians (Root, 1984, p. 13).

It must, of course, be remembered that neither Patty Hearst nor Jean Harris were acquitted, although Hearst was later released by act of clemency. Times have obviously changed and it is likely that while the realities of life for deviant and conforming women have changed very little, *perceptions* of deviant women have changed amongst the police, judges and the public.

Most sociologists of deviance have been so fascinated by the processes of defining deviance and becoming deviant that they have got over-excited. In this state they largely tend to ignore the much larger and more complex problem of the production of conformity. That problem is usually left to the experts in socialisa- tion, but in looking at women who deviate we have to link these two strands, first, because women are nearly always presented in dualis- tic terms as being both good and bad, saints and scrubbers. It is also vital to remember that women are involved in so little recorded crime and deviance that we need to look at their conformity as much as at their deviance. Models devised to explain societal reactions to male behaviour – the intellectual's lego of 'deviancy amplification' and 'feed-back-loops' – do not apply very well to women. Rosenb- lum has suggested that all women are 'primary deviants' – their subordinate social and sexual position makes this inevitable, but few stray into 'secondary deviance'. Rather control is maintained by the imposition of deep and damaging stigma on a small minority of women while for the rest a massive 'diversion' takes place as women are exhorted, cajoled and subtly coerced into conformity. Pictures and stories, poems and legends, advertisements for cleaning fluids, and soap operas all come laden with messages clearly saying 'the price of deviance is too high for women'. Once again, I must stress that I do not see a great male conspiracy behind this, nor invisible hands guiding it. It is instead probably an inescapable feature of patriarchal society (and most human societies are and have been patriarchal). At different times, for different groups the process takes different forms, but the general effect remains the same.

There are, however, a few signs of change. Some are depressing. There seems to have been something of a 'moral panic' reaction to the so-called 'new female criminal' who is probably little more than a myth. On the other hand, some women have begun to learn about and to confront the processes which subtly define and discipline behaviour. The Greenham Women who hung baby clothes and family pictures on the missile-camp wire fence were making subtle and ironic points as well as straightforward ones. Feminists have used terms like 'shrew', 'bitch', 'witch', etc. to name themselves. More women now have some kind of say in the media, in the production of public images, than ever before. Nevertheless, achieving the compliance of women is still a persistent theme in aspects of our culture. It is remarkable how little this has been commented on and even more remarkable (given how successful the process appears to be) that men do not try a little of the medicine on themselves.

6

Understanding female criminality

Social theories

Social theories have a central role to play in making sense of social reality. There is a well-established tendency to react against 'theory' which is seen as 'abstract' and therefore 'unreal' or distorted. Yet knowledge has to be fitted into a framework of some kind in order to be usable; it cannot, indeed be collected in the first place without assumptions being made about its use or the need to solve certain problems. Social theories are important and worth attention because they offer (or attempt to offer) coherent explanations of social happenings. Even if we reject the explanation as ill-founded, theories can be illuminating because their application has produced new and challenging material; few would now accept the ecological theories of the Chicago school, but its ethnographic studies remain fascinating. Finally, ideas do change the world, or at least parts of it. The influence of sociological concepts is frequently underestimated: they affect both the intellectual climate and social policies. Consider for instance, the impact of Bowlby's formulation of 'maternal deprivation' (Bowlby, 1953; Dally, 1982; pp. 97ff) or the idea of 'community' presented by nineteenth-century social theorists (Nisbet, 1966, Ch. 3).

Criminological theorising has been particularly abundant. A recent text describes its history as 'tumultuous', 'revolution after revolution', and 'this bewildering and extensive maze of quarrels and claims' (Downes and Rock, 1982, p. vii). Crime and deviance obviously have special characteristics which attract social theorists: they are key social issues, perhaps, after the economy, the major

110

issue. For sociologists, too, social order has been the central issue and the nature of crime is peculiarly problematic, confusing and ambiguous.

In this chapter, I want to look at the attempts which have been made to explain female criminality. As we have already seen, female crime as a subject has not been well-covered in criminological literature, despite the fact that it has certain distinctive and apparently challenging features. Indeed this neglect has generated its own commentary (Heidensohn, 1968; Smart, 1977). In more recent times there have been notable developments and there are articles and at least one text devoted to a critique of criminological theory and its bearing on women and crime (Naffin, 1981; Leonard, 1982). In these studies it is clear that it is difficult to impose a coherent pattern on the works discussed. Analyses of women criminals were very rare before the 1960s. They may therefore have to be studied in arbitrary isolation since they bear little relation to one another. The main schools of criminological thought have little or nothing to say about women offenders and so they have to be presented negatively or not at all. In order therefore to achieve what I hope will be a clear account of theories relating to women and crime, I have divided them into traditional, modern and feminist. In this chapter and the next I shall look at both the occasional 'classical' theories and modern criminology, and in the following one I shall discuss those more recent contributions which, while they differ markedly in approach and conclusions, have in common that women are the central focus of their work.

Traditional criminology

Criminology, mainstream and tributary, has almost nothing to say of interest or importance about women. This is as true of most major modern contributors as it was in the past. Writers on women and crime who have looked to the past, to 'classical' criminology have focussed on those few texts which do deal with women and tended to highlight them (Smart, 1977; Leonard, 1982). Even where Lombroso, Thomas *et al.* are placed in their intellectual and historical context as 'social Darwinist' or 'liberal paternalist' there is a tendency to overemphasise their distinctiveness because they actually wrote about women (and provide us with some detailed case histories and statistics) when their contemporaries were silent. What distinguishes writers on female crime is not only that they represent a particular criminological tradition, but that they seek to rationalise and to make intellectually acceptable a series of propositions about women and their consequences for criminal behaviour. Women, in this view, are determined by their biology and their physiology. Their hormones, their reproductive role, inexorably determine their emotionality, unreliability, childishness, deviousness, etc. These factors lead to female crime. Even a superficial examination shows up the contradictions here.

First, only women are seen as so particularly dominated by their biology. (Lombroso did, it is true, stress genetic factors in male criminals, but in later writings he modified this stress. Nor did he suggest that male sexuality or reproduction affected their criminality, although he believed that male criminals were much uglier than their female counterparts.) Any adequate explanation of female crime in biological terms has to explain why female but not male biology determines deviant behaviour. Moreover, such explanations are over-deterministic in that since most women experience the physiological changes discussed, a much higher crime rate should be predicted for women than for men.

A partial answer to questions about sex differences in criminality is given by all these theorists: not only are women biologically distinct and uniquely behaviourally determined, their deviance is peculiarly sexual. Thus they are seen as engaging in prostitution as an equivalent to normal crime in men (Lombroso, 1895) or as the key symptom of the 'unadjusted' girl (Thomas, 1923). Even apparently non-sexual actions such as assault or theft are redefined as evidence of sexual repression (Pollak, 1961, p. 142) or of the hysterical abnormality of the 'born female criminal' (Lombroso and Ferreros, 1895, p. 248).

Curiously, while stressing the innate, physically-based character of female deviance these writers also stress its pathology 'As a double exception, the criminal woman is consequently a monster – her wickedness must have been enormous' (Lombroso and Ferrero, 1895, p. 152). In other words, what occurs in nature, through atavistic inheritance or hormonal influences is at the same time unnatural and evil. A further duality can be noted in these writers' views of women. Women are both wicked and saintly, whores and mothers, the two images are frequently juxtaposed sometimes in very uneasy harmony. These three writers do differ in certain aspects as we shall see, but in these themes they have a great deal in common. What is most important, however, is that they expressed popular views about female crime and gave them mainly spurious scientific support. Far from being swamped by the modern criminological tides which have long washed away biological determinism these ideas have flourished in their intellectual rockpools, amazing examples of survival. Neo-Lombrosian studies of girl-delinquents were still being carried out in the 1970s, prostitution was still seen often as evidence of individual psychopathology rather than a rational economic choice for women in the 1980s (McLeod, 1982). Since their ideas have had great influence and are still with us it is worth looking at these writers in some detail.

Lombroso and Ferrero

Cesare Lombroso was the leading proponent of positivist criminology 'whose theories and writings have influenced the course of thinking more deeply than those of any other criminologists' (Mannheim, 1965, p. 213). Although his work with its biological – anthropological base is no longer accepted he played a crucial role in focussing research on individual offenders and their traits and characters. The monograph on women offenders which he published with his son-in-law Ferrero was a relatively late work. Although in other late works (Lombroso, 1913) he acknowledged social and economic factors in crime causation, these are discounted in *La Donna Delinquente*.

Applying the principles and methods of Lombroso's earlier work, he and Ferrero conducted detailed measurements of the skulls, brains and bones of women criminals and prostitutes, and studied their appearance from masses of photographs and their careers from a variety of life histories. Using this material they concluded that there were far fewer 'born female criminals' than males as judged by the characteristic signs of atavistic degeneracy and that prostitutes had more 'anomalies' than female offenders or normal women (Lombroso and Ferrero, 1895, p. 85). 'All the same' they observed it is incontestable that female offenders seem almost normal when compared to the male criminal, with his wealth of anomalous features' (Lombroso and Ferrero, 1895, p. 107).

Women, when they do degenerate into atavism, are more likely to become prostitutes 'whose types approximates so much more to that of her primitive ancestress'. According to Lombroso and Ferrero women commit less crime because they have not evolved to the same degree as men and are therefore more primitive and have less scope for degeneration. Really 'women are big children ... their moral sense is deficient' (Lombroso and Ferrero, 1895, p. 151). Women are much more likely to be occasional than born criminals; even so, the ordinary female criminal is perceived as particularly unnatural, she is masculine and virile and shows 'an inversion of all the qualities which specially distinguish the normal woman; namely, reserve, docility and *sexual apathy*' (Lombroso and Ferrero, 1895, p. 297, emphasis added). The Italian authors frequently asserted that maternity and female sexuality are mutually exclusive – 'her exaggerated sexuality so opposed to maternity'. 'In the ordinary run of mothers the sexual instinct is in abeyance' (Lombroso and Ferrero, 1895, p. 153).

Lombroso became famous as the father of 'scientific' criminology. In fact his work was fanciful rather than scientific. His detailed measurements were not subject to any tests of significance and his 'analysis' of photographs of 'fallen women' is as objective as an adjudication in a beauty contest. What this joint study sets out is an undoubtedly sincere attempt to justify certain beliefs and theories without submitting them to any kind of systematic enquiry. Thus Lombroso and Ferrero confronted the 'eternal anomaly of womankind' – that women could be madonnas but also prostitutes, and although women are 'revengeful, jealous inclined to ... cruelty' (Lombroso and Ferrero, 1895, p. 151), they nevertheless number few criminals amongst them. Like almost all the writers in this group and in others, Lombroso and Ferrero did not ultimately help our understanding of women and crime. What they did show us was the attempt to rationalise and justify the *status quo*, the existing position of women and the double standard of morals of their day.

Hence, although women are not very criminal, their 'evil tendencies are more numerous and more varied than men's' (Lombroso and Ferrero, 1895, p. 151) and by implication it is appropriate that they should be 'kept in the paths of virtue by ... maternity piety, weakness' (Lombroso and Ferrero, 1895, p. 152). Prostitution is the 'natural' state of regression for women and any women who are criminal are unnatural and more like men, lacking maternal feelings and carrying virile stigmata. In short Lombroso and Ferrero defined distinctive sub-species of women as 'good' and 'bad', 'natural' and 'abnormal' and equated these with conformity and crime. In this they reflected nineteenth-century attitudes to respectable and other women and add another footnote to the debates about 'separate spheres'. But they told us little about female criminality and more, much more about themselves and their ideas about women. Describing a bust of an old Palermo woman poisoner, they

> recall the proverbial wrinkles of witches and the instance of the vile old woman . . . of Palermo who poisoned so many . . . the bust of this criminal so full of virile angularities and above all so deeply wrinkled with its Satanic leer, suffices of itself to prove that the woman in question was born to do evil, and that, if one occasion to commit it had failed, she would have found others (Lombroso and Ferrero, 1895, p. 72).

Thomas

In studying the group of 'classical' criminological writers gathered into this chapter, we shall see how several central themes emerge in their work on women. These themes have remained important and influential in studying female crime, and indeed in its treatment. As scholars who produced full-length studies of women, they were exceptional, but they were not straying outside traditional territory. They used approaches already established and accepted in their fields. What does distinguish them, especially from the American sociologists of deviance at whom we shall look later, is the way in which they make certain ideas explicit.

Their view of women is heavily stereotyped. Women are defined according to domestic and sexual roles; they are dominated by biological imperatives; they are emotional and irrational. At the same time, irreconcilable ambiguities enter the picture. Women are uniquely qualified for motherhood and domestic tasks. It would be foolish and inappropriate to attack these writers for their unsurprising sexism. They were men of their age and subscribed to contemporary ideology and culture. Where they can be criticised is in their failure, despite strong claims of scientific rigour for and by them all

(Lombroso and Ferrero, 1895, p. xv; Thomas, 1923, p. xvi; Pollak, 1961, p. xv) to analyse any of their assumptions and to consider whether they might be changed or modified. They remain important then because they crystallise certain views scattered throughout criminology and also because, while they do not in the end help very much towards an understanding of women's crime, they themselves provide us with case study material to develop our own understanding.

W. I. Thomas was himself a pioneer of the use of case study material in social research. His *Unadjusted Girl* is a study of a series of such 'cases' designed to illustrate the dominance of four key 'wishes' in human behaviour: for new experience, for security, for response and for recognition (Thomas, 1923, p. 4). Thomas had earlier produced *Sex and Society* (1907) which was clearly influenced by Lombroso and Ferrero. Like them he assumed a 'natural' male – female dichotomy corresponding to 'active' and 'passive' states. As Smart noted, this was a narrowly selective view for Thomas to take 'as his major concern was the plight of immigrant, often peasant, women in the USA, who not only worked outside the home but often had to rear children single-handed' (Smart, 1977, p. 39). Klein (1976) has observed the close parallels between Thomas's early work and Lombroso's – 'they both delineate a biological hierarchy along race and sex lines'. Like Lombroso and Ferrero, Thomas asserted that men are further developed than women in evolutionary terms; 'Man ... (is) more ... specialised an animal than women' (Thomas, 1907, p. 36) just like the Italian positivists, Thomas linked women and children and 'the lower human races and the lower classes' as being tougher and less sensitive than white males.

Thomas did, however, live through a transitional period in the study of crime and delinquency and in his later work he was much more concerned with social influences and pressures. He still dealt with instincts, especially the maternal 'instinct' in women: 'the child is helpless throughout a period of years and would not live unless the mother were impelled to give it her devotion. This attitude is present in the father of the child also but is weaker, less demonstrative and called out more gradually' (Thomas, 1923, p. 18). What really interested him most, however, were the definitions of their situation which his subjects had. Thus subjective reality was more crucial than any 'facts' of a situation. Women, in Thomas's view, were more likely to be 'unadjusted' because they suffered more and were aware of their deprivations during a period of social change. The 'wishes' could and should be repressed as in the past:

> In the small and spatially isolated communities of the past, where the influences were strong and steady, the members became more or less habituated to and reconciled with a life of repressed wishes (Thomas, 1923, p. 71).

Mature women and young girls suffered in 'the modern revolt and unrest' because they were most excluded and felt most frustrated at their deprivations. 'Costly and luxurious articles of women's wear' Thomas wrote 'disorganise the lives of many who crave these pretty things' (Thomas, 1923, p. 71).

It is clear that Thomas largely equated female delinquency with sexual delinquency. Many of his case histories of unadjusted girls describe lives of promiscuity or adultery rather than of crime. Smart (1977) noted that in adopting anecdotal style he avoided theorising or indeed analysing women's social position. He noted the power of community and family in controlling and repressing women's behaviour in traditional societies, but he did not examine or extend this insight. Nor did he consider how female sexual misbehaviour was stigmatised, but male behaviour was not. Smart (1977) has linked his work with that of Konopka and with a whole school of social pathologists who individualise female delinquency, equating it with sexual delinquency and urging that the girl delinquent should be readjusted to society, to accept her role 'to co-ordinate the girl immediately with the large society in which she lives' (Thomas, 1923, p. 200). That the role assumptions or the prevailing morality might be changed are not ideas that Thomas ever contemplated.

The Unadjusted Girl differs from *La Donna Delinquente* and *The Criminality of Women* in that some 'real' women do appear in it. Thomas did not show the same distaste for his subjects that Lombroso and Ferrero and Pollak did. There is some compassion, albeit of a paternalist kind for the delinquent girls and little of the implicit fear of devious, dangerous femininity present in the other works. But Thomas did share their fears for the sanctity of the family:

> The bad family life constantly evident in these pages and the consequent delinquency of children as well as crime, prostitution and alcoholism are largely due to the over-determination of economic interests (Thomas, 1923, p. 256),

and throughout his work automatically took for granted the doctrine of 'separate spheres' – that the home is women's province, work and public life only for men. Nowhere did he consider that women too may have economic motivations as rational as those of men for their delinquent acts.

Pollak

Pollak's *The Criminality of Women* (1961) was originally published in the USA in 1950. It is the only full-length published study of this period which looks at women and crime. The post-war era did of course, produce a wave of criminological studies; (male juvenile delinquency was its especial focus in works by Cohen, 1955; Kobrin, 1951; Sykes and Matza, 1957, and Cloward and Ohlin, 1961). Pollak's study seems to have been inspired by his mentor, Thorsten Sellin (Pollak, 1961, p. vii) who with Reckless had 'drawn attention to this neglect of the study of the criminality of women'. Although written and published in the USA at a time of high creativity and debate in criminology, Pollak's work seems not to be part of that time at all.

In its careful but statistically unsophisticated handling of figures, its citation of long-dead European authors, its presentation of data from countries with their boundaries as well as their cultures twice dislocated in half a century, Pollak's book is closest to the works of European scholars such as Hermann Mannheim, but in some ways it seems to belong to a much older European tradition than that of the careful Central European scholar. The 1961 paperback edition has a binding with a crudely-coloured illustration of a witch beating a kneeling man.

Pollak's analysis of female crime has two main strands. First he examined data on recorded criminality in several countries and over time and endeavoured to show 'that female crime has been vastly under-estimated' Pollak 1961, p.153) and that indeed 'female crime is perhaps the outstanding area of undiscovered, or at least unprosecuted, crime in our culture and that its actual amount as well as its relation to male criminality has been greatly underrated' (Pollak, 1961, p.154). Second, and of greater theoretical interest, Pollak put forward a theory to explain this 'masking'. Here although a sociologist he used none of the existing repertoire of sociological explanations of crime. There are no references at all to Chicago school authors, to Tannenbaum or to Merton. Sutherland rated a passing mention (Pollak, 1961, p. 39), but his theory of differential association is not used. Instead Pollak put forward a view of women as inherently deceitful and vengeful, exploiting a flow of helpless victims and aided by men's besotted chivalry. Although Pollak stressed cultural variables his explanations are rooted in biological 'facts' and are profoundly ahistorical and unsociological.

Let us look first at Pollak's statistical chapters where his 'finding' of heavily masked female crime led him to put forward his theory. His main argument here is that the crimes women commit are more likely to be hidden or under-reported. In particular he cited criminal abortions and shoplifting as examples (Pollak, 1961, p. 44). He even produced figures which reduce the male : female crime ratio from 10 : 1 to 4.7 : 1 by including this under-recording. Of course he failed to take account of social and legal changes in abortion law: as successive nations have legalised abortion so illegal abortions have declined in incidence. With shoplifting as with illegal abortionists he made the unsupported assumption that almost all offenders are women. This is not so (see Chapter 1). Pollak was on even shakier ground when he discussed other 'hidden' female crimes: thefts by domestic servants, offences by prostitutes and domestic revenge: poisoning and violence carried out by women on their helpless families. It is hard to take this catalogue seriously, but it should be emphasised that Pollak remained quoted in texts – but uncritically – for nearly twenty years (Heidensohn, 1968) and that his ideas have been influential (Smart, 1977). Pollak's view that women were more criminal than men, more prone to 'revenge desires', somehow more evil seems to have been deeply-rooted. Thus he claimed repeatedly that domestic servants commit crimes frequently against their employers (Pollak, pp. 36, 111, 144, etc.) without offering any serious evidence for this. Further in order to refute the notion that men might also commit masked crimes on a large scale, he suggested (Pollak, 1961, p. 54) that male white-collar criminals, whom Sutherland had shown to be largely unprosecuted, employ female servants and therefore their offences cancel each other out! Again he offered no supporting evidence and totally failed to cite the enormous rise in white-collar employment especially amongst *women* in this century and the near-extinction of domestic service (Tilly and Scott, 1978). His discussion of prostitution is very selective. He accepted, as with abortion, the then current US definitions of sex offences of prostitution, adultery and fornication (Pollak, 1961, p. 55) and claimed that male customers are not party to any offence and therefore cannot be used to inflate male crime figures. But he ignored both crimes committed against prostitutes by their customers (the Yorkshire Ripper and his earlier namesake were only the most notorious perpetrators of these) and the whole range of traditionally male activities of pimp, landlord and tout associated with prostitution. In short, Pollak's approach seems rather more ideological than empirical.

It is, however, in his theoretical approach that Pollak's sexist assumptions are most obvious. Women, he argued, are more devious than men: 'for women deceit ... (is) ... a socially prescribed form of behaviour' (Pollak, 1961, p. 11). This is because women can fake an orgasm and still have sex whereas 'man must achieve an erection in order to perform the sex act and will not be able to hide his failure'. From what he considered physiological facts, Pollak moved on to social mores. Women were equipped to dissemble and they were also forced to do so by a society in which mention of menstruation, menarche, menopause and pregnancy are taboo. Smart has pointed out the dated sexual politics of Pollak's account and his unquestioning acceptance 'of folklore and stereotypical perceptions of women' (Smart, 1977, p. 48). His negative evaluation of all of the female reproductive cycle is very significant. Even 'pregnancy in a culture which ... fosters ... childlessness must become a source of irritation, anxiety and emotional upheaval' (Pollak, 1961, p. 58). He could find little evidence to link gynaecology with criminology (although some later authors have since taken up the challenge (Dalton, 1969): and in particular seems to confuse biological and cultural effects. Thus concealment of menstruation is by no means universal and changed sexual mores have long since made nonsense of his view of passive, receptive females brooding vengeance (Hite, 1977).

Pollak recognised the importance of women's domestic role in society and that women could be 'contained' in their homes in a special way. But he went on to contend that women use the home as 'cover' for a variety of crimes: poisoning their relatives and sexually abusing children. They can do this because they can conceal their crimes better than men, because their victims are vulnerable and unlikely to report them or co-operate with the police, because women use especially devious means such as poison and because men are chivalrous and cannot bear to prosecute or punish women. Once again social and biological factors are intertwined here. Women's domestic role in our society is not inherent in their reproductive role: it is based on economic and historical developments and is not always the same in all social classes. Pollak ignored too the possibility that personal privacy may hide much male crime such as rape and wife-battering and that women may be powerless to prevent these. Nowhere has he accounted for widespread male acceptance of huge hidden waves of domestic slaughter and indecency, nor given indications of its persistence.

Pollak saw women as automata (Smart, 1977, p. 52), impelled by their physiology, their hormonal cycles and their low self-evaluation to commit crimes which, he believed, total as much as those of men. He did not for a moment suggest that *male* criminality has a biological basis and can be explained by greater strength or aggression. Indeed the whole tenor of American criminology at this time stressed the social causation (and indeed function) of crime, its structural (Merton, 1949) or subcultural (Cohen, 1955) origins. Only women were presented in this way as a separate species whose behaviour could be explained in simple 'scientific' terms to which there still cling odours of witchcraft and demonology. Pollak wrote about women and crime, a topic ignored by his contemporaries. It did not fit readily into their sociological theorising and Pollak wrote as though this did not exist. He cannot be said to have helped our understanding of female crime, but his work has been influential because he lacked competitors and the topic interested no one else. As Leonard points out (Leonard, 1982, p. 5), while finding his work 'dismal' and 'ridiculous', issues raised by him recur in much subsequent discussion.

The European tradition

I have called this group of writers the 'European' tradition and have tried to show that in approach and methods they share certain common themes. I would not wish to stretch the parallels too far since each author saw himself producing a new and revealing work which broke with earlier traditions. What they did have in common were their assumptions that women are a different species from men, differently made and motivated. All of them confronted the duality in women's social roles and their moral natures (which they often confused). Women are 'madonnas' and 'magdalenes', 'witches' and 'good wives'. Pollak and Lombroso believed that women are more wicked than men. Rock has argued (Rock, 1977) that to examine the work of such theorists is to act like 'resurrection men' disinterring corpses of long-buried and neglected ideas. But only faint-hearted criminologists flinch at ghosts and ghouls. In fact the ideas of the old tradition have proved powerful and long-lasting.

First, it can be argued that they lend an intellectual respectability to very much older folk ideas about women and their behaviour. Unfortunately, these ideas are never questioned nor criticised in their work. Second, critical analysis of these studies was very limited until recently and the work of Pollak especially, accepted without reservation. Standard criminology textbooks quote him as 'definitive' (Reckless, 1961, p. 83) and as giving 'the lie to the current notion that women are less law-abiding than men' (Barnes and Teeters, 1951, p. 592). Both these texts also cite Lombroso's analysis of the specifics of female crime. Even far more modern texts are uncritical in their use of these sources (Clinard, 1968, p. 247). Mannheim was one of the earlier critics of Pollak, although he was very cautious:

> While many of Pollak's points may be valid, one gets the impression that in his efforts to show that the sex difference in crime rates is actually much smaller than generally assumed, he goes too much to the other extreme (Mannheim, 1965, p. 693).

A few pages on and he too was quoting Lombroso as an authority and moving into a magisterial condemnation of the inferior nature of the second sex:

> Political ideals . . . take second place in the female mind . . . [they] . . . lack respect for abstract ideas such as the state and its system of justice (Mannheim, 1965, p. 103).

Women, he asserted 'prefer shoplifting to looting' as they can then choose individual items which they want!

That this European tradition has influenced generations of criminologists is only too clear. Smart referred to 'their continuing influence on the development of analysis of criminality by contemporary criminologists' (Smart, 1977, p. 54) and Shacklady Smith pointed out that:

The predominant form of empirical research on the nature of female delinquency published over the last ten years ... owes a great deal to the sexist assumptions inherent in the classical studies of female criminality (cf. Lombroso and Ferrero, Pollak, Thomas). (Shacklady Smith, 1978, p. 75).

Cowie and his colleagues, for example, pinpoint characteristics of delinquent girls which sound remarkably like Lombroso's unattractive criminal women. 'They are ... oversized, lumpish, uncouth and graceless.' Cowie *et al.* (1968, p. 167). As Smart pointed out these factors are seen as constitutionally 'predisposing' girls to delinquency. Further, in this study it is the girls' biological nature and in particular their 'markedly masculine' traits (which they link to chromosome features) which lead them to delinquency. Smart has commented extensively (Smart, 1977, pp. 54–60) on their failure to question assumptions about culture, sex and gender, or indeed to consider whether the lumpish, ugly, delinquent girls they observed might have been suffering from the effects of a stodgy diet and lack of beauty aids. It is more pertinent to the present discussion however to note that a neo-Lombrosian study of delinquent girls could be produced in the late 1960s. No anatomist of the dismal history of female crime needs Burke and Hare if the 'corpse' is still alive and kicking!

Richardson, in a fuller and far more perceptive account of young girl delinquents, nevertheless also used Lombroso as a reference point and devoted extensive sections to the physique and appearance of her charges (Richardson, 1969, pp. 56–71). Her concern paled beside that of another professional, a member of the Massachusetts Parole Board who described some of her parolees thus:

The unmarried mother is usually a solitary being who has been wandering about seeking approval or affection. Many times she is extremely plain looking and her normal life has been marred by serious skin disease, partial blindness, or some other disfiguring physical handicap (Sullivan, 1956, p. 101).

The Foreword to Konopka's study of delinquent girls made quite explicit links to Thomas's work and even suggested that the

Foreword to that work 'might have been (written) of the situation and the need today, 42 years later, and of Dr Konopka's studies and purposes' (Ellington, 1966, p. viii). Konopka shared Thomas's liberal perceptions and her analysis of the emotional needs of women is close to Thomas's 'wishes'. She also used a similar method, avoiding statistical analysis and aiming at case histories and personal accounts. While Konopka claimed to avoid theory and let her girls speak for themselves, she did in fact have similar assumptions to those of Thomas about the role of biology in women's lives and the cultural significance of sexuality and reproduction. As Smart showed:

> Konopka can be seen (like Thomas) to be engaged in a process of weaving taken-for-granted assumptions about the female sex into an explanation of juvenile delinquency (Smart, 1977, p. 66).

Old ideas live on when they are not supplanted by new research enterprises nor by rigorous and thoughtful criticism. Old ideas about female criminality have had a remarkably sustained life. They largely failed to help to demystify female crime because they ignored clear evidence and rested on unexamined stereotypes. Female criminality, although studied in these few works, remained at the fringes of the criminological terrain, an intellectual Falklands remote, unvisited and embarrassing. In the major, dynamic areas of criminology which have flourished in the past half century, women were almost completely ignored within what I shall call the American tradition. Yet – and it is a most curious paradox – a central tenet of many of the theories of male delinquency which this tradition produced is based on assumptions about gender and gender difference.

7

Modern theories and female criminality

In this chapter I shall look at modern studies of deviance and, while picking out one or two studies which feature women, show that most ignore them. I shall try to explain why I think this happened. It may seem strange in a book on women and crime to devote a section to their absence from the stage, but I believe there are several crucial issues involved. First I want to show that traditional and, even more, 'new' criminology could not incorporate an adequate approach to women within its framework and hence a feminist criminology had to be invented. Second, I assume that most readers of this book will not only study crime and women at some point, but will meet crime in other contexts and be puzzled by the lack of 'fit' between analysis of female and of male crime. Finally, a central theme of many modern feminist contributions on female crime has been the comparative neglect of the topic (Heidensohn, 1968; Smart, 1977; Shacklady Smith, 1978, p. 74; Naffin, 1981, p. 70). Many of these contributors offer explanations for this neglect and these in turn – they include the low rate of female crime and the lack of public pressure – have had their impact on 'feminist' criminology. I believe that these explanations are inadequate and that it is important to try to understand the complex reasons which for so long limited the proper study of female crime.

Modern American sociology of deviance

The delinquent as hero

The classical studies we have just surveyed are the only major landmarks in the past century of orthodox criminological work.

Around them stand minor works, often in their shadows, and a number of clinical studies and personal accounts. Yet this was a period of massive criminological endeavour especially in the USA. Although major schools of this era are no longer taken as seriously as once they were, they are all still routinely 'on the syllabus' for the modern student of deviance.

'Anomie theory is distinctly out of fashion, perhaps permanently so. Like functionalism, from which it derives, it has become a routine, conceptual folly for students to demolish' (Downes and Rock, 1982, p. 94). It is significant that Leonard in her recent text on women and crime spent one brief chapter looking at the entire 'dismal history' of the topic and then devoted the rest of her book to a careful study of all the modern theorists of anomie, labelling, differential association subculture and Marxism (Leonard, 1982). She observed that they had almost nothing to say about women and crime and then tried to develop hypotheses which they might have constructed had they been interested. It is a noble attempt and one I shall not repeat here.

Instead I shall draw out some of the main themes of the sociology of deviance and show how, while they frequently depended on assumptions about gender, these assumptions went unexamined and unexplained until the advent of feminist criminology.

Several writers have examined the lack of interest in female crime in the work of criminologists (Pollak, 1961; Heidensohn, 1968; Smart, 1977; Leonard, 1982). So far, however, explanations of this gap have been very limited. Smart's argument is the fullest, and she argued that it was the apparently low level of offending amongst women which meant there was little official concern. In turn the

lack of interest in female criminality which is displayed by orthodox criminology has also had the effect of rendering it insignificant to more contemporary schools of thought within the discipline. There appears to have been no need to counter the conservative tradition with a more liberal perspective – largely because of the insignificance of female criminality in the 'old' criminology (Smart, 1977, p. 4).

But for much of the rest of her book Smart in fact contradicted her own argument. As we have already seen, she contributed to the comprehensive critique of 'orthodox' criminology by showing how important it was for both intellectual and policy reasons to 'counter the conservative tradition'. Further, as I shall suggest, developments in the sociology of deviance were precisely in directions which could have best linked with female crime. The move away from pathological explanations, for example, was particularly appropriate since, as we saw with Lombroso and Ferrero, women criminals had been dubbed doubly abnormal.

Women's exclusion for so long from paradigms of deviance demands, I believe, a more subtle and complex explanation. I am not altogether sure that I understand it entirely and here I offer a tentative account which depends on noting three broad trends in the sociology of deviance which I think, marginalised female deviance. In looking at these we also need to recall the context in which all deviance is studied and being dealt with, and who undertakes these tasks. Mannheim's summary cannot be bettered:

> Hitherto female crime has, for all practical purposes, been dealt with almost exclusively by men in their various capacities as legislators, judges, policemen; and ... the same was true of the theoretical treatment of the subject ... This could not fail to create a one-sided picture ... this centuries-old male predominance in theory (Mannheim, 1965, p. 691).

Three major linked but distinctive trends have characterised the growth of the sociology of deviance and these have led to the invisibility of girls and women in these studies. This development was not inevitable. As Leonard has shown, it is theoretically possible to take all these approaches and tease out of them some strands to link them with female crime (Leonard, 1982). That this did not occur was due to the contexts of state, society and culture in which they grew and the corresponding lack of a feminist critique.

Sociologists of deviance have, in this century, moved increasingly away from viewing deviant behaviour as inherently abnormal and therefore having pathological origins, and towards seeing deviance as a normal and even an admirable activity. Second, social structural approaches to deviance dominated for most of this century – anomie, subculture, Marxism. Finally, since the 1960s we have seen the rise of various West Coast or laid-back-spaced-out perspectives on deviance (labelling, interactionism, phenomenology) which made the process of becoming deviant problematic for the first time.

The 'end of pathology' can be traced through the contributions of the Chicago School, the work of E. H. Sutherland and W. F. Whyte and is clear in Merton's paradigm and those who followed him in the study of delinquency. Matza developed the appreciative stance but for its fullest flowering – enthroning the male delinquent as hero – we have to cross the Atlantic and examine recent British writers such as Willis and his colleagues.

Lombroso's distaste for the female offenders he studied was palpable. It was moral, physical and scientific, his solutions eugenic and Draconian. Fifty years later, Pollak expressed similar concern at female deviousness, although the physical horror had gone. But Lombroso was not so misogynistic; he had as much, if not more, horror of his male subjects (Lombroso, 1913). They were clearly not human to him, their motives irrelevant and uninteresting. The transition we noticed in Thomas's work was significant. In 1907 he too viewed criminals as if down a microscope, as unconscious objects; by 1923 he was at least quoting their words and noting their own definitions of the situation.

The 1920s saw at the University of Chicago one of the great creative explosions in modern sociology. The teeming city became the laboratory for a host of students who in particular examined the transitional zone and its many and manifest forms of deviance. Although loosely wedded to an ecological explanation of crime, there was little coherent theorising of crime (Short, 1963). Rather, what characterised the Chicago school was the ethnographic study of a group of type of deviants, a close and careful account of their characteristics. I shall use Thrasher's *The Gang* (1963) to illustrate the method, not only because it is a classic, but also because it already contained many of the traits which characterised later writers and led to the exclusion of women.

Far from rejecting his delinquent subjects or voicing distaste for them, Thrasher clearly admired them. Although the work is meant to be premised on the 'area theory' of crime, Thrasher very quickly made clear that the 'dreary and repellent ... external environment' (Thrasher, 1963, p. 3) produced 'life ... at once vivid and fascinating'. Thrasher did not approve of vice or violence any more than did his colleagues who studied slums or hoboes, but two crucial characteristics mark his work out from earlier studies of delinquency. First, twilight zones notwithstanding, he treated gangs as normal not abnormal phenomena to be studied in just the same way as normal social institutions:

Gangs, like most other social groups, originate under conditions that are typical for all groups of the same species (Thrasher, 1963, p. 4).

Play was crucial to Thrasher's understanding of his boy gang members, and he described the 'vigorous freedom of exciting gang life'. The second crucial aspect of Thrasher's approach is what Matza has called the 'appreciative' stance he took which brought him close to the gang members in sympathy and understanding:

To understand the gang boy one must enter into his world with a comprehension on the one hand of his seriousness behind his mask of flippancy and bravado and on the other, of the role of the romantic in his activities and in his interpretation of the larger world of reality (Thrasher, 1963, p. 96).

I think these aspects of the work lead to the exclusion of females from the discussion. Treating delinquency as normal made female delinquency problematic because it was both statistically unusual and also deemed role-inappropriate. Thrasher did deal very briefly with girls in gangs, and having assured us that the boys reject girls as members because:

They have interfered with the enterprises of the group, have weakened the loyalties of its members, or in demanding time and attention have impaired the gang as an effective conflict group (Thrasher, 1963, p. 157)

he asked how we may understand the role of girls in gangs.

The real explanation is that the girl *takes the role of a boy* and is accepted on equal terms with the others. Such a girl is probably a tomboy in the neighbourhood. She dares to follow anywhere and *she is ill at ease with those of her own sex who have become characteristically feminine* (Thrasher, 1963, p. 158, emphasis added).

Unusual female behaviour is thus (as by the classical criminologists) equated with inappropriate and 'unfeminine' behaviour. It is clear, I think, why Thrasher has to use this approach. He is defending an important 'normality of deviance' hypothesis. Girls present an anomaly and therefore have to be excluded or explained in terms of sex-role deviance. Women, in short, can only fit the model if they become sociological males.

Cases of this type indicate how a woman abandoning what are conventionally regarded as feminine traits may play the role of a man in a gang and be accepted on terms of equality with other members (Thrasher, 1963, p. 169).

The anthropological approach adopted by Thrasher and his colleagues with its close observation and appreciation of delinquents, while it produced a rich ethnography of downtown Chicago, obviously had certain limitations. As Thrasher implied, groups, such as girls 'even in urban disorganised areas, are much more closely supervised than boys and are usually well incorporated into the family group or some other structure'. In short contacts and study were harder for him and, though he does not say this, probably precluded by sex differences.

To E. H. Sutherland should properly go the credit for exposing the 'bad seed' fallacy in criminology. He treated criminal behaviour as learned behaviour, as a product of an excess of 'definitions favourable to violation of law over definitions unfavourable to violation of law' (Sutherland and Cressey, 1960, p. 77). In other words it was not qualitatively different from other forms of behaviour and did not need to have its origin ascribed to a bad cause. Sutherland – almost uniquely amongst criminologists of the time – claimed that his theory explained all crime and that differential association could show 'why males are more delinquent than females' (Cohen *et al.*, 1956, p. 19). But as Leonard crisply noted 'Unfortunately he did not pursue the matter' (Leonard, 1982, p. 106).

It seems to me that Sutherland largely ignored women in his theories and their application bacause like Thrasher he found that their inclusion would threaten and undermine his theory. Thus he would have needed an elaborate analysis of sex differences in socialisation to explain why males and females learn different behaviour patterns. He did hint at this but never explored it, suggesting that 'girls are supervised more carefully' because of fears of unwanted pregnancy (Sutherland and Cressey, 1960, p. 115), but as Leonard observed, this merely 'reflects socially constructed attitudes towards males and females' (Leonard, 1982, p. 110); it is not an adequate explanation at all.

Perhaps the best example of the effects of getting close to delinquent subjects is provided by W. F. Whyte's subtle and detailed account of his research for *Street Corner Society* (Whyte, 1955). Whyte spent three years in an Italian slum in an East Coast US city and his book describes those he met and lived amongst or more accurately the young men he met. The 'hero' of the book is 'Doc', leader of a corner boy gang, who is contrasted with 'Chick' Morelli a 'college boy'. Whyte clearly admired Doc and his loyalty to his gang and rather despised Chick who was more ruthless and self-seeking (Whyte, 1955, p. 108). In a fascinating account of his research methods in an Appendix to the second edition, Whyte outlined how close he became to 'Doc', how ' "Doc" had read every page of the original manuscript' (Whyte, 1955, p. 346) and he discussed in detail both his involvement in Cornerville and the impact of his book on its subjects after it was published. Whyte's book is exemplary of its kind. He was both participant and observer and his account is sympathetic and sociologically analytical. But as he himself engagingly admits, he could not study the girls of Cornerville who 'could not hang on street corners' (Whyte, 1955, p. 299). When girls do figure they are only observed through the eyes of the Nortons (the gang) and are not independent subjects. While being male prevented Whyte from close observation of Cornerville girls, his own preferences led him away from studying the family where he might have learnt something from them:

> I had done no systematic work upon the family. On the one hand, it seemed unconceivable that one could write a study of Cornerville without discussing the family; yet at the same time, I was at a loss as to how to proceed in tying family studies into ... the book ... I must confess also that for quite unscientific reasons *I have always found politics, rackets and gangs more interesting than the basic unit of human society* (Whyte, 1955, p. 324, emphasis added).

In short, the participant method used by Whyte meant that he could only study males and, since his own role and reactions as observer were so critical to his work, he focussed on the concerns that interested him and not those that would have given the broadest sociological perspective. However, I find the most important single thing about his work is that it marks the start of the long romantic attachment of sociologists of deviance to delinquents as heroes. This may not have been an inevitable outcome. It certainly meant that female delinquents and indeed females in any form other than sex objects did not enter into these accounts.

It is fairly easy to understand why urban anthropologists like Thrasher and Whyte were limited to studying male subjects. It is also understandable that they came, respectable, middle-class 'college boys' themselves, to admire their subjects. As gifted and sympathetic social observers they could identify much to admire in the energetic, lively delinquents with their group and communal loyalties. What is harder to understand is how this idealisation of the juvenile delinquent as folk-hero persisted and flourished among writers who were not as close to their subjects nor combating the fear and loathing of delinquents of the early twentieth century. But this model has remained dominant until the present day, although it has been joined by others more recently.

I do not think that it is exaggerating to say that celebrating the young, male delinquent became a consistent theme in the post-war sociology of deviance. Consider these examples picked almost at random; it is not an exhaustive selection:

> The delinquent is the rogue male. His conduct may be viewed not only negatively ... [but also] ... positively ... as the exploitation of modes of behaviour which are traditionally sumbolic of *untrammelled masculinity*, which are renounced by middle-class culture because incompatible with its ends, but which are not without a certain aura of *glamour* and *romance* (Cohen, 1955, p. 140, emphasis added).

Finestone's 'cool cats' – (young drug users) – are described almost reverentially:

> The cat seeks through a harmonious combination of *charm*, ingratiating speech, dress, music, the proper dedication to his 'kick', and *unrestrained generosity* to make of his day-to-day life itself a *gracious work of art*. Everything is to be pleasant and everything he does and values is to contribute to a *cultivated*

aesthetic approach to living (Finestone, 1964, p. 285, emphasis added).

Similar élite characteristics were observed by the Myerhoffs who give a

description of the delinquent as a kind of *aristocrat* – a *gentleman* of leisure – allowed to play, explore, test limits, indulge his pleasures and little else besides (Myerhoff and Myerhoff, 1972, p. 287, emphasis added).

All these descriptions define the delinquent as unmistakably and exclusively male. Indeed, when girls feature in these accounts it is to provide the appropriate counterpoints to the dominant male theme. There is no balance or equality in these accounts, female figures are whisked on and off the stage, a small cast of extras without whom the plot cannot go forward but who have no lines to say. Cohen's is the most explicit presentation. First he assures us of his own masculinity, curiously mixing biological and social sex differences:

My skin has nothing of the quality of down or silk, there is nothing limpid or flute-like about my voice, I am a total loss with needle and thread.

He then defines femininity in similar fashion,

I am reliably informed that many women ... often affect ignorance, frailty and emotional instability because to do otherwise would be out of keeping with a reputation for indubitable femininity (Cohen, 1955, pp. 137–8).

But Cohen only titillates us with these images; there is to be no analysis of female delinquency. It is different from the male version – 'it consists overwhelmingly of sexual delinquency' – but Cohen neither supports his assertions nor furthers his analysis:

Our task in this volume is to throw light on the delinquent subculture we have decribed and *not to explain* the kind of delinquency that is characteristically female (Cohen, 1955, p. 144, emphasis added).

British sociologists who looked at delinquency in the 1960s and 1970s have, if anything, elevated the male delinquent to an even higher status than their American counterparts. No doubt radical strains in criminology which have highlighted political aspects of deviance have contributed to this. The delinquent hero becomes a rebel delinquent hero.

The move from pathological to normal explanations of criminality and from there to hero-worship did bring with it a continued emphasis on gender roles even if the feminine part of the continuum was never studied. But when we look at the next key trend in the sociology of deviance, the emphasis on social structure, women disappear almost totally. Abstraction, in these explanations, tends to obscure gender. Thus Merton's anomie theory (Merton, 1949) functionalist and Marxist theories all deal with large, vague entities: American society, capitalism and the modern family. Perhaps this distancing, as well as possibly an uncomfortable awareness that their theories could be threatened, explains the gap. Leonard summarises the blanks:

Merton made no attempt to apply his typology to women – he has forgotten at least half the population with this formulation (Leonard, 1982, p. 57).

Taylor, Walton and young's massive [radical] criticism of criminology (1973) does not contain one word about women ... Quinney is all but blind to distinctions between the conditions of males and females in capitalist society (Leonard, 1982, p. 176).

Functionalism is perhaps a little redeemed by two studies, Davis's essay on 'Prostitution' and Grosser's seminal thesis on male and female delinquents which was often consulted but never published (Davis, 1963; Grosser, 1951).

Davis is not in practice really interested in studying prostitutes, rather, as Smart suggests:

His explanation serves to do no more than provide a legitimating gloss for the existing power structure which produces inequalities between men and women and social classes in contemporary society (Smart, 1977, p. 91).

Davis's argument is that prostitution is inevitable in society and indeed functions to preserve respectable women and their marriages. Sexual attractiveness is a scarce commodity and since 'Women must depend on sex for their social position much more than men do' because 'inevitably ... men (are) in control of economic means' (Davis, 1963, p. 345). They therefore exploit their attractions for economic reward. Smart points out the conceptual leap from the shortage of sexual attractiveness (surely at least as rare in men as in women) through the acceptance of an inevitable sexual imbalance of power to the assertion that only women need to prostitute themselves. That Davis is basically just rationalising the *status quo* becomes clear in his discussion of the different treatments of prostitutes and their clients. Punishing prostitutes does no social harm he argues, because they are:

1. social outcasts anyway;
2. only marginal to the economy and their loss does not disrupt production. Their clients are, however, much more valued.

To throw good citizens into jail for a vice that injures no one, would cause more social disruption than correcting the alleged crime would be worth (Davis, 1963, p. 340).

Downes and Rock's claim (Downes and Rock, 1982, p. 84) that 'Davis's analysis of prostitution ... is remarkably similar to the more recent demands for a "new deal" by prostitutes in the 1970s and before' is frankly astonishing. While it is true that Davis accepts prostitution as normal and functional to society, he also accepts and upholds the 'double standard' which punishes women but not their clients. Of the three leading organisations of prostitutes active in Britain in the 1970s *all* campaigned for the abolition of punitive measures against women (Expenditure Committee, 61–XIV, 1979), PROS (Programme for Reform of the Law on Street Offences) were also very clear about the injustice of the double standard while the English Collective of Prostitutes and PLAN (Prostitution Laws are Nonsense) quite explicitly linked their demands for 'the abolition of all laws on prostitution' (Expenditure Committee, 61–XIV, p. 286) with sexual discrimination: 'the rights of prostitutes are the rights of women'.

Grosser's unpublished study (Grosser, 1951) is one of the key 'hidden' texts of the modern American sociology of deviance.

Almost uniquely, Grosser studied boys *and* girls and saw delinquency as role expressive for both sexes. Male delinquency, however, he linked to the demands of the masculine gender role for
economic performance and to a direct participation in the market of
life, whereas for girls, delinquency was a function of their primarily
sexual nature. *Juvenile Delinquency and Contemporary American
Sex Roles* was never published and therefore never subjected to the
critical scrutiny that other texts in the delinquent subculture debate
received, but it is clear that it was very influential. (The list of
borrowers in the Harvard library copy is distinguished.) Cohen in
particular acknowledges his debt to it (Cohen, 1955, p. 193). What
Grosser's work seems to have done was to set the issue of female
delinquency to one side and allow another generation of
criminologists to avoid tackling it. Grosser suggested that female
sexual delinquency was the functional equivalent of male theft and
vandalism and gang behaviour. Cohen had endorsed this view and
though only an élite few made the effort to read Grosser's work it
was possible to believe that the issue was settled. Thus the many
major critiques of Cohen's 'provocative – monograph' question his
methodology (Kitsuse and Dietrick, 1959), his understanding of
working class culture (Miller, 1958), his empirical and theoretical
approaches (Sykes and Matza, 1957), but none questioned his
crucial handling of sex differences. Cohen's work and the critical
reaction to it largely determined the framework for the next generation of criminological work: in a standard textbook published in
1972 a high proportion of the selected readings are criticisms of, or
responses to, Cohen's original thesis.

Although assumptions about masculine and feminine gender are
crucial to this whole trend of criminological thinking these assumptions are nowhere examined nor empirically tested in the literature.
It was taken as self-evident that innate biological differences were
somehow translated into social, cultural and behavioural perfor-
mances related to delinquency. While one can perhaps understand
the research interests which led to the crop of studies after the
publication of *Delinquent Boys*, with their emphasis on delinquency, gangs and violence, it is much harder to explain the long gap on
the bookshelves which should have been filled with studies of
females. Whatever happened to 'Promiscuous Girls' or 'Lower
Class Culture and Teenage Prostitution'? We can only conclude
that the same limitations we observed in writers such as Thrasher

and Whyte still applied. Criminologists were still almost all male, limited by interest and experience from observing female behaviour. Moreover, a theory such as Cohen's which was actually based on gender difference could be easily undermined when its base was examined. It is clearly not true that girl delinquents are only or mainly sexually delinquent. They, like their brothers, are predominantly involved in property offences. Further, the Cohen hypothesis greatly over-predicts the incidence of female delinquency (Harris, 1977, pp. 8–9); with Grosser's thesis achieved but safely tucked away, perhaps it seemed possible as well as desirable to ignore the inconvenient problems of female delinquency for yet another decade.

Interactionist approaches to the sociology of deviance dominated the 1960s and early 1970s with Becker's *Outsiders* the key text. Much could reasonably have been expected of this approach with its emphasis on the process of becoming deviant, on the social audience for deviance, on the rule-makers rather than the rule breakers. There were new ways of looking at crime and deviance; interactionists were explicitly critical of previous positivist approaches – 'The study of crime lost its connection with the mainstream of sociological development and became a very bizarre deformation of sociology' as Becker put it. Within this framework there were, it is true, a very few tantalising interactionist studies of certain aspects of female deviance. Bryan's work on prostitution (Bryan, 1966) did something to remedy the odd lapses in Lemert's earlier work on the same topic. Bryan showed that prostitutes learnt their trade through apprenticeship and that their motivation was primarily economic while Lemert had seen prostitution as sexual deviation and concentrated on structural aspects not on societal reaction. Mary Owen Cameron's study of shoplifting certainly included men and women and showed how studying court reactions, differential prosecutions and convictions as well as differences in behaviour could be especially illuminating. She demonstrated more striking differences in court disposition between black women and white women than black men and white men although their thefts were of comparable value (Cameron, 1964, pp. 169–70). But these are rare examples. Cameron's work is curious because it appeared originally in 1964 at the same time as key 'labelling' studies, and has regularly been included in editions of the reader *Deviance: The Interactionist Perspective* (Rubington and Weinberg, 1968, 1973).

Cameron herself acknowledged more positivist inspiration for her work from Sutherland, Cohen, etc. (Cameron, 1964) and her study conducted in Chicago uses a classic Chicago school technique of plotting residence-patterns of offenders on city maps. Cameron was clearly interested in store theft and in extending the frontiers of criminolgical theory; issues of gender were not central concerns, to her. However gender was obviously central to the topic she studied and she brings this out well. Several key points are worth stressing here. They are developed in later discussion (Chapter 9).

First, Cameron pointed to the *private* policing of shoplifting by store detectives and discusses its importance (Cameron, 1964, pp. 61ff). She compared records of thefts by men and women and concluded that while 'on any one day women steal a greater number of articles than men', men on the other hand steal more valuable items, but as they steal fewer items they are therefore less at risk of arrest (Cameron, 1964, p. 84). In her interpretation of shoplifting, Cameron suggested that women shoplifters are of limited income and steal luxury goods for themselves which they would not expect to buy from the family purse (Cameron, 1964, p. 150). She stressed repeatedly that she found no support for the 'rich kleptomaniac' shoplifter (Cameron, 1964, pp. 156–8). Finally she noted that 'pilferers' who are more typically women than men, tend to deny any criminal or deviant identity before their theft or even during the processes of arrest and search (Cameron, 1964, p. 160).

Becker himself tossed a provocative thought into the air in *Outsiders* – 'it is true in many respects that men make the rules for women in our society (though in America this is changing rapidly)' (Becker, 1963, p. 17), but he did not catch the thought himself and nor did any other interactionist. This is particularly disappointing because so much new work was generated and the influence of this perspective was so important. As Leonard succinctly put it:

> There are conspicuous entry points where labelling might have begun a thorough analysis of women and crime, but once again this analysis was not forthcoming (Leonard, 1982, p. 81).

To the factors which I have already suggested inhibited the growth of interest in women and crime must be added in this case another one: exotic tastes. Liazos has analysed the way in which interactionists have focussed on a few somewhat marginal and exotic deviants such as drug-users and homosexuals and ignored the crimes of the powerful in favour of 'fascination with dramatic and predatory actions' (Liazos, 1972, p. 40). Liazos points out that this fascination with the 'nuts, sluts and perverts' prevents interactionists from looking *beyond* their deviant subjects either at the structures of society or more *deeply* into gender differences such as those that relate to stigmatisation of female prostitutes but not their clients.

The torch of subcultural theory passed during the 1970s from American to British sociologists who have appropriately enough, produced an athletically exuberant series of ethnographic and theoretical studies of youth culture with an emphasis on its deviant and rebellious aspects (for a discussion, see Cohen, 1980). 'The absence of girls from the whole of the literature in this area is quite striking, and demands explanation' remark the authors of an essay on 'Girls and Subcultures' (McRobbie and Garber, 1976, p. 209). But they are not, strictly speaking, accurate. Most of the work in this genre, like Cohen twenty years earlier, does acknowledge the importance of gender expressed in various forms of 'masculinity' to the (male) youth culture:

> We may see these three interrelated elements of territoriality, collective solidarity and 'masculinity' as being the way in which the skinheads' attempted to recreate . . . the community (Clarke, 1976, p. 102).

Girls do flit through the pages of these books and articles, but as in *Street Corner Society* they are perceived and portrayed through the eyes of the 'lads'. Thus Robins and Cohen in *Knuckle Sandwich* are supposedly writing about a working-class youth centre in London and its relation to the local community. Both boys and girls used the centre, but it is quite clear with whom the authors identify:

> The boys had, *of course,* classified all the girls into the *familiar* two categories: the slags who would go with anyone and everyone (they were all right for a quick screw but you would never get serious about it) and the drags who didn't but whom you might one day think about going steady with (Robins and Cohen, p. 58, my emphasis).

Earlier they have recounted the story of a conflict between boys and girls at the local youth club. The girls wanted pop groups booked at the club so that they could dance to them while the boys had 'more sophisticated tastes' and wanted to listen to progressive reggae and Rhythm and Blues.

But above all the *boys tended to appreciate more fully than the girls* the aspect of performance that the bands brought to the Black Horse (Robins and Cohen, p. 56, emphasis added).

I am not merely trying here to make simple points about crude sexism in these accounts. What I am trying to show is that in almost fifty years of theoretical and ethnographic work on deviant cultures from Whyte to Willis, *nothing* had changed. Skinhead girls in Smethwick, Sunderland or the East End were as 'invisible' to contemporary researchers as liable to be dismissed as mere sex objects as they had been in Boston.

There is this one difference. Whyte and Cohen were, as we have seen, aware of their gender and the limitations it placed on their research role. Modern male students of youth culture are aware of a feminist critique of their work, carried out in a parallel but quite separate sociological domain. They acknowledge this, albeit often in asides and footnotes:

At this stage I would hope that the reaction of many of the ladies (*sic!*) ... is fairly irate about my failure to mention girls at all ... this book follows the male-dominated sociological line of re-searching into ... male delinquency ... There is little real defence of this total exclusion of half the population from sociological research (Corrigan, 1979, p. 13).

Willis, having admired the 'rough *bonhomie*' and 'aggressively masculine' style of his tearaway bikers, admits to 'shared patterns of chauvinism between observer and observed' (Willis, 1978, p. 27). In his index to *Profane Culture* the sole reference under 'women' is 'attitudes *to*' (Willis, 1978, p. 212; added emphasis).

Several of these writers emphasise that, despite their awareness of sexism, bias and limitations in their work, they are *unable to remedy the situation:*

In this piece we have (in common with almost every other writer on youth culture) ignored women ... our notion of 'the working class kid' is a male one. *We have no excuse except ignorance* ... we know very little about the culture of teenage girls (Corrigan and Frith 1976, p. 239).

Even, then, in the late twentieth century, in a new approach to deviance which was consciously used to challenge conventional methods and theories it was still impossible to make women and girls 'visible' in studies of deviance. Willis's comments on his Walsall 'lads' could well stand for the sparse and limited nature of the descriptions of girls' behaviour in 'new deviancy theory' and in 'cultural studies':

Always it is their own experience and not that of the girl ... which is the focus of the stories. The girls are afforded no particular identity save that of their sexual attraction (Willis, 1978, p. 43).

I should like to suggest that at least four important strands in the development of the sociology of deviant behaviour are linked to this position. First there is the delinquent machismo tradition in criminology which has treated male working-class delinquency as heroic and romantic; Thrasher and Whyte were early examples, but the tendency is clear in subcultural theory and is shared too in the 'new' sociology of deviance which often becomes 'a *celebration* rather than an analysis of the deviant form with which the deviant theorist could *vicariously identify* – an identification by *powerless intellectuals* with deviants who appeared *more successful* in controlling events' (Taylor *et al.*, 1975, added emphasis). For Stan Cohen there is 'the obvious fascination with these spectacular subcultures' (Cohen, 1980, xix). Morgan, not himself a sociologist of deviance, catches the 'image of the male sociologist bringing back news from the fringes of society, the lower depths, the mean streets, areas traditionally 'off limits' to women investigators' (Morgan, 1981, p. 87). In short, it seems that the 'college boys' became fascinated by the 'corner boys'.

One cannot possibly criticise a perfectly legitimate intellectual interest of this kind. What is of concern to feminist social scientists is the second 'strand' in this particular pattern, that of male dominance in academic life. Oakley distinguished three crucial aspects of the male hegemony found in sociology. These are first, the 'founding *fathers*' origin of the discipline with their emphasis on male interests; second, the numerical and hierarchical preponderence of men in the academic profession, especially at the top and finally she referred to what she called the 'ideology of gender': a value system which involves constructing reality in sexually stereotyped ways – looking at delinquent boys and away from girls. As Oakley puts it 'a way of seeing is a way of not seeing'. Thus, at least until recently, it has been quite acceptable to study certain topics and not others and, more crucially, to present that viewpoint as the only or the total perspective. Whyte, for example, called his book *Street Corner Society* suggesting a fuller view than the study contained. With the exception of Cohen's *Delinquent Boys* nearly every major work which deals with crime and delinquency is exclusively about males but implies a wider relevance – *Outsiders, The Other Side, Delinquency and Drift, Becoming Deviant, The Delinquent Solution, The Gang* and so on.

There were also, I believe, important situational factors which were peculiar to the study of crime. Girls and women do undoubtedly have lower recorded crime rates (see Chapter 1). Moreover their official delinquencies tend to be of a relatively minor kind, lacking social threat and damaging their nearest and dearest rather than society at large (Heidensohn, 1970). Female crime has had therefore a low public profile, it has not seemed to be an acute social problem, needing solution, for which research funds might be forthcoming and upon which careers might be built. From the researcher's point of view these features have also meant that girl subjects have been more elusive, more thinly scattered; girls are located elsewhere than on the street corners or in the gangs. They are 'negotiating a different space' and this seems to be characterised by its privacy as McRobbie and Garber feelingly put it:

> Girl culture ... is so well insulated as to operate to effectively exclude not only other 'undesirable' girls – but also boys, adults, teachers and researchers.

Perhaps the most crucial factor explaining the Cinderella role which females played for so long in criminology concerns the central theories of the discipline. Most recent accounts of research on sex differences rightly stress that, on most measures, men and women are more alike than unlike in their behaviour (Maccoby and Jacklin, 1974; Nicholson, 1984). But recorded criminal behaviour remains – certain changes notwithstanding – a stubborn exception to this rule. Ironically, self-report studies which were originally seen as providing a truer picture of participation in crime on the whole confirm the sex-differential (Smith and Visher, 1980). For every hundred males convicted of serious offences there are only eighteen females so convicted. Age and sex remain the best predictors for crime and delinquency – better than class, race or employment status. It follows that any adequate theory of crime and delinquency must include an explanation of sex differences in crime rates. Most theorists take the sex differential for granted and do not develop adequate analysis. Thus theorists who locate crime causation in the social environment of the city, the structure of the society or the interaction process between public, police, courts and offenders need to make clear why these factors operate so much more effectively on males than females.

I believe they did not do so because they were able (as I have tried to show) to pursue an exclusive interest in male criminality in a comfortable world of academic machismo. There was for a long time no intellectual critique of this approach nor any strong social pressure because of political issues. Feminist criticisms of academic sexism were almost unheard of before the late 1960s. Theories of sex roles and sexual divisions were little more than assertions of stereotypes. Including the gender dimension, then, would have been uncongenial to masculinist scholars and could seriously have undermined key approaches:

> Sexist domain assumptions, in whatever specialized field of enquiry, do have consequences for the outcome of investigations and in many cases the final outcome would have been very different had the investigation taken account of questions of gender (Morgan, 1981, p. 87).

Moreover, the theoretical tools were lacking. As I hope to show in a later chapter, to understand female criminality fully we have to turn not to the formulations of sociologists of deviance but to the understanding of the control and oppression of women in family, work and public space which feminist analysis offer us. First, however, we turn to the development of so-called 'feminist' criminology which appeared as a highly comprehensible response to the 'sexist domain assumptions' about delinquency I have illustrated here.

I have dwelt at some length in this chapter on works which do not generally deal with female deviance. In doing so I have tried to show that both the paradigms of deviant behaviour and the methods of study of modern sociologists led to the exclusion of women as a central topic. Choice clearly played its part as is strikingly shown in the romanticisation and celebration of young male delinquents. Women are but shadows in these accounts, but they are vital shadows. Their social roles and positions are essential to all these explanations of crime since these depend on assumptions about 'masculine' and 'feminine' behaviour, on the nature of the family and women's role in it and even on variations on the Victorian doctrine of separate spheres for men and women. Where female deviance is discussed within a sociological framework it is only, and most significantly, prostitution which is examined. What is so striking about all these accounts is how little they examine the assumptions about sex and gender on which they base so much theorising. Definitions of deviance and normality may be problematic as are the processes by which these definitions occur but definitions of male and female, masculine and feminine are not challenged or examined. Within these terms female crime could simply not be studied nor understood. Feminist criminology became then the only way out of an impasse. I have, I hope, made clear how vital such a development was because some critics have suggested that feminist criminology is 'inadequate' (see Heidensohn, 1983) or have pointed 'to the dangers of a criminological separatism based on the issue of gender' (Greenwood, 1981). However, as I shall try to show in the next chapter, there really was no alternative to the development of feminist criminology.

8

Feminist criminology

The 1960s and early 1970s saw the growth of a new wave of feminism in the USA, in Britain and several European countries (Mitchell, 1971). One of the most interesting features of modern feminism was the impetus it gave to women's studies and studying women. While this was notable in fields such as literature and history, it was particularly marked in the social sciences, and the study of crime and deviant behaviour were not exceptions. In this chapter I shall try to map out the various developments often described as 'feminist criminology' and consider what importance they have for the understanding of female crime.

The feminist contribution to social science has covered a wide range of topics: housework and maternity (Oakley, 1974 and 1980), the welfare state (Land, 1976; Wilson, 1977). In their discussion of the subject Stanley and Wise (1983, pp. 13ff.) identify four themes of feminism and the social sciences:

1. the female critique: making women visible 'although women are frequently massively present within whatever is studied (they) but rarely appear in the end products of this';
2. that research should be on, by, and for women;
3. that 'non-sexist' methodologies should be employed;
4. finally that feminist research should be 'engaged' and therefore useful to the Women's Movement.

All these criteria are met by at least some of the feminist criminology which has appeared in recent decades.

I have already tried to show in the last chapter, that 'masculinism' was particularly strong in criminology. The likelihood of a feminist critique was probably higher in this area than in many others. To the traditional and near universal 'academic machismo' have to be added the dominance of the theme of the male teenage delinquent and the theoretical problems of fitting women in again. Feminist criminology began, then, very much as a critique of mainstream male criminology. That is its first, its most significant, and still its dominant characteristic and one at which we shall look next. The hypothesis most widely discussed in relation to modern feminist theory is that 'liberation equals crime'. In other words that the emancipation of women leads to their having more freedom to commit offences. Then I shall discuss the criticisms, both of that formulation and of other propositions from feminist criminologists. Finally, I want to look at the directions which feminist criminology is taking.

Feminist critique of criminology

Put very simply, the feminist criticisms of conventional criminology are (i) that women are largely 'invisible' and at best merely marginal, in its studies and (ii) that when women are studied, it is in a peculiarly limited and distorting fashion. In an article published in 1968 I focussed on this point:

> The most remarkable common feature of all the varied data on female deviance is the way in which it largely lacks consideration in the appropriate literature (Heidensohn, 1968, p. 164).

Strictly speaking, this is a pre-feminist paper: the term feminist does not occur in it, but the two key themes are already stated: the remarkable, indeed perverse, exclusion of females from consideration in criminological literature and the distortion of the experiences of women offenders to fit certain inappropriate stereotypes. Notable among these was the tendency to over-sexualise female crime, so that prostitution, for instance was seen only as sexual deviance and not as the rational choice for some women who need the financial support for themselves and their children (Heidensohn, 1968, p. 168). The only remedy for the neglect and distortion of 'female deviance is a crash programme of research which telescopes decades of comparable studies of males' (Heidensohn, 1968, p. 171). This article was, of course, published just as modern feminism was beginning to develop. However:

(Its) identification of a need for a criminology sensitive to the effects of women's every-day experience of their criminality therefore sparked off the new (sexual) political consciousness of women which had begun to cast doubts on the (to date assumed) functionality of a male-dominated society which limited its female members to the domestic sphere (Naffin, 1981, p. 71).

Klein's article was first published in 1973 (Klein, 1976, pp. 5–31) and it is remarkable how different is its tone even though approach and subject matter are broadly similar – she used terms such as 'feminist' and 'sexist' freely. Klein noted 'Female criminality has often ended up as a footnote to works on men that purport to be works on criminality in general'. She examined studies made by several major writers and their later (and lesser) followers and noted the continuity in their work:

The authors represent a tradition to a great extent. It is important to understand, therefore, the shared assumptions made by the writers that are used in laying the groundwork for their theories (Klein, 1976, p. 5).

These assumptions are 'uniformly based on implicit or explicit assumptions about the *inherent nature of women*' (Klein, 1976, p. 5, original emphasis).

She examined the works of Lombroso, Thomas, Freud, Davis and Pollak in some detail and then looked more briefly at Konopka, Vedder and Somerville, and Cowie *et al.*, in order to stress parallels: Lombroso's work has, as she points out, long been discredited, but is worth attention because later writers:

rely on those sexual ideologies based on *implicit* assumptions about the physiological and psychological nature of women that are explicit in Lombroso's work. Reading the work helps to achieve a better understanding of what kinds of myths have been developed for women in general and for female crime and deviance in particular (Klein, 1973, p. 8, original emphasis).

Lombroso characterises women, Klein argued, as passive both physically and emotionally – an idea also used by Freud and Thomas – he also saw them as adaptable and cold and calculating: themes which later surfaced in Freud, Thomas and Pollak. As Klein pointed

out, these ascribed characteristics contain considerable contradictions, especially when they are linked to the conventional view of
women's role as mother and homemaker which all these writers
took for granted. Thus if women are cold and calculating, how is it
that they are also more emotional and the most suitable carers for
children? Klein suggested that these writers should then take up a
dual notion of the nature of women. Women can be either 'good' or
'bad' women. 'Good' women are conventional socially and morally
and if they do transgress it is in ladylike and peculiarly feminine
ways (Pollak, 1961). 'Bad' women, on the other hand, are in some
ways more masculine in their behaviour.

All these writers Klein noted made two key unquestioned assumptions that feminist critiques have done much to undermine.
First, they took for granted a universal culture-, class- and history-
free feminine nature. In other words, they subscribed to a myth
about the 'forever feminine'. Second, they all emphasised sexual
factors in the aetiology of female crime, to the exclusion of
economic and social factors:

> [Thomas] shows ignorance of economic hardships in his denial of
> economic factors in delinquency. 'An unattached woman has a
> tendency to become an adventuress not so much on economic as
> on psychological grounds'.

This is an amazing statement in an era of mass starvation and illness!

> He rejects economic causes as a possibility at all, denying its
> importance in criminal activity with as much certainty as Lom-
> broso, Freud, Davis, Pollak and most other writers (Klein, 1976,
> p. 16).

Klein went on to link the main themes and assumptions of these
classical writers with later works which lie within the same tradition.
This work is deeply flawed by bias – 'further', she insisted '(these)
assumptions ... have served to maintain a repressive ideology with
its extensive apparatus of control' (Klein, 1976, p. 27). Finally she
pleaded for 'a new kind of research on women and crime' which
would have two characteristics – 'feminist roots and a radical
orientation' – and one that would recognise that 'it is necessary to
understand the assumptions made by the traditional writers and
break away from them' (Klein, 1976, p. 27).

Millman, too, took up the twin issues of the feminist critique, albeit with a slightly different emphasis. She noted that 'women have either been largely overlooked in the literature – or else regarded as deviant in only sex-stereotyped ... ways' (Millman, 1982, p. 279). She pointed out that not only have women been largely ignored in the sociological literature, but that when men write about male deviance they both glamorise it and identify with it, and especially when writing about deviant subcultures, give accounts only of, or from the perspective of, men.

She took two post-war writers, Bell and Becker, and showed how Bell 'portrays the racketeers and leaders of organized crime as not only loyal and helpful to their ethnic group, but also as brilliant, witty and personally appealing characters' (Millman, 1982, p. 255), while Becker 'tell(s) us sympathetically that jazz musicians consider themselves to be more sensitive, gifted and even sexier than ordinary men' (Millman, 1982, p. 256). Becker, she pointed out, did his research while working as a jazz musician. Millman denied a

> wish to say that sociologists should be criticized for their identifications and sympathies with their subjects (although these tend to create problems of omission . . .). My point is rather that it is only male deviants who have been studied with such empathy and appreciation (Millman, 1975, p. 257).

When male writers did tackle topics of female deviance, Millman argued that sexist stereotypes hampered both their research techniques and their understanding. Women are obviously present amongst alcoholics and drug users and in the criminal world, yet:

> The underworld and subcultures that Becker and Bell describe *apparently consist of men only*, and women appear in these worlds, and hence in these studies, only in degraded and unpleasant positions (Millman, 1982, p. 257, emphasis added).

Lack of glamour, she suggested, has deterred male social scientists from exploring any area of female deviance save that of prostitution. 'Prostitution is the only "female" recognized area of deviance that has the potential for presenting portraits of its subjects as exciting and fascinating as most male deviant occupations' (Millman, 1982, p. 258). But when men did study prostitution they studied the phenomenon and not the prostitutes themselves.

Moreover, they could not see the occupational wood for the sexual trees, ignoring the fact that prostitution is an important economic outlet for some women. Even Bryan, she noted, although he recognised the economic aspects of the profession, 'regards the pimps as authorities on prostitution' and quotes them extensively. 'Howard Becker' she observed 'certainly never asked the wives of jazz musicians what *they* thought about their husbands' occupations, much less quoted them as authorities on the subject'. (Millman, 1982, p. 260).

In conclusion, Millman noted that both the *form* and the *style* of female deviance have been restricted in sociological studies. Worse, however, is that 'certain aspects of social reality involving deviance and conformity are systematically ignored' (Millman, 1982).

Carol Smart's book was the first full-length contribution to this analysis; it is firmly subtitled 'A feminist critique' (Smart, 1977). Smart observed that she found 'a considerable silence surrounding the whole area' of female criminality. In the material she did collect, she detected the same 'uncritical attitude towards sexual stereotypes of women and girls' (Smart, 1977, p. xiii) as had Klein. Further she stressed the biological nature of the theories of the founding fathers (Lombroso, Thomas, Pollak *et al.*) and their emphasis on the 'biologically determined inferior status of women' (Smart, 1977, p. xiii). Smart concluded that a feminist critique and 'a new direction towards the study of female criminality' were essential and her book is focussed on achieving those ends. She did, however, raise two notes of doubt which, as we shall see later, have some resonance. First, the dangers of the ghetto: that if women and crime are treated discretely, this will remain a marginal topic and thus 'the discipline of criminology would remain unmoved by any feminist critique' (Smart, 1977, p. xiv). Her second fear was that in focussing on female crime she could draw attention to it and hence create a possible 'moral panic' by making a new social problem visible.

Smart began her critique with a systematic attempt to map the nature of female criminality, in order to compare that 'reality' with the traditional studies of women and crime. She was well aware that both the official data on recorded crime and most empirical studies are based on conceptually problematic bases. Thus, she noted, for instance, that an American study of young delinquents simply took for granted the 'sexual' nature of adolescent female delinquency and the consequent effects of this on referrals to social and welfare agencies. It is really 'the (differential) attitudes of welfare agencies and the judiciary to the delinquencies of girls compared with those of boys which are being measured and studied', she argued.

Smart went on to assess the contributions of the founding fathers to studies of female crime. While pointing to the same broad failures and distortions in these writings as did Klein: the crude stereotyping of female behaviour and the exclusion of socio-economic and other factors, Smart emphasised particularly the long-term and harmful effects that these writers had, not merely on the understanding of female crime, but also on the treatment of women criminals. Lombroso and Ferrero, she argued, set the agenda for most subsequent discussion of the topic. '[Their] work on female criminality has served to create an ideological framework in which later, more contemporary studies have developed ... variations on [their] beliefs ,.. all appear in later works on female criminality' (Smart, 1977, p. 36). Thomas, on the other hand, had had the most marked influence in Smart's view, on the treatment of young female offenders. His concern to treat 'unadjusted girls' in anecdotal, personal terms 'has encouraged the deflection of the study of female criminality from structural criteria to the realm of the individual emotional and psycho-physiological' (Smart, 1977, pp. 45–6). In her later chapter on treatment she directly linked the way in which 'policy-makers, like many criminologists, perceive female criminality as irrational, irresponsible and largely unintentional behaviour, as an individual maladjustment to a well-ordered and consensual society' to 'the failure of criminological theorists' (Smart, 1977, p. 145). The consequences, she concluded, are inappropriate and expensive facilities such as the 'new' Holloway and the reinforcement of certain types of stereotypical behaviour in young offenders in institutions.

Pollak she criticised most severely not so much for his direct impact on penal policy-making as for the way in which he took certain myths about women and about their crimes. She quoted him as suggesting that in our culture 'women have always been considered as strange, secretive and sometimes as dangerous' (Smart, 1977, pp. 52–3). Instead of dispelling 'these myths, rather he has incorporated them into his analysis and has thereby given folklore a pseudo-scientific status' (Smart, 1977, p. 53). Smart noted the absence of evidence for most of Pollak's assertions about the character of women, their 'masked' crime and the 'chivalry' of men towards women. He could also cite no real support for his assertions that males commit less 'masked' crime than females. Where Pollak did have statistical data, for example, on the sex ratios of imprisoned offenders committed for homicide and manslaughter, she showed that 'the comparisons he makes are, however, methodologically unsound and totally misleading' (Smart, 1977, p. 50). Like Klein, Smart linked the classical writers on women and crime to more contemporary authors like Konopka, Cowie *et al.* and Richardson and emphasised the continuity in their work.

In conclusion, Smart observed that women have not been entirely ignored in the study of crime and deviance. Rather, it is 'the quality of that work which does address the question of female criminality which leaves much to be desired' (Smart, 1977, p. 176). She contended that there are two categories of studies. In the first, while women are central there is 'a basic inadequacy in the perception of the nature of women and a reliance upon a determinate model of female behaviour' (Smart, 1977, p. 176). In the second category, 'the deviant, the criminal or the actor is always male' (Smart, 1977, p. 177). Women, if mentioned at all, remain at the margins. Smart linked women's exclusion from criminological studies as perpetrators of crimes with their invisibility as victims. Rape and wife-battering have been largely ignored in the literature and this, Smart suggested was because their victims were women. Women's absence from criminological studies has also led to injustice in their treatment as offenders, she claimed. Prisons and community homes reinforce the typical feminine role in women and girls. 'Such policies are geared to supporting the inferior position of women in society in the naive belief that femininity is the antithesis of criminality' (Smart, 1977, p. 182). Smart ended her book with a rather tentative plea for more research on women and crime, because it is too early yet to achieve 'the desired goal of a woman's perspective' (Smart, 1977, p. 183).

Since the mid-1970s several collections of articles have been published with a feminist approach on women offenders, women and criminal justice, and women and social control (for example, Smart and Smart, 1978; Crites, 1976; Mukherjee and Scutt, 1981; Hutter and Williams, 1981). They all contribute to the feminist critique of criminology, without taking it much beyond the initial outlines with which it began. However, these papers and others published in journals do add a little to balance the lack of studies of women and crime so much deplored by all these writers.

A recent book by Leonard extends the feminist critique into new territory by exploring the unused possibilities of modern mainstream theorists in relation to women and crime. After a very brief discussion of the 'dismal history' of some of the classical theorists (Leonard seemed to be taking the feminist critique of them for granted by now) she plunged into the task of 'putting women back in' to the theories of anomie, labelling, differential association, delinquent subcultures and critical criminology. It is an elaborate and to a large extent, unrewarding, task. Leonard set out the key concepts and examples of these approaches, listed important criticisms and then tried to apply them to women. She concluded that either these approaches offer potentially valuable insights (labelling theory and critical criminology) which have never been exploited or developed, or that there is no scope for applying the theory to women. 'The application of subcultural theory to women is extremely difficult primarily because these theories are aimed implicitly or explicitly at males' (Leonard, 1982, p. 138). 'Differential association, however, does not explain why the situation of men and women varies so profoundly ... It leaves us with essentially the same puzzling questions regarding women and crime' (Leonard, 1982, p. 114). 'The application of anomie theory to women and crime ... clearly illustrates this theory only applies to men and mainly to the goal of financial success' (Leonard, 1982, p. 61). Leonard ended her study by commending 'the utility of a feminist perspective' (Leonard, 1982, p. 192) within a structural analysis.

The feminist critique of criminology has been concerned with two outstanding features of the discipline: the *presence* of women in a very few seriously distorting stereotyping accounts and their more notable *absence* from most major studies and exclusion from all sociologically-based theories. The focus of feminists studying this area has been much more on the former, not just because they were the only topics to study, but because of the very considerable influence they are said to have had both on the later *study* of women and crime and the *treatment* of female offenders. To explain the neglect of women in conventional criminology, when gender is clearly such a crucial element, perhaps *the* crucial variable (Harris, 1977, p. 3), was a more complex task and one not as fully realised. (I have tried to take this critique a stage further in Chapter 7).

Direct criticisms of the feminist critique of criminology have been few. Indirectly, by making either a wincing acknowledgement of error (see Chapter 7) and then proceeding as before or by magisterially ignoring and failing to assimilate the critique, there have been many implied critics. Greenwood has attacked what she called the 'myths of female crime' perpetrated by feminist criminology. She suggested that feminists have partially accepted the traditional theorists and that without their sexism 'then the theories would at least by worthy of examination'. This hardly squares with the highly critical analyses which I have outlined which have focussed on the long-lasting and pervasive effects of inherently misleading and profoundly inadequate theories. More puzzling still is Greenwood's assertion that feminists accept 'existing theories about men's crime' (Greenwood, 1981, p. 77). There are clear references in several of these studies to the conventional stereotype of the young, male working-class delinquent and how this affects their behaviour (see, for example, Heidensohn, 1968 and 1970; Scutt, 1976). Smart pointed out, in a direct response to this paper, that Greenwood constructed a 'straw woman' of feminist criminology which she then criticised without explaining which writers she was criticising nor differentiating them from each other. While Greenwood's criticisms are unclear, I believe it is fair to suggest that a feminist critique of criminology has developed which has provided an important analysis of criminology. What Greenwood seems to have ignored is the considerable scope for change and progress in this field which a feminist perspective gives. I want next to explore some of the developments within the perspective and also to note its successful impact on a few theorists outside it who have taken it seriously.

Women's liberation and female crime

Growths in female crime rates have been linked to the emancipation of women for more than a century. Pike (1876) argued that as women grew more independent they would also grow more criminal. Bishop (1931) argued that there were already signs of increases in female criminality which he attributed to increasing emancipation. Since women could never be men's equals, improving their rights merely made them frustrated and discontented and ultimately delinquent. Pollak claimed that 'the total volume of female crime has increased as a result of the progressing emancipation of women in our society' (Pollak, 1950, p. 75).

These are, however, isolated examples of this view. The 1970s and 1980s saw the development and discussion of this proposition within a feminist perspective. It has proved a controversial debate and is one of the few aspects of the feminist approach to female criminality to have aroused broad interest, both from academics and from the popular media (Morris, 1981, pp. 64–6).

Bertrand, taking the developments in sex-role theory and crime, attempted to show, on an international basis, how women's self-perception, cultural stereotypes of female roles, penal codes and female emancipation would all be linked. Thus she argued that female crime rates vary with the degree of women's involvement with home and children, and that where women have well-established civil rights penal codes would not be discriminatory (Bertrand, 1969). In practice her hypotheses were not supported by her empirical studies.

Simon devoted a chapter of her book *Women and Crime* (1975) to the contemporary women's movement and concluded that although some of its members were socially defiant of conventions concerning women's traditional role, they had little connection with or influence on criminal women. 'Liberated' women were too well-educated, too upper-class to 'alter the behaviours, the perceptions, the beliefs, and the life styles of women already involved in criminal careers' (Simon, 1975, p. 18). The one way in which Simon did fear that the women's movement might have an influence is in making the treatment of women offenders at the hands of the police, the courts and prisons more 'equal' and therefore harsher.

Adler, however, was exuberantly convinced otherwise:

Women are no longer indentured to the kitchens, baby carriages or bedrooms of America . . . Allowed their freedom for the first time women . . . by the tens of thousands – have chosen to desert those kitchens and plunge exuberantly into the formerly all-male quarters of the working world . . . In the same way that women are demanding equal opportunity in fields of legitimate endeavour, a similar number of determined women are forcing their way into the world of major crimes (Adler, 1975, pp. 12–13).

Adler's arguments were that:

1. women have become increasingly emancipated in the USA and the Western world generally;
2. that this takes them into new 'masculine' areas of experience including crime and especially 'unfeminine' forms of crime such as violence;
3. the link between these two is proved by the rising tide of recorded female crime.

Both Adler's assumptions and her methodology have been heavily critised. Box suggested that 'women's social existence in our culture (is) bad enough without their collective attempts to achieve liberty and equality being viewed pejoratively as criminogenic' (Box, 1983, p. 188). Leonard pointed out that 'her assumption of rapidly increasing equality among men and women is highly debatable' and noted 'her naive idea of liberation ... (of) women using "guns, knives and wit"' (Leonard, 1982, p. 10). Smart and Leonard both criticised the interpretation of statistics with which she tried to show the dramatic rise in female crime rates. Much of Adler's data is from case studies whose provenance is not made clear enough. She quoted, for example, a 'London police officer' who believed that there was a trend toward widespread adolescent female violence:

These girls ... they're much smarter in their approach to this kind of thing ... the problem is they may eventually become better than men, and even more numerous, as street criminals (Adler, 1975, p. 101).

It is hard to take this seriously, nevertheless as Box put it 'There is a babble of voices over the emancipation ... leads to ... crime issue' (Box, 1983, p. 189) and it therefore merits some consideration.

While Adler's own argument is not soundly-based, other writers have endeavoured to contribute to the debate: Box cited over twenty relevant books and papers (Box, 1983, p. 191). Smart (1979) addressed herself to Adler and argued that:

To assess the proposition that there is a relationship between women's liberation and increases in female criminality two questions need to be asked. First, what changes, if any, are occurring in the criminal behaviour of women and girls? And secondly, what relationships exists between socio-economic and political changes in the position status and role of women and girls and a participation in crime? (Smart, 1979, p. 52).

In answer to the first, Smart suggested that 'dramatic rises in female criminality are not a new phenomenon': female crime rose sharply from 1935 to 1946. To the second, Smart replied that it is the socio-economic position of working-class women which needs to be considered and that while middle-class women have benefited from changes in the labour market, the position of black and working-class women may actually have deteriorated. Smart also criticised Adler's interpretation of the women's movement as 'unacceptable'.

Austin criticised Smart's statistical analysis, arguing that the period 1970–5 showed a 'a greater change in the female percentage (of all offenders)' (Austin, 1981, p. 372) and went on to suggest that there was 'clear evidence of a relationship between the movement and female criminality' (Austin, 1981, p. 373). Far from 'strengthening reactionary forces that would deny women the right to subordinate second-class status' (Smart, 1979, p. 58) he claimed that this approach lessens the power of genetic or biological explanations.

However, Box and Hale, stepping into the argument in the same journal, claimed that 'the Smart – Austin disagreement is based on analysis too weak to sustain either position' (Box and Hale, 1983, p. 37). They noted the considerable 'debate (which) is bewildering because rhetoric and anecdote are often substituted for vigorous analysis of relevant data (Box and Hale, 1983, p. 35) and proceeded to carry out just such an analysis for England and Wales. They pointed out five criteria which must be fulfilled by such a study:

1. the need to control for the 'at risk' female population aged 15–64;
2. the need to control for changing rates of male crime so that *relative* as well as *absolute* changes can be noted;
3. the need to breakdown the categories of crime;
4. the need to specify theoretically and measure rigorously the variables;
5. the need to test any observed changes or relationships for statistical significance (Box and Hale, 1983, pp. 35–6).

By these standards there are no adequate studies but three do come close to them (one of these was added by Box in his later reworking of this material (Box, 1983).

In a series of papers, Steffensmeier and colleagues 'concluded that female crimes of violence against the person have increased absolutely but not relatively to the male rate, whereas female property offences have increased faster than the male rate' (Box and Hale, 1983, p. 36), but this last point was due to 'non-occupational' frauds such as shoplifting. They summarised their extensive findings thus:

> The new female criminal is more a social invention than an empirical reality and that the proposed relationship between the women's movement and crime is indeed tenuous and even vacuous. Women are still typically non-violent, petty property offenders (Steffensmeier, 1978, p. 580).

The other two studies selected by Box and Hale and Box alone did, however, go some way to suggesting 'an association between female emancipation and female criminality, an increase in emancipation' (Austin, 1982, p. 423). Both Austin and Fox and Hartnagel (1979) tried to measure female emancipation in a more complex way than Steffensmeier *et al.*, and, using these indicators did find that they correlated with female convictions (Box, 1983, p. 193). Box concluded that these studies are contradictory and pointed out that, at present, the major focus of feminist criminologists is not the liberation-causes-crime hypothesis but the link between unemployment, stress and increased female crime – the economic marginalisation hypothesis.

Box and Hale proceeded to their own analysis of data for England and Wales. From this they 'find that females contributed hardly any more to crimes of violence than they did in 1951. On the other hand they do seem to have made a significant increase in the contribution they make to property offences' (Box, 1983, p. 195). They then constructed annual indicators for female liberation taking fertility, being single, higher educational experience and workforce participation as measures of emancipation. They found no support for the hypothesis for crime rates in general; there was no significant difference. Changes in convictions for violence were explained in terms of 'labelling'. Increases in property crimes were the result of economic marginality. The growing numbers of women police officers also had an impact on conviction rates.

Box and Hale ended their review and analysis with caution.

Although they could not find support for the 'liberation causes crime' theory they did make three caveats:

1. The relationship might hold with different measures of female emancipation;
2. Young women may feel the effects of the women's movement more keenly and this is not measured in Box and Hale's study;
3. Legal changes can affect the time series data. Box and Hale hoped, after their comprehensive reviews, that the 'best hope for understanding female crime rates (lies) . . . (away from) concentrating on the alleged criminogenic nature of female emancipation' (Box and Hale, 1983, p. 47).

But they underestimated the level of the 'moral panic' created by Adler's book (Chesney-Lind, 1980, p. 5; Morris and Gelthorpe, 1981, pp. 64–6). Roberts Chapman carefully reviewed the literature and concluded that the main determining factor in long-term trends of female crime is economic and that at most there is an indirect effect due to raised expectations (Robert Chapman, 1980, p. 63). Far from finding proof of the existence (and depredations) of the new tough female criminal, Chapman suggested that a more appropriate concept to describe the characteristic female offender in the current recession would be 'frayed-collar criminal'. If this is the case then as she herself asked:

Why have women offenders suddenly become visible again, after almost disappearing from the correctional scene. Why, particularly, is this visibility associated with an image of a woman with a gun in hand? (Roberts Chapman, 1980, p. 68).

She concluded that there are two reasons: first, women's crimes used to be invisible because the numbers were so small; when those numbers rose slightly, this was 'a sudden dramatic increase' because the percentage change was large. Second, there has been a complete switch in stereotypes about women's work from a previous assumption that all women were at home; it is now assumed that all women are working.

Chesney-Lind, however, sees a much more sinister design behind the moral panic over new, aggressive female criminals. 'In a classical example of "blaming the victim"' she argued 'the invention of the liberated female crook forced the female offender to bear the brunt of the hostility towards the women's movement' (Chesney-Lind, 1980, p. 15). This, she argued, serves two purposes:

First, it provided those opposed to the women's rights movements with apparently scientific evidence of the 'dark side' of liberation, and second, it deflected attention from the real problems within the criminal justice system (Chesney-Lind, 1980, p. 15).

She linked the 'moral panic' with past witch hunts and with the enforcement of sex-role-appropriate behaviour: 'the prevailing attitude toward women in the criminal justice system is basically enforcement of the female sex-role expectation' (Chesney-Lind, 1980, p. 28). She concluded

It is time to recognize clearly the notion of the liberated female crook as nothing more than another in a century-long series of symbolic attempts to keep women subordinate to men by threatening those who aspire for equality with the images of the witch, the bitch and the whore (Chesney-Lind, 1980, p. 29).

Her comments may be as exuberant as Adler's but her words reveal a central truth about the entire debate over liberation and crime. The central hypothesis has been extensively explored and tested, to no finally conclusive results – although it has been refuted to some degree. Its power as a concept is more than just scientific: it has a symbolic value to its proponents, its critics and the public. In a very real sense, then, and in the least helpful way to women offenders or women workers, one branch of feminist criminology has at last made female crime visible.

Developing feminist criminology

Women's studies are amongst the liveliest areas of the social sciences and feminist studies of crime have been one of the smaller blossoming branches. In the last section of this chapter I want to glance at trends in feminist criminology and where they might lead to.

Feminist criminology began with the awareness that women were invisible in conventional studies in the discipline. To a large extent that remains so. However, a few criminologists have assimilated the findings and approaches of feminists. Box discussed 'sexist ideology' and chivalry in his text book *Deviance, Reality and Society* (1981, p. 197) and he integrated discussions of female crime into his central arguments. In his later work he made his analysis of female crime and powerlessness a major part of his critique of conventional criminology (Box, 1983, p. 165). He did not go as far as Harris in suggesting that 'the continuing failure to consider women and consequently the sex variable' in criminology and thus 'purportedly general theories of criminal deviance are now no more than special theories of male deviance'. He goes on to look for a new interpretation of crime (his 'theory of type scripts') and concluded with a sweeping assertion: 'That the sex variable in some form has not provided the starting-point of all theories of criminal deviance has been the major failure of deviance theorizing in this century' (Harris, 1977, p. 14). There are few such reactions from male criminologists; perhaps there will be more.

More exciting, perhaps, from the feminist point of view has been the application of some of the insights of feminist criminology by women involved in crime to their own situations in the classic 'barefoot sociology' manner. In an earlier chapter I referred to McLeod's work with prostitutes and their self-help organisation. McLeod's description of the campaigns run by PROS show very clearly how the women have tried to destigmatise both themselves and their activities in order to get their occupation decriminalised: a true case of the application of delabelling techniques, and the application of the insights into the double stigma borne by deviant women. A film made for Channel Four television in Britain used a similar technique to present several women ex-prisoners in a very positive light. The image-changing purpose was made quite explicit (see Chapter 5). In another Channel Four programme, Carol Smart presented a discussion on prostitution as it linked to women's lives and their sexuality (*Images of Woman*, 1984). These are only tiny examples, but they do serve to show that studying women's crimes from a feminist perspective need not be a one-way process (Stanley and Wise, 1983, p. 23).

Feminist criminology began as a reaction; the reaction was against an old, established male chavinism in the academic discipline. Women were either invisible to conventional criminologists or present only as prostitutes or marginal or contingent figures. Further, when women were discussed it was in crude sexist stereotypes which were widely and thoughtlessly disseminated. Feminist criminology has been quite successful in developing and establishing this critique, although it has been much more difficult to get it taken into mainstream criminology. This was partly because no full explanation of the neglect of women and crime had been made. Without a map of the territory, it proved difficult to plan an invasion or even engineer a surrender.

All the contributors to the feminist critique have stressed the need for more research of the most basic as well as the theoretical kind. This call has not been very well-heeded. While there have been valuable studies of girl delinquents (Shacklady Smith, 1978; Campbell, 1981), female alcoholics (Hutter, 1981), a women's prison (Carlen, 1983), women offenders remain elusive. We have come a long way but there is still much to be done, not least in developing useful theories. I believe, as I try to show in Chapter 9 that we have to step outside the confines of criminological theories altogether and seek models from other sources in order to achieve a better understanding of women and crime from a feminist perspective.

9

Women and social control

'Social control' is a term which has become associated with two rather different approaches to the study of crime and deviance. In the first place, it is a key concept in the interactionist and other approaches to deviance. Numerous studies attest to the importance of examining the institutions (and their complex interrelationships) which form the 'control' apparatus of society: the police (Manning, 1977) the media (Cohen, 1980) and the courts (Carlen, 1976). These studies have demystified social control, showing, for example how attempts to combat crime by bringing in more policemen, can actually *increase* its recorded incidence, or that repeated imprisonment is very unlikely to 'reform' offenders. Second, a specific set of theories called 'control theories' has been developed over the past two decades which have emphasised bonding – in relation to family, peer group and school – as a control mechanism which reduces criminality. In further refinements, situational characteristics are linked to bonds to explain patterns of delinquency. Both approaches to social control have considerable salience for the understanding of female criminality and I want in this chapter to discuss the system, bond and situational aspects of control in relation to women. We have already seen how the criminal justice and penal systems affect women and also what impact the images of women depicted in various media have. We now turn to the structure of society itself.

The division of labour is crucial to the development of any society beyond the most rudimentary form. Sexual division of labour is the one universal, and apparently societally essential type. As Durkheim put it 'if the sexes were not separated at all, an entire category of social life would be absent. It is possible that the economic utility of the division of labour may have a hand in this, but, in any case, it passes far beyond purely economic interests, for it consists in the establishment of a social and moral order *Sui generis'* (Durkheim, 1933, p. 61). He had already observed 'Today, among cultivated people, the woman leads a completely different existence from that of the man' (Durkheim, 1933, p. 60). Durkheim's predictions of increasing sexual specialisation of role, function (and even of brain size!) have not been wholly fulfilled, but his words provide a sociological gloss on a doctrine and a debate which flourished in the Victorian era and which in modified guise, are still with us: the notion of 'separate spheres' for men and women. The appropriate spheres for men and women to control and influence are, for men, the realm of public life, while women should be confined to their proper place, the home. As Ruskin, a famous champion of this view put it:

'The man in his rough work in the open world, must encounter all peril and trial'

whereas

'the woman's power is for rule not for battle, and her intellect is not for invention or recreation, but sweet ordering, arrangement and decision' (Ruskin, 1865).

The concept of separate spheres was not merely a pretty Victorian conceit. It served to rationalise both the prevailing sex-role division of tasks and of power. Despite J. S. Mill's devastating attack on Ruskin's views (Mill, 1929) the concept remains with us as an ideology. It is also useful analytically in helping us to examine the parts men and women play in social control. In this section I want to look at the role women play in social control and then at the controls which constrain and modify women's behaviour.

Women in control

Women participate in a number of areas of society where their roles in the control of others are very important. These are:

1. the traditional domestic sphere of the home – 'the angel in the house';
2. the traditional community – the village street or tribe – 'the wisewoman and her kin';
3. the world of early modern welfare – what Hearn (1982) has called the 'patriarchal feminine';
4. the world of modern welfare, of the feminine semi-professional.

'The angel in the house'

Coventry Patmore's verses extolling the submissive, self-effacing wife are the poetic expression of an ideological view propounded by Rousseau and all-too-many other political philosophers (Elshtain, 1981). Women are the gentler, weaker sex. They bear and love children, they are also more childlike. It is therefore their duty to rear and nurture the next generation and to provide supportive services for their menfolk. Rousseau put it thus:

> Woman's reign is a reign of gentleness, tact, and kindness; her commands are caresses, her threats are tears. She should reign in the home as a minister reigns in the state . . .

and he of course advocated consequently differing educational paths for boys and girls. Sophie was to be educated to serve Emile and his children; girls must:

> early be accustomed to restraint. All their life long, they will have to submit to the strictest and most enduring restraints, those of propriety (Rousseau, quoted in Elshtain, 1981).

Elshtain summarised the importance of this concern for the female role for social control for, indeed, the stability of society itself:

> Women are a softening influence; they purvey moral values and sentiments to the young; they are the civilizers of children, and, sometimes of men. It follows . . . that when women are unchaste, unfaithful, unseemly, vain, or frivolous, *their ostensibly private behaviour is suffused with public implications.* Why? Because the basis of male public citizenship would disintegrate if his private world collapsed, as the citizen is also, necessarily a husband-

father, the head of a household (Elshtain, 1981, pp.161–2, emphasis added).

Rousseau's views are not as old fashioned and out of date even today as we might like to think. This was Sir John Newsom, distinguished educationist, writing only twenty years ago:

> The influence of women on events is exerted primarily in their role as wives and mothers, to say nothing of aunts and grand-mothers . . . this influence usually works by sustaining or inspiring the male . . . women . . . want to exert power both through men and also in their own right, and therefore this is almost impossible (Newsom, 1964).

Even if voices such as these are now rather quieter about what women *cannot* do especially in the 'public' world of men, the tasks women are required to carry out to ensure stability in civil society are awesome.

Amongst the most conspicuous are that women are charged with producing fit, healthy children who will grow up to be well-adjusted citizens, accepting their gender roles, capable of benefiting from education and of contributing to society (Dally, 1982; Badinter, 1981; Oakley, 1980; Ehrenreich and English, 1979). While rearing the next generation, women must maintain high (indeed increasing-ly high) standards of domestic order so that their husbands and children have clean, comfortable refuges to return to from the toil of the day (Oakley, 1974; Wilson, 1977; Land, 1981).

It is also assumed that marriage to a 'good woman' will limit the delinquent proclivities of young men and that, once settled into a situation where he is cared for and occupied, a young criminal will mature out of his misdeeds (Mannheim, 1940; Fyvel, 1963). In recent times, with the development of more humane policies for the treatment of vulnerable groups such as mentally ill, mentally hand-icapped, disabled and elderly people, a new set of expectations are being – implicitly at least – focussed on women in the home. As several writers have pointed out, without considerable changes and extra resources in official policies, 'community care' for these dependent groups means in practice, care by women in the home (Finch and Groves, 1980 and 1983; Parker, 1982). Women, of course, already do most of the tending of and caring for their close dependents within the family (Moroney, 1975). It is the additional burden resulting from changes in social policies which may leave burnt-out schizophrenics, the demented great-grandparent or the subnormal adult to the unsupported care of women at home which is at issue here.

Failure by women to comply with these expectations is finally blamed by numerous observers for increases in public disorder. Mothers who were absent or inadequate have been blamed for later delinquency in their children (Bowlby, 1946), working mothers for present misdemeanours in their 'latch-key kids'. Poor mothering has been specifically blamed by many writers for delinquency and promiscuity in daughters (see Barton and Figueira McDonough, 1984, for a review). Wives too are seen as culpable because they have incited husbands or lovers or sons to crime (Mannheim, 1940) or because some deficiency in their personalities or actions has 'driven' their menfolk to crime (Dalton, 1969; Pearson, 1973; Wilson, 1983).

Although women with family responsibilities have been working outside the home as well as within in increasing numbers for the past thirty years, neither domestic expectations of them nor their achievements have diminished. Women still carry a double burden of two roles with very little help from husbands or partners; if men do participate in child-rearing or household maintenance it is only in the lighter and pleasanter tasks and it is still construed as 'helping' the housewife (Oakley, 1974). Many families are now headed by a lone parent, nearly always the mother, who has inevitably to carry all the tasks of parenting and providing. Women, in short, in their roles as wives and mothers undertake the crucial basic tasks of care, containment and socialisation, crucial that is to the maintenance of order in society. Their investment, therefore, in that society's stability is clearly enormous despite, or perhaps because of the fact that their participation is within a context defined and dominated by men.

Wisewomen and their kin

We can distinguish at least four aspects of local community life in which women have played prominent and distinctive parts. The scripts they have followed have not had such prescriptive and exclusive moral requirements as those for the 'angel in the house'.

Nevertheless, women have played vital and significant parts for social order:

1. in the maintenance of informal social networks;
2. in tending the sick, the old, etc., in their own communities;
3. in various types of ritual and other informal social control;
4. in using specialised skills and crafts as midwives, wisewomen, etc., for the community's benefit.

A considerable array of moralists and social scientists have agreed that women are the primary producers of the bonds and fabric of society. It is women who maintain links with the extended family (Young and Wilmott, 1957 and 1960; Frankenberg, 1976) and who compensate for deficiencies in local provision, whether in housing, pre-school care of children or informal supervision of the old (Cohen, 1978; Hadley and Hatch, 1981; Caplan and Bujra (eds), 1978) with their own work in a voluntary and unstructured capacity. Social relationships are the basis of normative order in society and it seems to be agreed that women do much of the work of succouring and sustaining those relationships.

Caring in their own localities for those who cannot care for themselves is a task left largely to women and expected of them. With a return to 'community care' policies – a euphemism as I have suggested above, very often for 'domestic care by women' – there has been growing recognition that this is women's work and if women cannot or will not do it, serious problems will occur:

> Studies of individual client groups make it clear that the work of caring often falls largely on one person – typically a woman and can dominate her life (Hadley and Hatch, 1981, pp. 89–90).

Various proposals for 'community policies' – the radical chic solutions to social problems of the 1970s – ignored women's community role with unfortunate results (Hamner and Rose, 1980). Some commentators have suggested that current economic and social policies have as their goal the redomestication of women, so that forced out of the job market, women will once more do – without pay – those tasks of nurturing and minding in the community which at present some of them are paid to do (Segal, 1983). That the 'caring capacity of the community' comes down in practice, to *women's* willingness to look after other people for nothing has only recently been recognised. Yet this work and this kind of motivation are, as Titmuss saw, central to social welfare, that is, the maintenance of well-being in society and the solution of its problems (Titmuss, 1974).

Pressures on women to participate in the maintenance of order through social relationships and community care have probably not diminished in industrial society, although their character has altered. There have, however, been considerable changes in women's informal participation in the control and chastising of deviant behaviour in local communities. Social historians have contributed very interesting analyses of the various ceremonies used in pre-industrial and early modern societies to mock unruly or deviant behaviour or to prevent its continuance. Variously called 'hazing' 'charivari', 'skimmington' or 'skimmety' (as in Hardy's *Mayor of Casterbridge*), 'rough music' or *katzenmusik*, these rituals were directed at domestic disorders and disputes (Shorter, 1975, pp. 216–24) including increasingly, battering husbands who exceeded accepted norms of wife-abuse (Thompson, 1972). Men clearly played a part in these activities, though as Pearson notes, there were interesting acts of transvestism and 'misrule' in their participation (Pearson, 1983, pp. 197–202), but women's role was central to these rites in a way which largely ceased with the modern institutionalising of justice:

> Women had participated in the traditional forms of community regulation, but they were excluded almost completely from the formulation and administration of the new abstract forms of institutional control (Dobash and Dobash, 1981).

These activities, as all observers emphasise, took place within the structure of patriarchal society and were designed to reinforce traditional norms and re-establish traditional patterns of behaviour. Thus, henpecked husbands were particularly mocked, as were cuckolds and other men who had failed to assert their masculine authority (Shorter, 1975, p. 217). Wife-beaters were not generally punished in this way – 'community disapproval was reserved for men who beat their wives savagely and severely' (Dobash and Dobash, 1981, p. 568). Much disapproval was directed at women who deviated too. Pearson was inclined to see a subversive folk tradition 'saturated with fantasies of reprisal against the powerful and against existing moral codes' (Pearson, 1983, p. 196) in these rituals, but they seem to me to be rougher, albeit more popular versions of the enforcement of patriarchal authority which eventually replaced them.

Historical and literary references to charivari abound, even if it can prove difficult to disentangle just what happened to whom when the 'rough music' played. Much more shadowy and far harder to trace is the role played by women in the most informal community control through the passing on of advice and customs and the use of gossip and other devices to curb deviance. Rowbotham records the accounts of several Scottish wives who report pressures from older women in the early years of this century to conform to accepted norms of household management (Rowbotham, 1973). She also noted, as did the Dobashes, the fear and punishment of women (but not usually men) as 'scolds' (Rowbotham, 1973, pp. 5–6; Dobash and Dobash, 1981, p. 567). Several writers have noted the fears and disapproval, of 'experts' of the subversive feminine world of traditional knowledge. Oakley in particular has shown how this solidarity poses a threat to male hegemony and now it is dealt with (Oakley, 1980). That women have played a part in the maintenance of standards and tradition cannot be disputed, but that this is a part of their lives so far hidden from history is beyond doubt.

Far better documented are those contended areas of community life where traditional women's skills and craft roles have come into conflict with 'new men' who have sought to supercede them. Midwives were the original community health specialists, attending women in confinement and also overseeing aspects of child care. Several authors agree that medical men systematically conspired to down-grade and exclude the traditional midwife from obstetric care by establishing a paradigm of 'medical need' in childbirth. In order to achieve this, major assumption about what is 'normal' and 'natural' were redefined and the role of women themselves in childbirth was reinterpreted as passive and vulnerable, requiring medical help at every point (Donnison, 1977; Verschluysen, 1981; Graham and Oakley, 1981). 'Wisewomen' with similar knowledge and skills in healing were also ousted by medical men, although we know less of their history. 'Witch-hunts' may have been related to such disputes.

Two opposing trends can be noted in women's role in the maintenance of local communities. On the one hand industrialisation and the incorporation into formal, hierarchical structures of traditional customs led to women being excluded, except for a few middle class women, from activities to which they had once been central. On the other hand, the basic care and control tasks have increasingly been left to women who have been under growing pressure to shoulder them. Once again we can see both how vital a role women play, and have always played, in the ordering of communities and yet how little choice they have in practice as to the ways in which they act that role within structures devised, changed and dominated by men.

The patriarchal feminine and the semi-professions

So far we have looked at examples of women's role in social control without emphasising class distinctions. These, too, can sometimes be as important as gender differences in relation to the production of order; it is in the middle period of industrialisation that we can observe important trends emerging. Working-class women were increasingly excluded from the official public domain as working men fought for family wages and women became increasingly marginal and dependent in the labour market (Rowbotham, 1973, p. 59). As we have seen, they were also being excluded at this time from informal community activities by the institutionalising of abstract justice. Middle- and upper-class women on the other hand, although they lived under the same economic and political disabilities as their poorer sisters, were participating more and more in voluntary welfare work. This was, after all, the one extramural activity for women of which Ruskin thoroughly approved! In the United States middle-class women played particularly prominent roles in the anti-slavery campaigns, temperance movements and in various forms of social and educational reform (Banks, 1981).

Fraser (1973) has pointed out that the bountiful administration of charity could not deal with the basic problems of poverty and other ills that beset the urban working class. He suggested that as well as 'humanitarian concern for suffering' and certain psychological motives of the givers, the purposes of administering charity were clearly related to social control because of 'a fear of social revolution ... (and) a desire to improve the moral tone of the recipients'. Privileged women were, Thane pointed out, quite crucial to this enterprise:

The growing numbers of underemployed middle- or upper-class women, for whom unpaid charitable work was one of the very few socially acceptable occupation, supplied a willing and almost endless supply of volunteers for such activity, such as has been available at no other period of British history (Thane, 1982, p. 27).

Now it is clear that many Victorian feminists engaged in 'charitable' work, often with explicitly feminist aims and ideals (Hearn, 1982, p. 191; Banks, 1981, p. 25). As we saw in an earlier chapter, the women who campaigned against the Contagious Diseases Acts linked their concern for prostitutes and for 'respectable' women to feminist arguments about the relationships between men and women in society, but it was not true of the majority of charitable ladies that they sought the liberation of their sex. On the contrary, their work was primarily to gentle the masses, to make life for the poor a little more acceptable. Hearn in a very interesting analysis has shown how the development of what he called the 'patriarchal feminine' began in nineteenth-century voluntary organisations in which middle-class women served male professionals. Later, he argued, the semi-professions of nursing, midwifery, social work, etc., grew out of this basis, all retaining their subordination to male-dominated independent professions who still retain ultimate and true authority. Middle- and upper-class women have, then, some role and status in the public domain, but they are really, in Hearn's analysis, only able to keep these under the licence of patriarchal authority. In particular, he argued, reproduction and sexuality can thus be managed:

The male-dominated professions define the limits of action and ideology and so control both reproduction and the semi-professions, almost without having to be there (Hearn, 1982, p. 198).

It is women who overwhelmingly staff the socially-controlling semi-professions in health, education and social work, and it is usually women who hold the 'front-line' at the bedside, in benefit offices, the classroom, the courtroom or as 'gatekeepers' to welfare services. In that sense, these women and the public may believe that women are responsible for the system of social control. However, although the contribution made by women is immense – and it is, indeed impossible to imagine running welfare services without them – it is again true to say that women have been assimilated into the existing patriarchal system as professional handmaidens.

Women have in recent years been entering medical and law faculties in increasing numbers and there are more women police officers, who are no longer a separate force within a force but part of the main policing system. Nevertheless, women are still virtually unrepresented at the top of the 'controlling' professions and occupations. There are two main positions which women occupy in these institutions. First, they can take symbolic positions as head of church or the armed forces, as the Queen does in Britain or as the blindfolded, feminine figure of justice does. Presumably the strength and power of tradition is undiluted here by female presence. Second, and far more important, women are interposed between the state and people, strategically softening the sternness of its power. This is, of course, as true in non-capitalist as in capitalist societies.

I began the analysis of social control in this chapter with the part that women play in it, in order to show their considerable stake in, and commitment to, the maintenance of social order. Women of all social classes have often been assumed to be more conservative than men because of their supposedly greater physical fragility and dependence and their consequently greater need for order and stability (see Randall, 1982, pp. 49–53 for a discussion). What is much less often pointed out is that women through participation in social control at all the basic levels in society have an enormous stake in perpetuating that society and its institutions. I have suggested that this role is, of course, carried out in structures dominated by men; but it is hardly surprising that, apart from the work of feminists, there has been little acknowledgement, let alone criticism of this state of affairs. All human societies are so organised and it is very difficult to bring about the seismic shocks necessary to alter that. Just consider the history of the women's refuge movement. Inevitably and reasonably this feminist-based cause had provided help for battered wives and their children, but of course the *real* problem lies in the men themselves and the patriarchal culture of which they are part – and they are far too significant a group to tackle. Whatever licence women have to practise social control, they are not as a general rule permitted to exercise authority over fit, adult men.

The control of women

At the beginning of this book I suggested that we needed to explain female conformity as much, if not more than, female deviance in looking at female criminality. Criminologists have, in general, looked too little at conformity, but this neglect is particularly striking with regard to women. I have already suggested in the previous section that women are burdened with heavy responsibilities and demanding duties in social control at domestic and informal levels. Preoccupation with these tasks can, in itself, obviously act as a form of constraint; burglary is rendered more difficult when one is encumbered with a twin baby-buggy and its contents; constant care of a demented geriatric is not a conducive situation in which to plan a bank robbery. But while women may be constrained to some extent by their part *in* social control, this pales beside the complex but enormously limiting forces which operate *upon* women. I shall look at the control of women on somewhat similar levels to those I used in the previous section, that is:

1. at home;
2. in public;
3. at work;
4. in social policies.

1. *Domestic constraint*

In a briskly polemical article entitled 'The coercion of privacy' Dahl and Snare argued that women are privately and domestically imprisoned within the home:

> The nuclear family represents a prison comparable to the public institution carrying this label (Dahl and Snare, 1978, p. 22).

> on a quantitative basis many more women are controlled through informal methods. A woman's seclusion fosters close control by children, husband and neighbours. Sociologically speaking the dominant tool is primary rather than secondary social control (Dahl and Snare, 1978, p. 21).

They went on to argue that women are too heavily supervised in the home to commit much crime and that this 'supervision' by husbands and family members is sanctioned, but not itself supervised. They seemed to mean preventive detention, rather than imprisonment as punishment, as women's sentence in the home because they suggested:

It can be argued that women are segregated and locked in their 'cells', the nuclear family, where they are hindered from having their own personal life due to lack of mobility, cash and free time. In particular a housewife with small children can not regulate her own time ... one can propose that through material and ideological bonds, women are kept 'out of circulation' [out of] ... a life in the public sector where men [of the ruling class] are now in control! (Dahl and Snare, 1978, p. 22).

Now to see the domestic life of women as a form of detention which constrains them from committing crimes may seem extreme, but consider this three-page advertisement which appeared in the glossy magazine *Options* in March 1984. It is headed 'Have you sentenced yourself to a life of hard labour?' In the centre is an authentic 'mug-shot' and 'prison record' of a young woman whose 'crime' is given as 'housewife' and whose sentence is listed at '77 hours housework per week for life'. The copy then reads as follows:

Next time your old man staggers home from the pub complaining about how hard he works, let him into a little secret. Which is that you probably work nearly twice as hard as he does. Because the average British housewife puts in a 77 hour week! No one should have to work that hard and no one needs to: some women manage to have plenty of free time. So what keeps your nose pressed firmly to the grindstone? In a word: You ... you're kept hard at it by a collection of attitudes and prejudices you're probably not even aware of!

The advertisement then offers a quiz designed to test how *angst*-ridden about her feminine role the respondent is and then ends with some sensible suggestions about minimising household tasks and maximising personal potential. These include making more use of tinned foods since the advertisement is not for a feminist publishing house or book, but is a promotion by the Canned Food Advisory Service!

That a bastion of commerce concurs in a feminist analysis of women's domestic oppression does not make that analysis correct, but it is a very significant congruence. Moreover, similar perspectives on women's lives can be derived from many other sources. Mill, of course, saw the subjection of women as the result of their seclusion in the home and consequent inferior education and power. Gavron (1966) called her study of young women burdened with domestic tasks for the first time, *The Captive Wife*, and set in train a series of studies which Oakley reviewed under the heading 'the prison-house of home' (Oakley, 1981, p. 173).

In one sense, women can be seen as in private, solitary, domestic confinement, unlikely to stray because of both the role-constraints of motherhood and housewifery and the time-consuming nature of their tasks. Yet as many writers have pointed out, and feminists have increasingly stressed, women do not have the autonomy within the home that the term 'privacy' normally implies. If there are 'separate spheres' for men and women, this means in practice that women are banned from men's clubs, not that men are banned from clubbing women at home.

'Prison' is perhaps more a meaningful metaphor for women's domestic position than an actual description of it, but many women are clearly disciplined and dominated in the home by domestic violence in ways which enormously constrain and confine what they can do. Indeed, many observers confirm that wife-battering is in fact, an assertion of patriarchal authority. Historically, husbands did have the right to chastise their wives. Only in the latter part of the nineteenth century was that right gradually undermined by legal changes (Dobash and Dobash, 1979, ch. 4). Its survival in folk memory, however, can be attested. As the Dobashes starkly put it:

> For a woman to be brutally or systematically assaulted she must usually enter our most sacred institution, the family. It is within marriage that a woman is most likely to be slapped and shoved about, severely assaulted, killed or raped (Dobash and Dobash, 1979, p. 75).

They went on to emphasise that it is in the exercise of male power that wives get beaten:

> It cannot be stressed too much that it is marriage and the taking on of the status of wife that make a woman the 'appropriate

victim' of violence aimed at 'putting her in her place' and that differential marital responsibility and authority give the husband both the perceived right and the obligation to control his wife's behaviour and thus the means to justify beating her (Dobash and Dobash, 1979, p. 93).

Marsden and Owens in a study of battered wives in Essex found that, 'Most felt that their husbands showed an unreasonable wish to dominate them ... due to old-fashioned and authoritarian attitudes' Marsden and Owens 1975).

Pahl found that many battered wives had also been kept in submission by having no access to spending money of any kind. They were so impoverished as well as so battered before coming to the Women's Aid Refuge that they, and their children, were better off on the lowest level of supplementary benefit (Pahl, 1980, p. 328). As Wilson succintly phrased it:

> Wife-beating is therefore not about the under-socialized who had too few lessons in social skills at school ... or [could not] communicate with a spouse. Domestic violence was about power. It was not – any more than was rape – an explosion of testosterone – wife-battering was often planned or semi-planned, and in many cases amounted to quite systematic and deliberate torture (Wilson, 1983, p. 119).

Carlen made very clear and telling links between women's isolation in the family, domestic violence and women's crimes in Scotland. After marriage, she argued, the women in her study were increasingly isolated and dependent, yet they were expected to maintain children and household order, often without resources:

> Women who had entertained the romantic notion that marriage would give them protection, full adult status and companionship had found instead that it gave them the triple burdens of increased responsibility, increased dependency and a deadening sense of increasing isolation from the world outside the home! (Carlen, 1983, p. 45).

Many of these women had been battered but Carlen suggested marital violence was just one part of the 'non-penal and informal disciplining of women' (Carlen, 1983, p. 44). The family relationships of women, she observed, were full of contradictions; yet the ultimate contradictions were reached when the women stepped outside the 'discipline' and protection of family life into alcoholism and crime. They were then much more likely to be punished formally if they were defined as 'outwith', in Carlen's term, family structures and control, *despite the fact* that all the sheriffs, prison staff and social workers agreed that the women's home conditions were often intolerable (Carlen, 1983, pp. 66–7). The final irony Carlen observed is that, once they are imprisoned, the penal system attempts to reimpose a domestic form of control on the female inmates:

> Thus the woman's place in the family is constitutive of, and conditions, the meanings of her imprisonment from the sentencing stage onwards. Many Scottish working-class women, like their contemporaries elsewhere in Great Britain, have not had the opportunity to negotiate a public realm of existence (Carlen, 1983, p. 86).

The main prison block at Cornton Vale she noted, is called, 'Papa'!

It is not my intention to suggest that the majority of women spend their lives locked into the domestic equivalent of Parkhurst with gaolers who are likely to beat or terrorise them into submission. I am proposing an ideal-typical analysis of family life and social control which involves very different meanings for men and for women within the same institution. While most women may not experience direct violence, nor collapse under intolerable burdens, domestic life is constituted as an elaborate series of constraints and expectations for women, supported by a very pervasive value system (see Chapter 8). To fail in their required tasks can involve either the informal 'disciplining' of women or the acknowledgement of role- and identity-failure.

Several writers have attempted to explain the continued subordination of women by men in societies which differ in economic and social organisation. All begin with the domestic relationship. Bell and Newby suggested that the traditional dominance of wives by husbands is maintained by what they called 'the deferential dialectic' (Bell and Newby, 1976, p. 154). They noted that its keynotes are legitimacy (via tradition) and stability. They analysed various factors which contribute to the persistence of domestic deference:

these include the 'totality' of the domestic situation and the social milieux which surround it and they noted:

An additional and fundamental reinforcement comes of course from the whole culture of industrial societies as reflected in the mass media (Bell and Newby, 1976, p. 158).

In much of their argument they laid stress on 'ideological hegemony' fortified by hierarchy and tradition:

The relationship between husband and wife is a deferential one in that it is traditionally legitimated and hierarchical. It appears both natural and immutable. *It has also become – because it has been in the interests of those in the superordinate position – a 'moral' order* (Bell and Newby, 1976, p. 164, added emphasis).

Finally, they acknowledged the threat behind the suburban curtains:

Should, however, the deferential relationship between husband and wife begin to break down . . . behind the morally charged, traditionally legitimate domination is savage force (Bell and Newby, 1976, p. 165).

Young and Harris began their analysis of the cross-cultural subordination of women by looking at violence. They suggested that while women are subordinated by men in all societies, the form and degree of subordination varies with the development of productive force. While in simpler societies 'the mechanism appears to be that of unmediated physical violence . . . gang rape is the example', in more settled and complex societies ideological and economic forms become paramount with violence being threatened but 'masked as individual men become responsible for the good conduct of their "own" women' (Young and Harris, 1982, pp. 470–1).

Of considerable interest here are various studies which have considered mental illness in women in relation to marriage and deviance. There are many complex arguments involved, which extend well beyond the scope of this volume (see Smart, 1977, ch. 6, for a review) but a theme of much of the discussion has been the heavy 'costs' to women of marriage and domesticity which are apparent in the higher incidence of neurosis and depression amongst housewives. Brown and his colleagues found in the community study in London that working-class women isolated at home with children were particularly prone to depression and distress. 'Life-threatening' events other than marriage, such as maternal death or separation, increased vulnerability to illness, as did having three or more young children at home. These conditions can also of course be construed as isolating the woman further in her home. One of Brown and his colleagues' most interesting findings was that having a job outside the home afforded the women some 'protection' from stress (Brown *et al.*, 1978). Weissman and Paykel (1974) reported similar findings from the USA. Procek has suggested that some women may take refuge in mental illness and in the shelter this 'sick role' affords, as their way of handling the asymetrical power battles within the family:

> Women's mental illness is the form taken by their power struggle within the personal space of the family (Procek, 1981, p. 29).

Depression and neurosis are in her view, ways for some women to resist the controls imposed upon them and that because of the private, personal nature of the male dominance of women, it is only through the medicalisation of the problem that it can be manifested.

Marriage and domesticity provide powerful controlling mechanisms to ensure the good behaviour of adult women. They are all the more powerful since they can largely be imposed with the willing, even eager, acquiescence of women themselves. Before leaving the home behind, it is worth noting that domestic containment does seem to be differentially applied to sons and daughters – albeit somewhat marginally as well as to their mothers.

Most observers today agree that boys and girls are handled in disciplinary terms in fairly similar fashion, even though they are socialised ultimately into appropriate gender roles (Lloyd and Archer, 1982, ch. 9; Nicholson, 1984, pp. 18–19). Boys tend on the whole to be more severely punished (but perhaps their behaviour is worse). More striking are the different degrees of freedom allowed to male and female children, especially as they reach adolescence. Not only are girls expected to 'keep close' at home far more than boys and much more discouraged from venturesome play, but it is also assumed, especially in working-class households that girls will take on domestic tasks both of child-care and housework; stark evidence of this can be found in the higher accident mortality rates for young boys aged 5 – 15; the differential is particularly marked in social class V.

2. *Public propriety*

Western women are not confined by the institution of purdah, nor do they wear the *chador* in public. Nevertheless, it can be argued that appropriate behaviour for women in public is both differently defined *and* more narrowly circumscribed than it is for men. One only has to consider that the term 'public men' refers to leaders of the establishment whereas 'public women' means prostitutes. Lingering remains of the doctrine of separate spheres can lead to there being no proper place in public for women at all.

It is useful to distinguish three aspects of the control of women's public behaviour. All (since we are now in the public realm of observed behaviour and formal control) are related to forms of officially-determined deviance. They are:

1. the male quasi-monopoly of force and violence
2. the notion of reputation and 'name'
3. the ideology of separate spheres.

1. *Male violence* Men have almost total power over both legitimate and illegitimate means of force in our society. Legitimate force is of course, meant to be used in the defence of vulnerable women, children and the old, not against them. (Modern and past history show that this is an optimistic view.) However, women are unlike some powerless groups in that they have traditionally neither used legitimate 'force' or illegal 'violence' to attain their ends. The typical victim of public violent attack appears to be young, fit and male (Hough and Mayhew, 1983, p. 17). However, the same Home Office study which reported this finding also noted the discrepancy between actual risk of street violence and perceived fears:

> Around third of women (but only 5 per cent of men) said they sometimes avoided going out on foot after dark in their neighbourhood for fear of crime. (Hough and Mayhew, 1983, p. 23)

In inner citys areas more than half the female respondents expressed such fears. Clarke and Lewis also found much stronger fears of
victimisation among elderly women than elderly men and they cited
several other studies which support their findings (Clarke and
Lewis, 1982, pp. 55–6). These authors also suggested that victimisation rates among women and the old may be lower *because of*
their fears, which prevent them from going out – especially at night,
– or in inner city areas (see Harrison, 1983, pp. 339–46 for some
sadly graphic case histories of victims).

To general fears of crime and lawlessness in public places, women
have to add the fear of sexual assault. Brownmiller has suggested
that rape and the fear of it are forms of sexual oppression:

> It is nothing more or less than a conscious process of intimidation
> by which *all men* keep *all women* in a state of fear (Brownmiller,
> 1973, p. 15, emphasis added).

This view has been criticised by other feminists (Wilson, 1983,
pp. 73–6) as overemphasised, but almost all writers on the subject
agree on the degree of fear which is engendered in women of sexual
violence and rape and the consequence of this for their activities:

> Rape is an abomination because it is an assault on freedom
> (Toner, 1982, p. 256).

> Rape *is* an act of violence against women. It is a hostile and a
> sadistic act. It is a violation of a woman's autonomy and a
> negation of her independence (Wilson, 1983, p. 78).

Attempts by groups of women to reassert their right of access to
public places after dark, following sexual attacks and murders have
been expressed in 'Reclaim the Night' marches.

Hanmer has observed what a powerful conditioning and controlling effect such anxiety can have on women:

> In a woman's life fear of violence from men is subtle and
> pervasive. At a subliminal level fear is experienced as unease, a
> concern to behave properly (Hanmer, 1977, p. 5).

She suggested that, in our cities:

The central institutions the places of power, prestige, or influence where the most significant transactions of the community are carried out are effectively closed to women as a group. . . . Women do not have full use of the city rather 'their paths are studded with keep-out signs and danger signals'. . . Urban space for women is compartmentalised, to deviate from women's allotted space is to run the risk of attack by men (Hanmer, 1977, p. 20).

Statistically, the true risk of being sexually assaulted or raped may be quite low, lower, for example, than the risk of injury in a traffic accident. But it is the fear and the consequent helplessness that are traditionally engendered in women which are relevant here. Undoubtedly these act as controlling agents on women's behaviour. They can hardly do otherwise when the reporting of sexual crimes tends to be so lurid and sensational and when there appears to be a tendency for police and the courts to 'blame the victim' (Smart, 1977, pp. 117–28; Toner, 1982, pp. 224–54). A woman's public activities are then controlled by a double fear: of actual unprovoked assault and of unknowingly provoking such an attack by her dress, demeanour or 'contributory negligence'. Hanmer explicitly linked private and public violence to women with the role of the state in maintaining marriage. She bleakly asserted that:

The view that the purpose of male violence to women is to control them parsimoniously explains both acts of public and private violence (Hanmer, 1977, p. 18).

Only very recently have women themselves begun both to understand this and to organise to protect themselves.

2. *The fear of ill-repute* Women who parade in public may run the risk of being regarded as public women. Image and reputation have traditionally been very important to women of all social classes who wished to be defined as 'respectable'. As we shall see, it is not merely Jane Austen's heroines who fear the loss of their 'good name' but a range of women from urban teenagers to Scottish housewives and young brides in the Welsh borders. 'Keeping your reputation' then becomes an aim for women which will inhibit their behaviour, particularly in front of public audiences.

The attentive reader of this chapter will not be surprised to learn that it is largely men, with some support from the feminine community, who control female reputations. One of the best-documented examples of this is the way in which teenage working-class males define females publicly in terms of their sexuality, and how this inhibits the latter's behaviour, or as Lees economically put it: 'How boys slag off girls' (Lees, 1983, p. 51). Whyte long ago recorded the taxonomy of the sex code operated in the Boston slums: girls were either 'good' or various kinds of 'lays'. The street-corner boys wanted to sleep with lays, but marry good girls, and according to Whyte they, of course, were able to determine which was which (Whyte, 1943).

Willis also found that the 'lads' in his study distinguished between 'girl friends' and 'easy lays':

> The model for the girl friend is, of course, the mother and she is fundamentally a model of limitation. Though there is a great deal of affection for 'mum' she is definitely accorded an inferior role (Willis, 1978, p. 45).

Willis notes the power that controlling girls' reputations gives to boys:

> The resolution amongst working-class girls of the contradiction between being sexually desirable but not sexually experienced leads to behaviour which strengthens 'the lads' sense of superiority.

This resolution leads the girls in only one direction to 'the respectable values of the home and monogamous submission' (Willis, 1978, p. 45).

One of 'the lads' with all the usual and ineffable charm pictured the present and future well-ordered fate of a good 'bird':

> Her's as good as gold. She wouldn't look at another chap. She's fucking done well, she's clean. She loves doing fucking housework. Trousers I brought yesterday, I took 'em up last night, and her turned 'em up for me . . . she's as good as gold and I wanna get married as soon as I can (Willis, 1978, p. 45).

Frith has suggested that marriage and preparation for marriage are a girls 'career' and that this explains relative absence of girls from youth cultures as they prepare to 'go out' or stay at home to guard their reputations (Frith, 1976, p. 66).

Women researchers have got rather closer to teenage girls and actually recorded their views. The end result however, is, depressingly similar. Wilson found that her sample of working-class inner-city girls did not fully share Whyte's slum sex code, but they too differentiated between permissible and improper levels of sexual activity. She claimed that these girls themselves defined and monitored the sex codes and conduct. It is apparent, however, that they only did so within a framework policed and controlled by boys and by parents. Boys punished deviant girls by getting 'the girl's name . . . passed around the streets as being easy' (Wilson, 1978, p. 71). Wilson noted that the girls she observed in the juvenile courts having supervision orders imposed were 'concerned with sexual activities or rather the *suspicion of sexual activity*'. For these girls, too, loss of reputation might prove disastrous for the future:

> It was essential therefore for the girls to safeguard their entry into the mainstream of adult social life – namely marriage – by adhering to the neighbourhood code of sexual conduct (Wilson, 1978, p. 72).

Lees has given a very vivid account of girls' vulnerability and powerlessness to control their own reputation. For boys sexual reputation is not important, but 'for a girl, the defence of her sexual reputation is crucial to her standing both with boys and girls' (Lees, 1983, p. 51). Lees observed that girls cannot fight back when boys call them 'bitch, slag, slut'. Girls have no such vocabulary of male-abusing labels, and in any case, while boys may label girls wrongly and unfairly and be believed, the reverse is not true. Keeping a good reputation is extremely difficult 'The girls tread a very narrow line'. They must have the right kind of dress, demeanour, make-up and even speech. The effects on behaviour in public places is absolutely crucial:

> Behaviour towards boys is, of course the riskiest terrain. You mustn't: hang out too much waiting for boys to come out . . . talk

or be friendly with too many boys; or the wrong boy; or someone else's boy; or too many too quickly; or even more than one boy in a group; or just find yourself ditched (Lees, 1983, p. 52).

Next to being called a 'slag' the girls hated to be labelled 'tight bitch' often in arbitrary and wholly undeserved fashion. As Lees pointed out, with the power that boys can exert over girls' reputations and futures, it is hardly surprising that 'some girls see boys as simply dangerous' (Lees, 1983, p. 53) and fear them. Several stayed at home just with girl friends in what McRobbie and Garber have called the 'culture of the bedroom' in which girls can be themselves and are 'safe'.

There are no risks involving personal humiliation or degradation, no chance of being stood up or bombed out . . . [it] can be seen as a kind of defensive retreat away from the possibility of being sexually labelled (McRobbie and Garber, 1976, p. 219–20).

Other forms of labelling of females by males have not been as fully anatomised. There is, however, considerable evidence of similar processes at work in the lives of adult women. Whitehead (1976), for example, in her account of 'sexual antagonism in Herefordshire' described incidents of abuse, horseplay and scandal-mongering in a border village. She noted how rumours and hostile encounters 'Can be seen as situations in which joking abuse is used by men to control the behaviour of women' (Whitehead, 1976, p. 179). Stanley and Wise recorded their own experience of receiving obscene and vituperative phone calls when their telephone was the contact number for a lesbian group, 'These calls dominated our lives in the sense that they could, and did occur at all times'. They then went on to express some sympathy:

For the vast majority of women we have known, it is not being able to envisage people's reactions to lesbianism – or being able to envisage these *only too well*. These women feared rejection, abuse, biblical scenes of denunciation, or even physical attack (Stanley and Wise, 1983, p. 78, emphasis added).

For some women, of course, loss of reputation is not merely an anxiety which limits their social and sexual lives. For prostitutes, for some women alcoholics and for some 'bad' mothers the consequences of being labelled deviant are far more serious than once they were for 'witches'. As we have already seen, defining a prostitute as such depends on her being 'known' to the police and her offence of soliciting is only an offence if she is a known and cautioned common prostitute. Prostitutes themselves have resisted this system of control (McLeod, 1982) both for its dual standard of morality and also because of the arbitrary nature of the labelling involved. During the campaign against the Contagious Diseases Acts it was clear that many working-class girls and women feared the terrible consequences of wrongful designation. A tragic suicide which followed such an episode helped to stimulate the campaigns.

Carlen (1983, ch. 7) and Otto (1981) both pointed out that drinking is less acceptable for women than men. Heavy drinking and alcoholism are therefore much more damaging to a woman's good name and she is likely to be regarded as far more delinquent and much less acceptable. Otto suggested that this has to do with women's role as mothers, 'No one likes to believe that the hand that rocks the cradle might be a shaky one' and that 'A woman who had deserted her feminine roles sufficiently to be an alcoholic has deserted respectability in all areas (Otto, 1981, p. 156).

Carlen showed that alcoholic women in Scotland are given no help and no hope because they are regarded as so much more reprehensible than men and Otto reported similar findings. Carlen also catalogued the experience of women who have, through drink or crime or a combination of the two, become defined as bad mothers. It is they who are the most likely of all women to slip from the net of informal or unofficial control by men at home or in public into the bonds of imprisonment.

3. *Separate spheres and a woman's place* It is, I hope, clear from the foregoing that even in our own society today, women's behaviour in public places is bound by different rules from that of men. The chief difference is that men monitor and control women's behaviour, giving and taking away names and reputations whether they are boy-friends, drinking partners, officials or just the anonymous freemasonry of men in groups, in pubs, or on street corners. We have to come back, I think, to the notion of separate spheres to understand this.

Women, strictly speaking, are only supposed to be 'at home' at home. The public domain is men's and they control access to it and behaviour in it. Nothing illustrates the force of this doctrine better than the message, consistently reinforced in headlines, cartoons and jokes that the women at Greenham Common should not merely stop protesting, but that they should be *at home* carrying out their allotted, role – appropriate tasks in their proper place.

What is ultimately most 'controlling' about the separation of spheres is that the insulation and isolation of private domestic life prevents (or has done so until recently) personal issues becoming political ones and real changes which could improve the status of women being achieved. Thus wife-battering was a secret crime until recently, and even now victims get little support from the police. Loneliness and depression, child-care problems and health have also, until recent years, been either ignored and invisible or treated individualistically as aspects of medical- or psycho-pathology. The doctrine of separation of private and public itself has become part of the system that subtly and sometimes brutally contains and confines women. In all these circumstances, it is hardly surprising that women's deviant behaviour takes the rather modest form that it does.

I have, I hope, now established the additional, formidable and distinctive forms which the social control of women takes in both the private and public realms. I want now to look rather more briefly at the three remaining areas which straddle the public and private domains. I shall do so in rather less detail since I hope we can now take for granted the apparatus of control in the home and outside and I want now to touch on particular factors which oblige women to follow certain prescriptions.

3. *At work*

Three notable factors about women's work today add to the already strong normative constraints under which they have to manage their lives:

1. most women carry the burden of two roles – they have to cope with home and work;
2. although job segregation means that most women work with other women at women's work, most of their supervisors are men;
3. sexual harassment at work.

1. *Dual roles*   It is generally agreed that while women have very considerably increased their commitments to paid work outside the home over the past thirty years, men have not put in any extra compensating activity in the home (Land, 1981). Women in consequence, do as much housework whether they go out to work or not and achieve great feats of ingenuity in fitting work and home responsibilities together. It is clear, too, that most married women have gone to work because of family needs. Many more families would have suffered poverty, had it not been for women's wages. While paid work outside the home can keep women from being miserable and depressed, its main function is to provide extra resources, not lighthearted recreation. It can therefore be seen as another form of constraint which limits women.

2. *Hierarchies at work*   In economic literature much is made of job segregation by sex and the way in which this prevents better pay for women because they have no well-paid male comparators working beside them. However, while women do not work alongside men, they certainly work under them. Much as in the domestic sphere, men hold the controlling powers and authority as foremen, supervisors and managers. Trade union officials too are usually male and have been sharply criticised for the way in which they have manipulated, controlled or prevented women's collective action (Cunnison, 1983). Lown summed up succinctly the process of dominance in the workplace as 'Not so much a factory, more a form of patriarchy' (Lown, 1983, p. 28) and added:

> Adult men – capitalists or workers emerged from mechanisation and factory organisation with authority and control in varying degrees and types over female kin and non-kin, and over younger males. New hierarchies took shape with the factory itself becoming an embodiment of 'family' ideals and the employer as father/patriarch at the head. Patriarchal relations were being reformulated in both the home and the workplace (Lown, 1983, p. 43).

3. *Sexual harassment*   Recognition of the problem of sexual harassment of women at work is not new. Engels long ago noted the power of the mill-owner to make his mill his harem. Nowadays, however, there is a growing awareness that many women at work

endure sexual harassment which ranges from whistles and catcalls and the fixing of pinups and soft porn pictures, to physical approaches and attacks which could be defined as possibly indecent and criminal. There are now numerous accounts of the problem and suggestions as to how it can best be handled (Hadjifotiou, 1983). Trades unions are gradually being made aware of the problem and persuaded to help in handling it (though of course, they are often very much part of the problem). What is of interest in the context of this discussion is what exposure of this issue reveals about control exercised over women at work by their male colleagues and supervisors.

Proponents of the 'liberation equals crime' argument have tended to assume that in moving more into work outside the home, women were 'liberating' themselves. In so far as women have gained some financial autonomy that is true, although women still earn less than men and contribute their earnings to the family's budgets. However, it is important to stress how little autonomy women have at work. They tend to fill the lowest levels in the pecking order, to be supervised and not be supervisors. Sexual harassment is also another constraint which operates to confine and inhibit women's activities at work. Many women report having left jobs they liked because of constant harassment (Hadjifotiou, 1983) while others have been made acutely ill or depressed and have their promotion chances affected and their working lives made miserable. It is a myth that these encounters are part of the 'natural urges' of *homo sapiens*, longed for and reciprocated. For most women workers they constitute another dimension of male dominance, a further assualt on their freedom.

By exercising power in this way, men reinforce and maintain their authority and control in the workplace (Hadjifotiou, 1983).

The incidence of such harassment appears to be high – 60 per cent of women interviewed in one survey reported at least one incident. Surveys have failed to find serious examples of men sexually harassed by their female colleagues (Hadjifotiou, 1983, pp. 10–11).

4. Social policies

The forms of social control both informal and institutional which define and limit the behaviour of women are extremely diverse. They range from the subtle pressures to be a good wife and mother at home with her children in her proper place, which emanate from mass media and from deepest cultural assumptions to the crude hostilities of the open office of the factory floor, where women may be kept 'in place' by sexual taunts or silent displays of pin-ups which remind them that they are defined as mere sexual objects. Of all the subtler constraints on the way women act and are supposed to act, few are more complex than the workings of social policies.

Social policies are not usually regarded as instruments whose prime purpose is the definition and enforcement of prescriptions about gender roles, especially for women, but a growing body of analyses shows that such prescriptions underpin, or are an effective part of certain policies. Several areas of policies assume that gender-roles, especially in the family, take particular forms for both men and women. On men, for example, falls the obligation to maintain their wives and children and indeed their common-law partners. What notably characterises the way women's roles and actions are prescribed in welfare provisions is that since these tend to regard married women and some single women as 'dependent', constraints applied to women are reinforced. Thus some women have not been able to claim benefits in their own right nor for their dependents. Legislation varies over time and place but, for example, in the UK, until the mid-1980s, the national insurance and the tax system treated women as their husbands dependents. It is still the case that unemployed married women are 'lost' in official counts. The ways in which social security systems define women's role, discourage work outside the home for some groups of women and assume that others will look after dependents within the home, are very complicated and can change with time. Land (1976 and 1981) and Wilson (1977) have analysed the ways in which women's compliance with certain role assumptions and prescriptions are achieved. Land quoted Elenor Rathbone who understood the nature of the issues at stake very well:

The economic dependency of the married woman is the last stronghold of those who, consciously or unconsciously, prefer woman in subjection, and that is perhaps why the stronghold is proving so hard to force (Land, 1976, p. 129).

I have tried in this chapter to sketch out some of the key aspects of the control experienced by women in our society. First of all there is the primary distinction of women's proper place: in the privacy of home. This can make women's public lives, whether in public places or at work problematical – simply by being outside the home they run the risk of formal sanction, of moral disapproval or of unprovoked assault. Even within 'her' home, a woman is not private nor autonomous – domestically, publicly and at work, women are subject to the control and approval of men. Much of the pattern of nurture and care, of rewards and sanctions which comprise the moral fabric society are designated as 'women's work', but again, women have relatively little choice or autonomy in performing such actions. A great variety of institutions and customs comprise the 'system' that keeps women in their place.

These ideas and their relation to women's criminality are necessarily speculative for the moment. I would suggest that when women do become criminal it is in the context of the structure of conformity and constraint that we should see them and relate to them. The awareness of women with convictions of the vast pressures to conform is considerable. Those who defy 'man-made' laws may well have perceived the bias of the system and decided to push against it. Class differences in female crime can be related both to the more limited resources which working-class men can employ to contain and 'protect' their womenfolk and also to the fact that, once outside that 'protection' and any command over its resources, working-class women are particularly vulnerable because they are so economically exploited. Numerous autobiographies of prostitutes demonstrate that the street was the only place to earn reasonable money.

Women are not merely automata reacting as if pre-programmed to a robotic control system. Rather, the pattern of bonds, attachments and constraints I am trying to picture is a subtly-woven web which women themselves help to weave. Their adherence to their bonds is close, their attachment profound. The system is highly successful, since far fewer women than men commit crimes particularly of the predatory sort. Women who do commit crimes and are apprehended and stigmatised are often those on whom constraints, or their inherent contradictions were all-too effective: such as women who steal since theft is more profitable than ill-paid work, or who solicit for the same reason.

Some empirical work has been done by control theorists to test the validity of narrower, but similar versions of the ideas which I have put forward here. In Hirschi's original formulation (1969) he suggested that social bonding was crucial in preventing delinquency. Without such ties 'delinquent acts results when an individual's bond to society is weak or broken'. Bonds consist of attachment, commitment, involvement and belief. As Downes and Rock (1982) noted, 'the strength of Hirschi's work however, is empirical rather than theoretical' and the propositions of control theories have been tested repeatedly, although mainly on teenage populations and usually in relation to infractions which would not be reckoned serious criminal offences in an adult.

Nevertheless, these studies do provide some support for the ideas expressed here and are also interesting for the attempts made by several proponents to make sex differences in delinquency central to their theories and their testing (see Box, 1983, pp. 178–81 for a review). In these studies, the authors agree that social bonds that attach young people so deeply to family, friends and schools prevent them from becoming delinquent. Those who do become delinquent either have only weak ties, or these are damaged in some way. Most reports further suggest that 'the social locations of females typically contains more of those factors which act as constraints on delinquent behaviour' (Box, 1983, p. 179). In a Canadian study, Hagan *et al.* found some evidence for this amongst high-school girls and concluded that women were 'over-socialized – over-controlled'. They also observed that there was 'a larger stratification system – a system which makes women the instruments and objects of informal social controls, and men the instruments and objects of formal social controls' and that 'in the world of crime and delinquency, as in the world of work, women are denied full access to the public sphere through a socialization sequence that moves from mother to daughter in a cycle that is self-renewing' (Hagan *et al.*, 1979, p. 34). Box further suggested that girls' response to blocked opportunity structures is likely to be different from boys in that they will 'internalise blame' since 'they have been socialised to *endure* the female's lot in life'. In consequence, he agreed with Clinard and Piven that:

In a patriarchal society like ours, women's disorganized and spontaneous 'protests' are more likely to be channelled away from innovative criminal behaviour and into retreatist and self-defeatist adaptations (Box, 1983, p. 181).

Figueria-McDonough and her colleagues (1981) tried in a series of papers to develop a 'gender-integrated theory of delinquency'. Their argument is that gender-specialised delinquency is a myth and that from their self-report studies and from the relationships they found in their 'inclusive model of bond theories (they) produced very similar results for both genders' (Barton and Figueria-McDonough, 1984). The conclusion is that similar attachments and their opposites, predict male and female delinquency. However, what their model cannot explain is the very considerable differences in offence-behaviour between boys and girls. The sexes had similar patterns on trivial matters such as 'lied about age' and 'loitered at school' but showed dramatic differences on more serious offences. This would seem to suggest that although the bonds are the same for both boys and girls, they are more effectively applied to girls. It may also be that additional factors, of the kind I stressed earlier which attach girls and women more successfully to the social bonding system are at work.

Hutter and Williams in a perceptive essay which brings together ideas about normal and deviant women observed that:

As daughters, wives, mothers, workers and friends, we, as other women, have experienced various forms of control. We are only beginning to realize the extent to which we have taken for granted this picture of what is normal, to grasp the all-pervasiveness of the controls and the extent to which the various forms of control are related . . . controls embodied a notion of normality that specifically referred to women rather than to people in general. They sought to contain their behaviour not only in one capacity, for example as childbearer or purveyor of sexual services, but in many other aspects of their lives. It usually has to be claimed that men are less than adult, psychopaths, have inadequate personalities . . . before justifying such extended control. With women it is sufficient justification that they are women (Hutter and Williams, 1981, pp. 9–10).

I have tried to demonstrate the nature and force of this pervasive control in this chapter.

In both the widely-expressed values of our society and in the structure of that society are embodied particular notions of normal women and controls to ensure their production and conformity.

This all works very 'successfully' despite many inherent contradictions and the very considerable costs to individual women. That is why understanding the control of women is so important to our appreciation of their criminality. Obviously since women are, in Hagan's term, 'over-controlled' they commit less crime and fewer serious and repeated offences. Even when they do deviate they do so within a particular man-made framework of controls. Some women may correspond to conventional stereotypes of female crime – wicked, evil and beyond reason: the witch of myth and legend. Others may be sexually deviant: the harlot of ancient tradition. Even if women are not in fact conforming to stereotypes, the chances are that their behaviour will be so defined by the media, by the agents of control and perhaps even by the women themselves. That most criminal women are, in fact trivial property offenders whose crimes, as Box pointed out appear, to be related to their powerlessness and economic marginalisation is hardly recognised at all (Box, 1983, p. 199). Of course, if there were a simple equation that 'poverty and powerlessness equals criminality' girls and women would be the leaders in crime waves. That they are not leads us to consider the highly-effective system of controls and bonds which make criminality a damaging and difficult course for women to take. Barbara Wootton pointed out many years ago that if men behaved like women the courts and prisons would be empty. Strictly speaking, that is not true, but it is very interesting to speculate on the reversal of the present system of social order. Could boys and men be contained as comprehensively as women have been? I have not dealt in this chapter with the ways in which some women have begun to circumvent those constraints and tried to loosen some of the knots on the silken bonds. If nothing else, the analysis that has been engendered helps us look at women in public and in private, the normal and the deviant, and to see how these interact. It is a considerable and formidable enterprise to try to understand, let alone to change, the system. As Hutter and Williams put it:

The pervasiveness of controls over women suggest that, as a group their attempts to free themselves from their unequal position in society offer a particularly strong threat to existing social arrangements (Hutter and Williams, 1981, p. 11).

10

Conclusion: towards a feminist understanding

As far as I know, no one has yet written a book called 'Men and Crime', although as I have already suggested most books about crime, delinquency and deviance do in fact turn out to be only about males. Only the bulkiest American texts claim to give a comprehensive account of crime as a topic and most focus on one group such as juveniles, or on a male perspective. To try to tackle the whole range of possible perspectives on women and crime is a formidable assignment and I hope the patient reader will forgive the pace at which we have had to cover the requisite ground.

I have posed a number of questions in the course of the book and tried to provide at least some partial answers. We began with description: what are women's crimes and how do they feel about them, how are they treated by the criminal justice and the penal systems? As we saw, women commit relatively few crimes and relatively few of those women are repeated or serious offenders. Those women who do become involved in crime tend to disavow their deviant status even when, as with prostitution, they have chosen their deviant profession. That this strenuous disavowal is a reasonable reaction can be seen in the images of deviant women prevalent in society. These are all profoundly damaging to the role and status of conventional women, not least to their position as 'proper' wives and mothers. Moreover, as we could see in looking at social control, women had little say themselves in deciding what is appropriate behaviour. The codes they follow in public and in private are set by men, even though women themselves may play a part in enforcing them. It is one of the more exquisitely painful ironies of this whole topic that young delinquent males, often depicted as the social rebels, the iconoclasts of their generation play such a large part in the repression and control of 'their' girls.

Women are not especially indulged by police, courts or prisons. It is reasonable to suggest that their low representation amongst convicted sentenced prisoners is because of their less serious offending pattern. Some American studies do suggest that adult women receive a little chivalry, but other US data shows young women being punished for sexual misdemeanours which go unpunished in either young men or adult women. Those few women who go to prison suffer the usual pains of imprisonment but are also penalised because they are so few in a system designed for and focussed on men.

Studying criminal women was a task tackled by very few criminologists and the results, when it was undertaken were very odd. Indeed the whole area stayed locked in a time-warp until the late 1960s when a feminist critique began to offer a new approach. Ultimately the best way to understand women and crime seemed to be not through feminist criminology as it has developed so far, but in using the insights into the role, position and social control of women which can be derived from other studies of women's oppression.

That for the moment, is, about as far as I think we can take the argument. We have telescoped a good deal into the past decade and a half, but there is still a long way to go. Women involved in crime are only just finding their own voices. On the other hand, many more women do perceive the outlines of the system under which they live and if they have not changed it they have certainly mocked and exposed it.

Towards a theory

Involvement in crime must be the outcome of a variety of social, economic and other pressures. 'Crime' is itself a social construct, and a fairly wobbly construct at that. Most contemporary crime consists of offences concerning motor vehicles, or thefts from self-service stores: acts which have only been made possible by modern developments in technology and retailing. There are no *a priori* reasons for believing that female crime should be very different from male and indeed it is clear that women can and do emulate men in committing all types of crime. But the sexes differ markedly in the frequency and seriousness of their offences and in the respective social consequences of being labelled an offender.

After recent contributions to the study of crime commission (Clarke, 1984) we can say that carrying out deviant acts which break the law must be related to:

1. opportunity
2. time
3. space
4. scope
5. available role models
6. deviant images and stigma.

Being observed, caught, cautioned or convicted will in turn depend on how agencies of control operate and use:

1. values and ideology
2. agency practices
3. formal rules and laws
4. conventional behavioural stereotypes (of race, sex, etc.).

I should like to suggest that women face distinctively different opportunity situations and to some extent with agencies of control, the main point with the latter being that women face an additional series of controls. They are the one section of society whose policing has already been 'privatised', even though they have not ceased to be publicly controlled as well.

Messages and insights

I have tried to provide some food for thought for several groups of people in this book. For women who are themselves involved in crime I hope it may provide some coherence in what can seem like a fragmented 'meaningless' experience, but I am really more in their debt than the other way round. For feminists, I shall be pleased if this book makes it possible to uncover a realm of women's experience which has previously been hidden and to make a kind of sense of it as part of a feminist analysis of the world. For students who, if they are anthing like my own, always want 'just one key book', I hope this for the moment may be it. I have tried hard to pack in as much information, from as many sources as I could.

Professionals, too, should take away a series of messages. There is no 'new' female criminal. Girls, on the other hand, are still being defined into stereotypically sexually-delinquent roles and then being 'punished' or protected for their own good. Penal treatment of women does not meet their needs and is even less defensible on its present scale than the treatment of men which it so anomalously emulates and inverts.

It is too much to hope that conventional criminology will at any foreseeable future time address the questions raised by the gender issue in crime and put its house in order. For women and crime this may not really matter very much. After all, as I have tried to show, the systematic critique of female exclusion and distortion in its work is well developed, as are alternative approaches which place women more centrally in the analysis. It is of course, the study of *male* crimes which suffers and is most distorted by the failure to consider, let alone build in, the dimension of gender in crime.

It is conventional to assert the need for more research when concluding studies of topics such as this where large gaps in our knowledge still remain. We have very little on women, race and crime although several authors have suggested that this is an important variable (Hartz Karp, 1981; Greenwood, 1981). While it would be valuable to have more information of this kind, there are particular problems which must be stressed. First, as Smart (1977) noted there is the danger of a moral panic about female crime. It does seem to be the case that some of the increased interest in women offenders in the early days of feminist criminology was associated with a backlash against them (Chesney-Lind, 1980) and see Gibbens (1981) for a classic example of misunderstanding. There are difficulties too caused by secrecy and disavowal of deviancy. Women and girls do not readily take on deviant identities, their lives are much more private than men's and while women researchers can more easily reach them, there remain considerable problems (McRobbie and Garber, 1976).

These are just some of the reasons which seem to me to justify a considerable shift in perspective in the study of female crime. If we start from the broader issues of conformity and control and observe and analyse how these affect *all* women to some degree and *some* groups of women more than others, we can then learn rather more about those who become involved in crime as compared with other kinds of activities which might be available to them. This would, I think, show that female crime is not a particularly homogeneous category: thus some groups of women have deliberately broken the law to expose the contradictions in the social and legal position of their sex and to make political statements. Others, constrained by socio-economic pressures, commit crimes because alternative sources of income for them and their dependants are poor. For others, especially young girls, there will be subcultural pressures to conform to group or gang norms. Whatever the respective controls and constraints on roles and actions, the arena in which women's behaviour occurs will be similar for most groups of women and affect the outcomes in terms of their criminal careers.

In short, I am arguing for a perspective that is not primarily criminologically-based, nor even one located in the sociology of deviance (which has proved still more disappointing as an approach) but one which uses the interesting and challenging analyses of family life, male dominance and separate spheres which feminist theory and studies have to offer. I once thought that by a crash programme of research we might enable studies of female crime to catch up those of male and that we could then 'reintegrate the study of male and female deviance'. That day now seems further off than ever and less enticing as a prospect. For the moment, let us settle for an autonomous approach.

Bibliography

F. Adler (1975) *Sisters in Crime*, McGraw-Hill, New York.
F. Adler (ed.) (1981) *The Incidence of Female Criminality in the Contemporary World*, University Press, New York.
F. Adler and R. J. Simon (eds) (1979) *The Criminology of Deviant Women*, Houghton Mifflin, Boston.
Anon (1959) *Streetwalker, An Autobiographical Account of Prostitution*, Bodley Head, London.
J. Archer and B. Lloyd (1982) *Sex and Gender*, Penguin, Harmondsworth.
P. Arrowsmith (1970) *Somewhere Like This*, Panther, London.
R. Austin (1982) 'Women's Liberation and Increases in Minor, Major and Occupational Offences', *Criminology*, vol. 20.
R. L. Austin (1981) 'Liberation and Female Criminality in England and Wales', *British Journal of Criminology*, vol. 21, no. 4.
P. Bailey (1983) *An English Madam*, Fontana, London.
E. Badinter (1981) *The Myth of Motherhood*, Souvenir Press, London.
J. Baldwin and M. McConville (1980) 'Juries, Foremen and Verdicts', *British Journal of Criminology*, vol. 20, no. 1.
O. Banks (1981) *Faces of Feminism*, Martin Robertson, Oxford.
M. Banton (1984) 'Keeping the Force in Check' in *Times Higher Education Supplement*, 13 January 1984.
H. E. Barnes and N. K. Teeters (1951) *New Horizons in Criminology*, Prentice-Hall, New York.
W. Barton and J. Figueira-McDonough (1984) 'Gender Attachments and Delinquency' in *Deviant Behaviour* (forthcoming).
H. S. Becker (1963) *Outsiders: Studies in the Sociology of Deviance*, Macmillan, London.
J. Becker (1977) *Hitler's Children*, Michael Joseph, London.
C. Bell and H. Newby (1976) 'Husbands and Wives: The Dynamics of the Deferential Dialectic' in D. L. Barker and S. Allen, *Dependence and Exploitation*, Longman, London.
J. Berger (1973) *Ways of Seeing*, BBC Pelican, London.
M. A. Bertrand (1969) 'Self-Image and Delinquency: A Contribution to

the Study of Female Criminality and Women's Image', *Acta Criminologia*, January.

V. Binney *et al.* (1981) *Leaving Violent Men: A Study of Refuges and Housing for Battered Women*, Women's Aid Federation, London.

L. Biron (1981) 'An Over-view of Self-reported Delinquency in a Sample of Girls in the Montreal Area', in Morris and Gelsthorpe (eds).

C. Bishop (1931) *Women and Crime*, Chatto & Windus, London.

R. K. Blyth (1971) 'New Plans for Treatment in the New Holloway', paper given to the Howard League.

G. Boccaccio (1964) *Concerning Famous Women* (transl. G. Guarino), Allen & Unwin, London.

J. Bowlby (1946) *Forty-four Juvenile Thieves, Their Characters and Home Life*, Baillière, Tindall & Cox, London.

J. Bowlby (1953) *Child Care and the Growth of Love*, Penguin, Harmondsworth.

S. Box (1981) *Deviance, Reality and Society*, Holt, Rinehart & Wilson, London.

S. Box (1983) *Power, Crime and Mystification*, Tavistock, London.

S. Box and C. Hale (1983) 'Liberation and Female Criminality in England and Wales', *British Journal of Criminology*, vol. 23, no. 1.

A. M. Brodsky (ed.) (1975) *The Female Offender*, Sage, London.

G. W. Brown and T. Harris (1978) *Social Origins of Depression*, Tavistock, London.

S. Brownmiller (1973) *Against Our Will*, Penguin, Harmondsworth.

J. H. Bryan (1966) 'Occupational Ideologies and Individual Attitudes of Call Girls', *Social Problems*, vol. 13, no. 4.

A. Buckle and D. P. Farrington (1984) 'An Observational Study of Shoplifting', *British Journal of Criminology*, vol. 24, no. 1.

J. Buxton and M. Turner (1962) *Gate Fever*, Cresset, London.

M. O. Cameron (1964) *The Booster and the Snitch*, Free Press, London.

A. Campbell (1981) *Girl Delinquents*, Basil Blackwell, Oxford.

P. Caplan and J. Bujra (1978) *Women United, Women Divided*, Tavistock, London.

K. Carey (1977) 'Police Attitudes to Women Offenders', unpublished paper presented to British Sociological Association (mimeo).

P. Carlen (1976) *Magistrates' Justice*, Martin Robertson, Oxford.

P. Carlen (1983) *Women's Imprisonment*, Routledge & Kegan Paul, London.

M. Casburn (1979) *Girls Will Be Girls*, Women's Research and Resources Centre, London.

M. Chesney-Lind (1973) 'Judicial Enforcement of the Female Sex Role: The Family Court and the Female Delinquent', *Issues in Criminology*, vol. 8, no. 2.

M. Chesney-Lind (1980) 'Rediscovering Lilith: Misogyny and the "New Female Criminality"', in C. Taylor Griffiths and M. Nance (eds) *The Female Offenders*, Simon Fraser University.

M. Churchill Sharpe (1928) *Chicago May*, Macaulay, New York.

D. Clark (1984) 'Police out of Step in Kerb Crawl Clean-up', *The Observer*, 26 February.

J. Clarke (1976) 'The Skinheads and the Magical Recovery of Community' in S. Hall and T. Jefferson (eds).

A. H. Clarke and M. J. Lewis (1982) 'Fear of Crime Among the Elderly', *British Journal of Criminology*, vol. 22, no. 1.

R. V. Clarke (1984) 'Opportunity-based Crime Rates', *British Journal of Criminology*, vol. 24, no. 1.

D. Clemmer (1958) *The Prison Community*, Holt, Rinehart & Winston, New York.

M. Clinard (1968) *The Sociology of Deviant Behaviour* (3rd edn), Holt, Rinehart & Winston, New York.

R. Cloward and L. Ohlin (1960) *Delinquency and Opportunity*, Collier-Macmillan, London.

A. K. Cohen (1955) *Delinquent Boys*, Free Press, London.

A. K. Cohen *et al.* (eds) (1956) *The Sutherland Papers*, Indiana University Press, Bloomington.

G. Cohen (1978) 'Women's Solidarity and the Preservation of Privilege' in Caplan and Bujra (eds).

S. Cohen (1977) 'Introduction and Postscript' in Probyn.

S. Cohen (1980) *Folk Devils and Moral Panics*, Martin Robertson, London.

A. Cook and G. Kirk (1983) *Greenham Women Everywhere*, Pluto Press, London.

P. Corrigan (1979) *Schooling the Smash Street Kids*, Macmillan, London.

P. Corrigan and S. Frith (1976) 'The Politics of Youth Culture' in S. Hall and T. Jefferson (eds).

J. Cowie, V. Cowie and E. Slater (1968) *Delinquency in Girls*, Heinemann, London.

D. R. Cressey (ed.) (1961) *The Prison*, Holt, Rinehart & Winston, New York.

N. Crisman (1976) 'Female Offenders', American Civil Liberties Conference, Penn., USA.

L. Crites (ed.) (1976) *The Female Offender*, D. C. Heath, Lexington, Massachusetts.

J. Cunnison (1983) 'Trade Union Activity' in E. Garmanikow (ed.).

T. S. Dahl and A. Snare (1978) 'The Coercion of Privacy' in C. Smart and B. Smart (eds).

A. Dally (1982) *Inventing Motherhood*, Burnett Books, London.

K. Dalton (1969) *The Menstrual Cycle*, Penguin, Harmondsworth.

K. Davis (1963) 'The Sociology of Prostitution' in R. Merton and R. Nisbet (eds) *Contemporary Social Problems*, Hart Davis, London.

S. Dell (1971) *Silent in Court*, Bell, London.

J. Ditton and J. Duffy (1983) 'Bias in the Newspaper Reporting of Crime News', *British Journal of Criminology*, vol. 23, no. 2.

R. E. Dobash and R. Dobash (1979) *Violence Against Wives*, Open Books, London.

R. Dobash and R. E. Dobash (1981) 'Community Response to Violence against Wives: Charivari, Abstract Justice and Patriarchy', *Social Problems*, vol. 28, no. 5.

G. Donaldson (ed.) (1976) *Women in Crime*, Phoebus, London.

J. Donnison (1977) *Midwives and Medical Men*, Heinemann, London.
D. Downes and P. Rock (1982) *Understanding Deviance*, Clarendon, Oxford.
E. Durkheim (1933) *The Division of Labour in Society*, Free Press, New York.
S. Edwards (1981) *Female Sexuality and the Law*, Martin Robertson, Oxford.
B. Ehrenreich and D. English (1979) *For Her Own Good*, Pluto Press, London.
J. Ellington (1966) Foreword to G. Konopka, *The Adolescent Girl in Conflict*, Prentice Hall, New Jersey.
J. B. Elshtain (1981) *Public Man, Private Woman*, Martin Robertson, Oxford.
M. Evans (ed.) (1982) *The Woman Question*, Fontana, London.
Expenditure Committee (1978–9) Education, Arts and Home Office Sub-Committee of the Expenditure Committee: 14 volumes of oral evidence and written submissions contained in vols. 61–i to 61–xiv.
F. Farmer (1974) *Will There Really be a Morning?*, Fontana, Glasgow.
D. P. Farrington (1981) 'The Prevalence of Convictions', *British Journal of Criminology*, vol. 21, no. 2.
D. P. Farrington and T. Bennett (1981) 'Police Cautioning of Juveniles in London', *British Journal of Criminology*, vol. 21, no. 2.
D. P. Farrington and A. M. Morris (1983) 'Sex, Sentencing and Reconviction', *British Journal of Criminology*, vol. 23, no. 3.
D. Faulkner (1971) 'The Development of Holloway Prison', *Howard Journal*.
C. Feinman (1980) *Women in the Criminal Justice System*, Praeger, New York.
M. Ferguson (1983a) 'Learning to be a Woman's Woman', *New Society*, 21 April 1983.
M. Ferguson (1983b) *Forever Feminine*, Heinemann, London.
W. Feyerheim (1981) 'Measuring Gender Differences in Delinquency: Self-Reports Versus Police Contact' in M. Q. Warren (ed.).
E. Figes (1970) *Patriarchal Attitudes*, Faber & Faber, London.
J. Figueira-McDonough *et al.* (1981) 'Normal Deviance: Gender Similarities, in Adolescent Subcultures' in M. Q. Warren (ed.).
J. Finch and D. Groves (1980) 'Community Care and the Family: A Case for Equal Opportunities?', *Journal of Social Policy*, vol. 9, pt. 4.
J. Finch and D. Groves (eds) (1983) *A Labour of Love*, Routledge & Kegan Paul, London.
H. Finestone (1964) 'Cats, Kicks and Colour' in H. Becker (ed.) *The Other Side*, Free Press, New York.
F. Finnegan (1979) *Poverty and Prostitution*, Cambridge University Press, London.
C. J. Fisher and R. L. Mawby (1982) 'Juvenile Delinquency and Police Discretion in an Inner City Area', *British Journal of Criminology*, vol. 22, no. 1.
C. Follett 'Mixed Prison Experiment', *The Times*, 12 January 1981.

J. Fox and T. F. Hartnagel (1979) 'Changing Social Roles and Female Crime in Canada', *Review Canadian Sociology and Anthropology*, vol. 16.

R. Frankenberg (1976) 'Sex and Gender in British Community Studies' in D. L. Barker and S. Allen (eds) *Sexual Divisions and Society*, Tavistock, London.

D. Fraser (1973) *The Evolution of the British Welfare State*, Macmillan, London.

B. Friedan (1963) *The Feminine Mystique*, Dell, New York.

S. Frith (1978) *The Sociology of Rock*, Constable, London.

T. R. Fyvel (1963) *The Insecure Offenders*, Penguin, Harmondsworth.

E. Garmarnikow *et al.* (eds) (1983) *Gender Class and Work*, Heinemann, London.

H. Gavron (1966) *The Captive Wife*, Penguin, Harmondsworth.

R. Giallombardo (1966) *Society of Women: A Study of a Women's Prison*, Wiley, Chichester.

R. Giallombardo (ed.) (1972) *Juvenile Delinquency: A Book of Readings* (2nd edn), John Wiley, New York.

R. Giallombardo (1974) *The Social World of Imprisoned Girls*, Wiley, New York.

T. Gibbens (1981) 'England and Wales' in Adler (ed.) (1981).

T. C. N. Gibbens (1971) 'Female Offenders', *British Journal of Hospital Medicine*, vol. 6.

T. C. N. Gibbens and J. Prince (1962) *Shoplifting*, Institute for the Study and Treatment of Delinquency, London.

S. and E. Glueck (1934) *Five Hundred Delinquent Women*, Knopf, New York.

E. Goffman (1976) *Gender Advertisements*, Macmillan, London.

E. Gomme (1976) see T. Middleton and M. Gold (1970) *Delinquent Behaviour in an American City*, Wadsworth, Belmont.

H. Graham and A. Oakley (1981) 'Competing Ideologies of Reproduction' in H. Roberts (ed.).

V. Greenwood (1981) 'The Myth of Female Crime' in Morris and Gelsthorpe (eds).

G. Grosser (1951) *Juvenile Delinquency and Contemporary American Sex Roles*, unpublished Ph.D thesis, Harvard University.

Guardian (1983) M. Dean, 'Holloway's Fast Lady Keeps to her Course: Catalogue of Conflict over Holloway Governor'; 'Holloway's Blind Alley'. (leader) 25 July 1983.

N. Hadjifotiou (1983) *Women and Harassment at Work*, Pluto Press, London.

R. Hadley and S. Hatch (1981) *Social Welfare and the Failure of the State*, Allen & Unwin, London.

J. Hagan, J. H. Simpson and A. R. Gillis (1979) 'The Sexual Stratification of Social Control: A Gender-based Perspective on Crime and Delinquency', *British Journal of Sociology*, vol. 30.

S. Hall and T. Jefferson (eds) (1976) *Resistance through Rituals*, Hutchinson, London.

J. Hanmer (1977) 'Violence and the Social Control of Women', British Sociological Association, mimeo.

J. Hanmer and H. Rose (1980) 'Making Sense of Theory' in P. Henderson *et al.* (eds) *The Boundaries of Change in Community Work*, Allen & Unwin, London.

A. Harris (1977) 'Sex and Theories of Deviance', *American Sociological Review*, vol. 42:1.

M. Harris (1984) 'On the Crawl', *New Society*, 1 March.

P. Harrison (1983) *Inside the Inner City*, Penguin, Harmondsworth.

M. Hartman (1977) *Victorian Murderesses*, Robson Books, London.

J. Hartz-Karp (1981) 'Women in Constraints' in Mukherjee and Scutt (eds).

J. Hearn (1982) 'Notes on Patriarchy, Professionalization and the Semi-professions', *Sociology*, vol. 16, no. 2.

P. Hearst (1982) *Every Secret Thing*, Doubleday, New York.

F. M. Heidensohn (1967) 'Delinquent Girls', unpublished paper, London School of Economics.

F. M. Heidensohn (1968) 'The Deviance of Women: A Critique and an Enquiry', *British Journal of sociology*, vol. XIX, no. 2.

F. M. Heidensohn (1969) 'Prison for Women', *Howard Journal*.

F. M. Heidensohn (1970) 'Sex, Crime and Society' in G. A. Harrison (ed.) *Biosocial Aspects of Sex*, Blackwell, Oxford.

F. M. Heidensohn (1975) 'The Imprisonment of Females' in S. McConville (ed.) *The Use of Imprisonment*, Routledge & Kegan Paul, London.

F. M. Heidensohn (1981) 'Women and the Penal System' in Morris and Gelsthorpe (eds).

F. M. Heidensohn (1983) review of E. B. Leonard, *Women, Crime and Society*, *Sociology*, vol. 17, no. 3.

A. E. Hiller and L. Hancock (1981) 'The Processing of Juveniles in Victoria' in Mukherjee and Scutt (eds).

M. Hindelang (1974) 'Decisions of Shoplifting Victims to Invoke the Criminal Justice Process', *Social Problems*, vol. 21, no. 4.

M. Hindelang (1979) 'Sex Differences in Criminal Activity', *Social Problems*, vol. 27.

T. Hirschi (1969) *Causes of Delinquency*, University of California Press, Berkeley.

S. Hite (1977) *The Hite Report*, Summit Books, London.

Home Office (1970) *The Treatment of Women and Girls in Custody*, HMSO, London.

Home Office/J. Davies and N. Goodman (1972) *Girl Offenders Aged 17 to 20 years*, HMSO, London.

Home Office (1975) *Further Studies of Female Offenders*, HMSO, London.

Home Office (1979) *Report of the Work of the Prison Dept.*, HMSO, London.

Home Office (1980) *Prison Statistics: England and Wales 1979*, HMSO, London.

Home Office (1982a) *Report on the Work of the Prison Dept. 1981*, HMSO, London.

Home Office (1982b) *Prison Statistics: England and Wales 1981*, HMSO,

London.

Home Office (1982c) *Criminal Statistics: England and Wales 1981*, HMSO, London.

Home Office (1983a) *Criminal Statistics: England and Wales 1982*, HMSO, London.

Home Office (1983b) *Criminal Statistics: England and Wales Supplementary Tables, 1982*, HMSO, London, vol. 4.

R. Hood (1962) *Sentencing in Magistrates' Courts*, Stevens, London.

M. Hough and P. Mayhew (1983) *The British Crime Survey*, Home Office Research Study no. 76, HMSO, London.

B. Hutter and G. Williams (1981) *Controlling Women*, Croom Helm, London.

M. Hyde (1972) *The Other Love*, Mayflower, London.

M. Ignatieff (1978) *A Just Measure of Pain*, Pantheon, New York.

H. Kalven and H. Zeisel (1966) *The American Jury*, Little, Brown, Boston.

J. Kelly (1967) *When the Gates Shut*, Longman, London.

J. Kitsuse and D. Dietrick (1959) 'Delinquent Boys: A Critique', *American Sociological Review*, vol. 24.

D. Klein (1976) 'The Aetiology of Female Crime: A Review of the Literature' in L. Crites (ed.).

G. Konopka (1966) *The Adolescent Girl in Conflict*, Prentice Hall, New Jersey.

S. Kobrin (1951) 'The Conflict of Values in Delinquency Areas', *American Sociological Review*, vol. 16.

C. Kruttschnitt (1981) 'Prison Codes, Inmate solidarity and Women: A Re-examination' in Warren (ed.)

H. Land (1976) 'Women: Supporters or Supported?' in D. Leonard Barker *et al.* (ed.).

H. Land (1981) *Parity begins at Home*, Equal Opportunities Commission and Social Science Research Council Joint Panel on Equal Opportunities, London.

S. Landau and G. Nathan (1981) 'Juveniles and the Police: Who is Charged Immediately and Who is Referred to the Juvenile Bureau?' *British Journal of Criminology*, vol. 21, no. 2.

S. Landau and G. Nathan (1983) 'Selecting Delinquents for Cautioning in the London Metropolitan Area', *British Journal of Criminology*, vol. 23, no. 2.

C. Larner (1981) *Enemies of God*, Chatto & Windus, London.

S. Lees (1983) 'How Boys Slag off Girls', *New Society*, 13 October.

D. Leonard Barker and S. Allen (1976) *Sexual Divisions and Society*, Tavistock, London.

E. B. Leonard (1982) *Women, Crime and Society*, Longman, London.

D. Lewis (1981) 'Black Women Offenders and Criminal Justice: Some Theoretical Considerations' in M. Q. Warren (ed.).

A. Liazos (1972) 'The Poverty of the Sociology of Deviance: Nuts, Sluts and Preverts', *Social Problems*, vol. 20, no. 1.

C. Lombroso (1913) *Crime, its Causes and Remedies*, Heinemann, London.

C. Lombroso and W. Ferrero (1895) *The Female Offender*, with an introduction by W. D. Morrison, T. Fisher Unwin, London.

J. Lown (1983) 'Not So Much a Factory, More a Form of Patriarchy: Gender and Class During Industrialisation' in Garmarnikow *et al.* (eds).

E. Maccoby and C. Jacklin (1974) *The Psychology of Sex Differences*, Stanford University Press, Stanford.

H. Mannheim (1940) *Social Aspects of Crime in England Between the Wars*, Allen & Unwin, London.

H. Mannheim (1965) *Comparative Criminology*, Routledge & Kegan Paul, London, vols. I and II.

P. Manning (1977) *Police Work*, Cambridge, Massachusetts.

D. Marsden and D. Owens (1975) 'The Jekyll and Hyde Marriages', *New Society*, 8 May.

H. Martineau (1865) 'Life in the Criminal Class', Edinburgh Review, pp. 363–8.

J. Matthews (1981) *Women in the Penal System*, National Association for the Care and Resettlement of Offenders, London.

D. Matza (1964) *Delinquency and Drift*, Wiley, Chichester.

R. Mawby (1980) 'Sex and Crime: The Results of a Self-report Study', British Journal of Sociology, vol. 31, no. 4, December.

R. I. Mawby (1981) 'Women in Prison: a British Study' (mimeo).

D. May (1977) 'Delinquent Girls Before the Courts', *Medicine, Science and the Law*, vol. 17.

P. Mayhew (1977) 'Crime in a Man's World', *New Society*, 40, 560, 16 June.

S. McConville (ed.) (1975) *The Use of Imprisonment*, Routledge & Kegan Paul, London.

S. McConville (1981) *A History of English Prison Administration*, Routledge & Kegan Paul, London, vol. I.

M. McIntosh (1978) 'The State and the Oppression of Women' in A. Kuhn and A. Wolpe (eds) *Feminism and Materialism*, Routledge & Kegan Paul, London.

E. McLeod (1982) *Women Working: Prostitution Now*, Croom Helm, London.

A. McRobbie and J. Garber (1976) 'Girls and Subcultures' in S. Hall & Jefferson (eds).

Y. McShane (1980) *Daughter of Evil*, W. H. Allen, London.

J. McVicar (1974) *McVicar by Himself*, Arrow, London.

L. Melvern and P. Gillman (1982) 'The Woman who Cannot Face the Truth', *The Sunday Times*, 25 April.

R. K. Merton (1949) *Social Theory and Social Structure*, Free Press, New York.

T. Middleton and T. Dekker (1976) *The Roaring Girl*, Benn, London.

J. S. Mill (1929) *The Subjection of Women*, J. M. Dent, London.

W. B. Miller (1958) 'Lower Class Culture as a Generating Milieu of Gang Delinquency', *Journal of Social Issues*, vol. 14.

K. Millett (1977) *Sexual Politics*, Virago, London.

M. Millman (1982) 'Images of Deviant Men and Women' in M. Evans (ed.).

J. Mitchell (1971) *Women's Estate*, Penguin, Harmondsworth.

D. Morgan (1981) 'Men, Masculinity and the Process of Sociological Enquiry' in H. Roberts (ed.) *Doing Feminist Research*, Routledge & Kegan Paul, London.

R. M. Moroney (1975) *The Family and the State*, Longman, New York.

A. Morris and L. Gelsthorpe (1981) 'False Clues and Female Crime' in Morris and Gelsthorpe (eds).

A. Morris and L. Gelsthorpe (1981) (eds) *Women and Crime*, Cambridge, England, Cambridge Institute of Criminology.

R. Morris (1965) 'Attitudes towards Delinquency', *British Journal of Criminology*, vol. 5.

J. Mott (1983) 'Police Decisions for Dealing with Juvenile Offenders', *British Journal of Criminology*, vol. 23, no. 3.

S. K. Mukherjee and Fitzgerald (1981) 'The Myth of Rising Crime' in Mukherjee and South *et al.* (ed.).

S. K. Mukherjee and J. A. Scutt (1981) *Women and Crime*, Allen & Unwin, London.

H. Myerhoff and B. Myerhoff (1972) 'Field Observations of Middleclass Gangs' in Giallombardo (ed.).

National Association for the Care and Resettlement of Offenders (1978) 'Memo to House of Commons Enquiry into Women and the Penal system'.

National Association for the Care and Resettlement of Offenders (1982) 'Women in Prison'.

N. Naffin (1981) 'Theorizing About Female Crime' in Mukherjee and Scutt *et al.* (eds).

I. Nagel *et al.* (1980) 'Sex Differences in the Processing of Criminal Defendants' in D. Kelly Weisberg (ed.) *Women and the Law: The Social Historical Perspective*, Schenkman, New York.

I. Nagel (1981) 'Sex Differences in the Processing of Criminal Defendants' in Morris and Gelsthorpe (eds).

J. Newsom (1964) *The Observer*, 11 October.

J. Nicholson (1984) *Men and Women*, Oxford University Press, Oxford.

R. A. Nisbet (1966) *The Sociological Tradition*, Heinemann, London.

A. Oakley (1974) *The Sociology of Housework*, Martin Robertson, Oxford.

A. Oakley (1980) *Women Confined: Towards a Sociology of Childbirth*, Martin Robertson, Oxford.

A. Oakley (1981) *Subject Women*, Martin Robertson, Oxford.

R. Omodei (1981) 'The Myth Interpretation of Female Crime' in Mukherjee and Scutt *et al.* (eds).

S. Otto (1981) 'Women, Alcohol and Social Control' in Hutter *et al.* (eds).

J. Pahl (1978) *A Refuge for Battered Women: A Study of the Role of a Women's Centre*, HMSO, London.

J. Pahl (1980) 'Patterns of Money Management within Marriage', *Journal of Social Policy*, vol. 9, pt. 3.

C. Pankhurst (1912, 1913, 1914) quoted in E. Sarah, 'Cristabel Pankhurst: Reclaiming her Power' in D. Spender, *Feminist Theorists*, Women's Press, 1983, London.

H. Parker , M. Casburn and D. Turnbull (1981) *Receiving Juvenile Justice*, Blackwell, Oxford.

R. Parker (1982) 'Family and Social Policy' in R. N. Rapaport *et al.* (eds) *Families in Britain*, Routledge & Kegan Paul, London.

T. Parker (1965) *Five Women*, Hutchinson, London.

J. Pascal and F. Pascal (1974) *The Strange Case of Patty Hearst*, New American Library, New York.

P. Patullo (1983) *Judging Women*, National Council for Civil Liberties, London.

S. Pearce (1984) 'Witch – That's What They Branded Me', *'Woman's Own'*, 31 March.

R. Pearsall (1969) *The Worm in the Bud*, Penguin, Harmondsworth.

J. Pearson (1973) *The Profession of Violence*, Panther, London.

G. Pearson (1983) *Hooligan: A History of Respectable Fears*, Macmillan, London.

R. Pearson (1976) 'Women Defendants in Magistrates Courts', *British Journal of Law and Society*, Winter.

G. Petrie (1971) *A Singular Iniquity*, Macmillan, London.

L. O. Pike (1876) *History of Crime in England*, Smith & Elder, London.

J. Place (1978) 'Women in *Film Noir*' in E. A. Kaplan (ed.) *Women in Film*, British Film Institute, London.

E. Player (1981) 'A Female Subculture', paper given to the British Society of Criminology.

K. Plummer (1979) 'Misunderstanding Labelling Perspectives' in D. Downes and P. Rock (eds), *Deviant Interpretations*, Martin Robertson, Oxford.

Policy Studies Institute (1983) *Police and People in London*, London, vols. I–IV.

O. Pollak (1961) *The Criminality of Women*, A. S. Barnes, New York.

M. Pratt (1980) *Mugging as a Social Problem*, Routledge & Kegan Paul, London.

Prison Matron, A (1862) *Female Life in Prison*, (cited in McConville, 1981).

W. Probyn (1977) *Angel Face*, Allen & Unwin, London.

E. Procek (1981) 'Psychiatry and the Social Control of Women' in Morris and Gelsthorpe (eds).

Radical Alternatives to Prison (1972) *Alternatives to Holloway*, Christian Action Publications, London.

V. Randall (1982) *Women and Politics*, Macmillan, London.

W. Reckless (1961) *The Crime Problem*, Appleton Century Crofts, 3rd ed. New York.

H. J. Richardson (1969) *Adolescent Girls in Approved Schools*, Routledge & Kegan Paul, London.

D. Robbins and P. Cohen (1978) *Knuckle Sandwich*, Penguin, Harmondsworth.

H. Roberts (ed.) (1981) *Women, Health and Reproduction*, Routledge &

Kegan Paul, London.
H. E. Roberts (1973) 'Marriage, Redundancy or Sin: the Painter's view of Women' in Vicinus (ed.).
J. Roberts Chapman (1980) *Economic Realities and the Female Offender*, Lexington Books, Lexington.
P. E. Rock (1977) 'A Review of Carol Smart's Women Crime and Criminology'. British Journal of Criminology, vol. 17.
C. H. Rolph (1955) *Women of the Streets*, Secker & Warburg, London.
J. Root (1984) *Pictures of Women*, Pandora Press, London.
H. Rose and J. Hanmer (1975) 'Community, Participation and Social Change' in D. Jones and M. Mayo (eds) *Community Work Two*, Routledge & Kegan Paul, London.
K. Rosenblum (1975) 'Female Deviance and the Female Sex Role: a Preliminary Investigation', *British Journal of Sociology*, vol. 25.
R. Roshier (1973) 'The Selection of Crime News by the Press' in S. Cohen and J. Young (eds) *The Manufacture of News*, Constable, London.
J. J. Rousseau, quoted in Elshtain (1981).
S. Rowbotham (1973) *Hidden from History*, Pluto Press, London.
E. Rubington and M. Weinberg (1968, 1973) *Deviance: The Interactionist Perspective*, Macmillan, New York. (1st and 2nd edns).
J. Ruskin (1865) *Sesame and Lilies*, Allen & Unwin, London.
A. Sachs and J. H. Wilson (1978) *Sexism and the Law*, Martin Robertson, Oxford.
R. Sarri (1976) 'Juvenile Law: How it Penalizes Females' in L. Crites (ed.).
J. Scutt (1976) 'Role-conditioning Theory: An Explanation for Disparity in Male and Female Criminality', *Australian and New Zealand, Journal of Criminology*, vol. 9, no. 1.
J. A. Scutt (1981) 'Sexism in Criminal Law' in Mukherjee & Scutt *et al.* (eds).
L. Segal (ed.) (1983) *What is to be Done About the Family?* Penguin, Harmondsworth.
L. Shacklady Smith (1978) 'Sexist Assumptions and Female Delinquency' in Smart and Smart (eds).
S. Sharpe (1976) *Just like a Girl*, Penguin, Harmondsworth.
R. G. Shelden (1981) 'Sex Discrimination in the Juvenile Justice System: Memphis Tennessee 1900–17' in Warren (ed.).
J. F. Short (1963) Introduction to Thrasher's *The Gang*.
E. Shorter (1975) *The Making of the Modern Family*, Fontana, London.
M. Simms (1981) 'Abortion: The Myth of the Golden Age' in Hutter and Williams (eds).
R. J. Simon (1975) *Women and Crime*, Lexington, London.
C. Smart (1977) *Women, Crime and Criminology*, Routledge & Kegan Paul, London.
C. Smart and B. Smart (eds) (1978) *Women, Sexuality and Social Control*, Routledge & Kegan Paul, London.
C. Smart (1979) 'The New Female Criminal: Reality or Myth', *British Journal of Criminology*, vol. 19, no. 1.
C. Smart (1980) 'Patriarchal Relations and Law', paper given at Social Science Research Council Conference, University of Kent.

C. Smart (1981) 'Law and the Control of Women's Sexuality', in Hutter and Williams (eds).

A. D. Smith (1962) *Women in Prison*, Stevens, London.

S. Smith (1982) 'Victimisation in the Inner City', *British Journal of Criminology*, vol. 22, no. 4.

D. A. Smith and A. C. Visher (1980) 'Sex and Involvement in Deviance/Crime: A Quantitative Literature of the Empirical Literature', *American Sociological Review*, vol. 45.

L. Stanley and S. Wise (1983) *Breaking Out*, Routledge & Kegan Paul, London.

D. I. Steffensmeier (1978) 'Crime and the Contemporary Woman', *Social Forces*, vol. 57.

R. Strachey (1978) *The Cause*, Virago, London.

K. Sullivan (1956) *Girls Who Go Wrong*, Gollancz, London.

R. Sullivan (1975) *Goodbye Lizzie Borden*, Chatto & Windus, London.

A. Summers (1981) 'Hidden from History: Women Victims of Crime' in Mukherjee and Scutt *et al.* (eds).

E. Sutherland and D. Cressey (1960) *Principles of Criminology*, Lippincott, Philadelphia.

G. M. Sykes (1958) *The Society of Captives*, Princeton University Press, New Jersey.

G. Sykes and D. Matza (1957) 'Techniques of Neutralization: A Theory of Delinquency', *American Sociological Review*, vol. 22.

I. Taylor *et al.* (1975) *Critical Criminology*, Routledge & Kegan Paul, London.

R. M. Terry (1970) 'Discrimination in the Handling of Juvenile Offenders by Social Control Agencies' in P. Garabedian and D. C. Gibbons (eds) *Becoming Delinquent*, Aldine Press, Chicago.

P. Thane (1982) *The Foundations of the Welfare State*, Longman, London.

D. A. Thomas (1970) *Principles of Sentencing*, Heinemann, London.

K. Thomas (1959) 'The Double Standard', *Journal of History of Ideas*, vol. 20, no. 2.

W. I. Thomas (1907) *Sex and Society*, Little, Brown, Boston.

W. I. Thomas (1923) *The Unadjusted Girl*, Little, Brown, Boston.

E. P. Thompson (1972) 'Rough Music' quoted in Shorter (1975).

H. Thompson (1966) *Hell's Angels*, Penguin, Harmondsworth.

F. M. Thrasher (1963) *The Gang*, Phoenix Press, Chicago.

L. Tilly and J. Scott (1978) *Women, Work and Family*, Holt, Rinehart & Winston, New York.

R. M. Titmuss (1974) *Social Policy*, Allen & Unwin, London.

C. R. Tittle (1969) 'Inmate Organisation: Sex Differentiation and the Influence of Criminal Subcultures', *American Sociological Review*, vol. 34, August.

P. G. Tjaden and C. D. Tjaden (1981) 'Differential Treatment of the Female Felon: Myth or Reality?' in Warren (ed.).

B. Toner (1982) *The Facts of Rape*, Arrow Books, London.

D. Trilling (1981) *Mrs Harris*, Hamish Hamilton, London.

M. C. Verschluysen (1981) 'Midwives, Medical Men and "poor women labouring of child"': Lying-in Hospitals in Eighteenth-century London', in Roberts (ed.).

M. Vicinus (ed.) (1973) *Suffer and Be Still,* Indiana University Press, Bloomington and London.

J. Walkowitz (1980) *Prostitution and Victorian Society,* Cambridge University Press, Cambridge.

D. A. Ward and G. G. Kassebaum (1966) *Women's Prison,* Weidenfeld and Nicolson, London.

J. Ward (1982) 'Telling Tales in Prison' in R. Frankenberg (ed.) *Custom and Conflict in British Society,* Manchester University Press, Manchester.

M. Q. Warren (ed.) (1981) *Comparing Male and Female Offenders,* Sage, London.

M. Q. Warren (1981) 'Gender Comparisons in Crime and Delinquency' in Warren (ed.).

D. Webb (1984) 'More on Gender and Justice: Girl Offenders on Supervision', *Sociology,* vol. 18, no. 3.

S. and B. Webb (1963) *English Prisons Under Local Government,* Cass, London (new edition).

M. Weissman and E. Paykel (1974) *The Depressed Woman: A Study of Social Relationships,* Chicago University Press, Chicago.

S. Welsh (1981) 'The Manufacture of Excitement in Police–Juvenile Encounters', *British Journal of Criminology,* vol. 21, no. 3.

A. Whitehead (1976) 'Sexual Antagonism in Herefordshire' in D. L. Barker and S. Allen (eds) *Dependence and Exploitation in Work and Marriage,* Longman, London.

W. F. Whyte (1943) 'A Slum Sex Code', *American Journal of Sociology,* vol. 49.

W. F. Whyte (1955) *Street Corner Society,* University of Chicago Press, Chicago, 2nd edn.

P. Willis (1977) *Learning to Labour,* Saxon House, London.

P. Willis (1978) *Profane Culture,* Saxon House, London.

P. Willmott and M. Young (1960) *Family and Class in a London Suburb,* Routledge & Kegan Paul, London.

D. Wilson (1978) 'Sexual Codes and Conduct' in C. Smart and B. Smart (eds).

E. Wilson (1977) *Women and the Welfare State,* Tavistock, London.

E. Wilson (1983) *What is to be Done About Violence Against Women?,* Penguin, Harmondsworth.

E. Windschuttle (1981) 'Women, Crime and Punishment', in Mukherjee and Scutt *et al.* (eds).

Wolfenden Committee Report (1957) *Homosexual Offences and Prostitution,* HMSO, London.

K. Young and O. Harris (1982) 'The Subordination of Women in Crosscultural Perspective' in M. Evans (ed.).

M. Young and P. Willmott (1957) *Family and Kinship in East London,* Routledge & Kegan Paul, London.

Index